Aidan McQuade
Ethical Leadership

De Gruyter Transformative Thinking and Practice of Leadership and Its Development

Edited by Bernd Vogel

Volume 2

Aidan McQuade
Ethical Leadership

—

Moral Decision-making under Pressure

DE GRUYTER

ISBN 978-3-11-074574-0
e-ISBN (PDF) 978-3-11-074584-9
e-ISBN (EPUB) 978-3-11-074588-7
ISSN 2701-4002

Library of Congress Control Number: 2022932948

Bibliographic information published by the Deutsche Nationalbibliothek
The Deutsche Nationalbibliothek lists this publication in the Deutsche Nationalbibliografie;
detailed bibliographic data are available on the internet at http://dnb.dnb.de.

© 2022 Walter de Gruyter GmbH, Berlin/Boston
Cover image: Mirrorpix / Kontributor / Getty Images
Typesetting: Integra Software Services Pvt. Ltd.
Printing and binding: CPI books GmbH, Leck

www.degruyter.com

For my parents, Eilish (RIP) and Gerry, my first ethical leaders

Suspect too much sweet talk, but never close your mind.
— Seamus Heaney, *The Cure at Troy*

Acknowledgements

> Piglet noticed that even though he had a Very Small Heart, it could hold a rather large amount of Gratitude.
> – A.A. Milne

This book has been a long time in gestation. Many of the ideas at its core started life during my doctoral research in Strathclyde University almost 20 years ago. So, my first thanks must go to my supervisors Dr Phyl Hughes and Prof Gerry Johnson for all their advice and support in the course of that often tortuous thinking and writing process. I would also like to thank the Friday Night Philosophy Club of Peter Keenan, Suzanne Bunniss, Andy Kelly, Marie Macrae and Hannah Hesselgreves for all their support and encouragement throughout this process. Peter McInnes and Paul Hibbert were unfailingly generous with their time and friendship, and Val Turner was a lifesaver at repeated points in the process, not least with her demon transcribing skills. I would also like to say special thanks to Dave Pratt, Anne Douglas and Steve Gibson, who kept me going through some very dark moments. Beyond the University I must express huge gratitude to Kathleen Rankin, Billy Kirkwood and Mark Nelson for keeping me sane, more or less.

All the participants in my doctoral research were gracious with their time, patiently answering my sometimes quite ignorant questions: The extended McAlinden clan in Belfast were exceptionally hospitable in this regard.

However, this book would not have seen the light of day without the very specific prodding and encouragement of Dr Joanne Murphy of the Centre for Leadership, Ethics and Organisation at Queen's University Belfast. Her inspiring words, "You'd be an awful eejit if you didn't write it", were what started the process. So particular thanks to her are in most especial order.

Bernd Vogel, Steve Hardman, and Jaya Dalal have been insightful and patient guides through this writing process. Suruthi Manogarane has shown the patience of a saint helping me understand the wonders of modern publishing technology. Natalie Wills has given wise advice on the sometimes daunting matter of book promotion.

My brains trust of Harriet Dodd, Karin de Jonge, Kate Halff, Meena Varma, Andrew Bovarnick and Mil Nielpold have been the source of vital advice at various points. Professor Mo Hume was extraordinarily kind with her insights and her memories. Luke Wilde, Jo Berry, Charles Mathais, Victor Riega and Richard Brindle were enormously generous with their time and thoughts on the challenges facing leaders striving to be ethical, and on the nature of leadership itself.

Finally, my wife, Klara, who in addition to being a patient reader and a tenderhearted critic, has, more than usual, had to put up with my extra messiness and frequent distractedness as I've finalised this text from behind an ever-growing mountain of books and papers. So, my biggest thanks go to her, with all my love.

Foreword

> ... ethical leadership – the effort to optimise life-affirming choices that seek to protect human rights and advance environmental restoration – no matter how inhospitable the political, social or professional environment: the future of the planet depends upon it.
> – Aidan McQuade, *Ethical Leadership: Moral Decision-making under Pressure* (2022, p. 1).

When Aidan approached us with this book proposal ...
... I was immediately captivated and thought: "It would be a privilege to have this book in the series!" I start above with a quote from the book that encapsulated why I got hooked and why I think this is relevant and generative for every person engaging in leadership, which, by the way, in my understanding is everybody!

For years I have been fascinated by the theme of constructive dissent, and thankfully others, better equipped than myself, have written about this. Such as the work by Ira Chaleff on intelligent disobedience, or the book *I Object* by Ian Hislop and Tom Hockenhull accompanying the exhibition with the same name at the British Museum a few years ago. And then a book comes along about choices under pressure and staying the course. What a gift.

Some might think: "Dealing with slavery, corruption, war zones, or life and death decisions as a doctor is far away from my remit at work and my other spheres of life. What has that to do with me?" This is a book for all circumstances. To me the same ideas apply everywhere. We are also somewhat very quickly connected to this theme of ethical challenge when we consider our typical daily activities and decisions for a moment.

Hence, *Ethical Leadership: Moral Decision-making under Pressure* addresses an age-old and contemporary pressing issue that is at the core of thinking and practicing leadership for a desirable world – all the time.

This is a challenging book. That is why it is in the series!
When you start reading the book, to some this will be uncharted territory. However, that is an opportunity to reframe our own leadership practice and thinking.

At its core the book will equip you to lead more ethically and to make difficult choices when you face those moments that profoundly challenge your identity, beliefs and who you think you are.

Asking why some people, professionals, or managers continue to do the "right" thing in situations of adversity is a generative avenue. And a counterpoint to the seeming urge and guilty fascination of focussing on people when they get it wrong. The latter is an important avenue. However, enabling practicing managers to positively deviate in testing times is often overlooked and a day-to-day task, that many of us face.

It is helpful to explore that managers and organizational members can face some form of dynamic balancing between, on the one hand, the level of freedom they have about their own choices and, on the other hand, the social conditions and circumstances that also impact them. The Cruciform of Agency model is a generative and accessible way to engage with this interplay of the individual and the social in our decision-making and leading. I envision the Cruciform of Agency model to become a guide for managers and humans in those situations.

The second theme that struck a chord with me is the idea of assonance. Admittedly a difficult term, but I have started to embrace it already. Moral assonance sits the middle ground – when things are not clear cut and managers and professionals have doubts or are uncertain about what is the right course of action. Don't you face situations regularly, where it is ambiguous what is ethically right and how to assert human dignity in your world of work and leadership?

This book is not only for the broadsheet attracting cases and situations. It is for everyday leadership, where people are facing ethical struggles. This book is challenging, but make no mistake, life and work are difficult. Therefore, the book provides fundamental guidance on ethical leadership for practicing managers, professionals and humans in all spheres of life – from the moment you start reading, reflecting, and translating this book toward action in your context.

We do not have the luxury any more to ignore in our day-to-day activities in practice and science how every piece of insight and learning can shape a desirable future for our planet.

And if you are not convinced of the practicality of the book, why don't you read page 134, the second-to-last paragraph as a teaser? That is something I try hard every day, hopefully at least sometimes with success. Aidan, thanks so much for reminding us.

Bernd Vogel
Henley-on-Thames, UK
March 2022

Contents

Acknowledgements —— IX

Foreword —— XI

Chapter 1
Introduction —— 1
  A resumption of war —— 1
  Learning from Archie on his work experience —— 3
  Lighting a candle rather than cursing the dark —— 4
  Purpose of the book —— 5
  Outline of the book —— 6

Chapter 2
The intellectual terrain of ethical leadership —— 9
  Evasions of responsibility —— 9
  The political economies of exploitation —— 11
  Rule of law and ethical practice —— 14
  Moral exemplars in business —— 16
  Responsibilities to stakeholders —— 17
  Some moral guidance for international business —— 19
  Conclusion —— 20

Chapter 3
Philosophers: What do they know? —— 22
  Introduction —— 22
  Freedom versus determinism —— 24
  Illuminating moral philosophy with social science —— 25
  Why do good people do bad things? It's determinism stupid! —— 25
  Why do good people do bad things? Maybe it's just bad people? —— 27
  Why can't everybody just be nice? —— 29
  Conclusion —— 30

Chapter 4
The Cruciform of Agency —— 32
  Introduction —— 32
  Social aspects of human agency —— 34
  The private self —— 36
  The Cruciform of Agency —— 37
  Implications of the Cruciform of Agency —— 41

Chapter 5
Exploring some narratives of moral choice —— 45
Introduction —— 45
Executive on a mission: Saving the planet —— 46
The conscience of the Colonel —— 47
"You can't eat a flag" —— 50
Malawi's fearsome chief, terminator of child marriages —— 53
"The Whistleblower" —— 55
"This is a fight for human rights" —— 57
"I have a duty to serve my community" —— 59
Ethical choice: Acting in accordance with (even impeded) values —— 61

Chapter 6
Just what the doctor ordered —— 64
Introduction —— 64
All in a day's work —— 65
End of life —— 65
Abortion —— 67
Introducing the concept of "assonance" —— 68
Treatment of patients against their will —— 70
Child protection —— 71
Is the system more important than the patient? —— 72
The professional value of doubt —— 73
Elements of a code of conduct —— 75
Professional maturation —— 76
Conclusion —— 79

Chapter 7
Becoming an ethical leader —— 80
So where have we got to? —— 80
Agency and ethical leadership —— 82
Still not my problem! —— 84
Personal responsibility —— 86
Moral guidance for ethical leadership —— 88
A code of conduct for ethical leaders —— 91
Myanmar: Fumbling towards ethical leadership —— 91

Chapter 8
Towards a movement for ethical leadership —— 95
Corporate governance: A tragedy —— 95
A new hope? —— 98

Chapter 9
Towards an agenda for action —— 102
    But didn't Wilberforce and Lincoln put an end to all of that? —— 103
        A short story from India —— 103
        Advocacy for change —— 105
        Older than Troy —— 106
        Reforming the political economy of slavery —— 109
        Elements of an agenda for action, part one —— 112
    It's getting hot in here —— 116
        Slavery and the environment —— 116
        Two minutes to midnight —— 117
        The collapse of civilisations? —— 119
        In the absence of environmental justice —— 120
        Elements of an agenda for action, part two —— 122
    Some human consequences of inaction —— 124
    Conclusion —— 126

Chapter 10
Final reflections —— 129
    The consequences of leadership —— 129
    Summing up —— 131
    A word of advice —— 134
    Numberless diverse acts of courage and belief —— 135

References —— 137

Further reading —— 147

About the author —— 149

About the series editor —— 151

Index —— 153

Chapter 1
Introduction

> It is from numberless diverse acts of courage and belief that human history is shaped. Each time a [hu]man stands up for an ideal, or acts to improve the lot of others, or strikes out against injustice, [they send] forth a tiny ripple of hope, and crossing each other from a million different centers of energy and daring, those ripples build a current that can sweep down the mightiest walls of oppression and resistance. – Robert Francis Kennedy

In which . . . the author explains the origins of this book in his experiences as a leader in a humanitarian crisis, and the importance of ethical leadership – the effort to optimise life-affirming choices that seek to protect human rights and advance environmental restoration – no matter how inhospitable the political, social or professional environment: the future of the planet depends upon it . . . and an outline of what is in the rest of the book.

A resumption of war

In January 1999 I hitched a ride with the International Committee of the Red Cross (ICRC) on the first civilian aid flight to the city of Kuito in central Angola since the resumption of the war the previous month.

The city had been the scene of intense fighting over the previous weeks. UNITA[1] forces, attacking the city in one of their last major offensives of the civil war, had advanced to within a few kilometres of the city centre before being turned back amid much bloodshed. When I arrived, there was still a great deal of tension following the battle, and the city, already devastated by previous rounds of fighting, was choking with people from other parts of the central highlands who had fled from UNITA's advance.

I had been concerned about getting back into the city as soon as the news of UNITA's defeat was learned. I had Angolan colleagues there who I, as director of Oxfam GB's Angola programme, had failed to evacuate at the beginning of the battle. I knew the influx of displaced people would also mean an urgent demand on the water and sanitation resources of the city. The provision of these was my organisation's raison d'etre in Angola and in their absence a public health crisis threatened.

I recall the bombed-out basketball court in the city. It had become home to some of the new arrivals, luckier than others in that at least they had some shelter. In the midst of that I remember the look of complete exhaustion on the faces of some of the old people sitting uncomplaining in the ruins.

---

[1] *União Nacional para a Independência Total de Angola* – National Union for the Total Independence of Angola.

This sort of aftermath was common across Angola until the end of the war in 2002. It was only one of a number that I encountered during the time I worked there. The tide of misery ebbed and flowed across the country in direct relationship to the movement of the armies. So, a central part of my job was to identify where humanitarian operations should be placed to alleviate some of the misery of the civilian population and to manage operations in a way that minimised the risk of death or injury to my subordinates.

The early stages of the war in Angola were driven by ancient interethnic disputes exacerbated by the trans-Atlantic slave trade. This had pitched the peoples of the coastal regions against those of the interior who they had captured to be trafficked to the plantations of the Americas. These bitter divisions lived on into the anticolonial era when they were further exacerbated by the politics of the Cold War. The USSR backed the governing MPLA,[2] which had most support on the coast, while the United States backed UNITA, a movement that had grown up amongst the people of the interior.

With the end of the Cold War and emergent peace processes in Namibia and South Africa the geopolitical logic of the war dissipated. Yet the war in Angola continued in large part due to the megalomania of Jonas Savimbi, the UNITA leader,[3] and because the means to fight were facilitated by international trade. Oil (Global Witness, 1999) and diamonds (Global Witness, 1998) funded the war machines of the two opposing factions and enriched the elites of the country.

The causes of the war and humanitarian catastrophe that it brought are matters that came to dominate my mind in the years that I worked in Angola. The question of how to mitigate the consequences of all of this became my principle professional objective. Continually reminded of various aspects of the war from simply living in the country, I found the matter came to pervade all my thinking.

During those couple of days in Kuito I met an older English man, an engineer working on a short contract for another nongovernmental organisation (NGO). He reckoned that given the increased war-displaced population of the city, there was no way it would be possible to develop enough sealed wells to provide safe water for everyone before the rains. This was the approach towards water supply that we had been using up to that point. However, this engineer thought, no matter how durable and appropriate this technology was in normal times it simply could not be deployed rapidly enough in the current situation. That meant a considerable risk of disease for the whole city.

---

[2] *Movimento Popular de Libertação de Angola* – People's Movement for the Liberation of Angola.
[3] One diplomat who was involved in the Angolan peace process told me that Savimbi had once told him that the conflict would end either with his total success, or with his death, a position, which my friend observed, did not leave a lot of room for compromise (personal communication, summer 1998, Angola).

Instead, he thought, if enough hand-dug, open wells were excavated in the makeshift camps and treated with chlorine on a regular basis, it would be possible to increase a relatively safe water supply to a level sufficient to stave off a surge in water-borne disease amongst the war-displaced. As I was from Oxfam, with a greater specialism in water and sanitation than his own organisation, he reckoned this should be our job.

Over the course of an afternoon, we scribbled together plans and, over the next couple of weeks, my team organised the money and personnel to implement them. There was some scepticism amongst my team whether this would have the necessary impact. But it was not as if we had many other ways to cast the die. So, we put the plans into effect.

It is not uncommon, I have found, for people who have never worked in humanitarian response to think it a rewarding job. I have rarely found it so. Rather it is typically one of the most extreme experiences of managing insufficient resources to meet extraordinary levels of need under the constant threat of violence. No matter how well you do your job it is never enough. The work is meaningful, but it can also be bleak.

Nevertheless, as the weeks passed, and the inventory of wells across Kuito began to swell, the records kept by colleagues in health-focussed NGOs indicated that the Englishman's prediction was coming true. Cases of water-borne and water washed diseases were not rising.

Sitting at my desk one afternoon towards the end of the rainy season I realised that the feared public health crisis would not materialise because of the work of my Angolan and international colleagues in the city.

It was the single moment of pure professional satisfaction I had in the five years I worked in Angola.

Learning from Archie on his work experience

Years later, when I was director of Anti-Slavery International, I spent an afternoon with a young man called Archie.

Archie had come from his school to do work experience for a week in our office. He spent that week with enormous good humour doing all sorts of the more boring and routine sort of office work, from photocopying to filing. Towards the end of the week Susan, the office manager who had been supervising him, thought it might be a bit more interesting for him if I brought him along to a meeting that I had to attend to talk about law and policy on the issue of contemporary slavery.

As we chatted on the underground journey into the city Archie asked me an arresting question: Who was the most inspiring person I had ever met?

I had to think about that for a minute.

I have had the occasional conversation with undoubted giants of Irish and African history. But it was not anything they said or did that kept me going during the proverbial dark nights of the soul that have cropped up occasionally in my life and career, such as in those grindingly exhausting years in Angola.

Archie's question made me reflect, rather, that it was family, friends, and colleagues who inspired my choices and sustained my endurance in those trying times. The sort of people who knew my weaknesses and flaws but who still stuck around to say at key "moments of truth" – when my hopes and values were challenged by the difficulties of the situations I faced – "Keep at it", or, "We expect better of you", or, "Don't let the bastards grind you down".

Archie's question also made me remember that English engineer again, a stranger to me then and someone, to my regret, whose name I cannot recall. Perhaps I was merely a convenient person onto whom he could shift the responsibility for a problem he didn't want for himself. But I don't think so. In any event he inspired me to see a way through what was up to that point probably the biggest professional challenge of my career. He did this by using his experience and imagination to empower me with new choices and an idea for a path through a looming crisis with which I could lead my colleagues. In doing so he helped stave off death and illness for thousands.

What this collective of friends and colleagues demonstrated was an expectation that when responsibilities fell towards me, irrespective of the circumstances, that I would make the necessary choices that would aim for the better, that would, in some extreme instances, save their lives or those of others, and that if, sometimes, I failed or made a mistake that I would try to learn enough to do better the next time.

Simply put, they were the people who expected and encouraged me to lead ethically.

Lighting a candle rather than cursing the dark

Martin Luther King thought that "the arc of the moral universe is long, but it bends towards justice" (Ellis, 2011). But, if we are to consider the current historical trajectory of humanity, we appear to be skewing towards environmental crisis, and the millions of children, women and men currently exploited in different parts of the international supply chain, must still be wondering when justice will present itself in their lives.

It is important to remember that if this is the way of the world, it is not the result of impersonal forces. It is the result of numberless human choices through history and across the planet deciding on unsustainable and exploitative courses of action. Often these choices will be made because the decision-maker thinks that it is simply not their problem. Sometimes they will be made because they promise profits irrespective of which laws they contravene or who they hurt. Sometimes it will be made because the decision-maker simply has not thought about it enough to consider an alternative.

Anyone who works as a leader knows that their choices matter. They matter in relation to the lives of their subordinates and in relation to the lives of those that their organisation impacts. Leaders who act to optimise the positive impact of their decisions on human life and environmental sustainability are ethical leaders. It is because, at all levels of society, not enough leaders make life-affirming decisions that the planet is in such peril environmentally, and why so many individuals are in abject poverty and exploitation.

By logical extension, if more leaders strived to act more ethically and make life-affirming choices in the face of prevailing injustices, then there may be a better prospect of retilting King's "moral arc" towards justice and environmental sustainability.

Given the scale of the crisis, this is a worldwide leadership challenge of some urgency.

Purpose of the book

This book aims to equip professionals to lead more ethically when they face their own "moments of truth" that test who they are and what they truly believe. It seeks to do this by deepening the reader's understanding of how decisions are made in a *Cruciform of Agency*: the process by which an individual contemplates choices posed by the social world, such as a professional environment, in relation to personal moral values and hopes. The Cruciform of Agency helps explain how some leaders have succeeded in making moral choices in challenging environments. Drawing on examples of such ethical leadership the book outlines elements of an explicit moral code for leaders, and elucidates some of the key moral challenges facing our planet that cry out for ethical leadership by citizens and professionals alike.

Not all work environments are as personally testing or morally complex as managing humanitarian operations in a war. But most leaders know the challenges posed by situations when they need to make decisions without sufficient information. Leaders also know about having to make choices between comparably deserving demands because there are not enough resources to satisfy all stakeholders. Furthermore, leaders know that their decisions matter: the lives and livelihoods of others often depend upon them. So, understanding how they can make better decisions, and how these decisions can make a difference in the social world also matters.

Many volumes have been written on diverse perspectives of what is "good" leadership. This book grows out of reflections on the moral obligations of leadership, originating during the Angolan civil war. It asserts the possibility of *ethical* – life-affirming – leadership in the complex and sometimes morally ambiguous contemporary world.

Moral decision-making in complex multi-stakeholder environments may always be difficult. But some leaders manage to do the "right" thing despite such circumstances. If the world is to survive, more will need to urgently do so.

Outline of the book

Chapter 2 is a survey of the existing terrain of the predominant thinking on leaders' ethical responsibilities in relation to the contemporary political economy. These form a significant part of the intellectual environments within which leaders' ethical choices will be made. It is important for leaders to be aware of the diverse perspectives on the ethical challenges that they will face and so be better equipped to meet them.

As noted, constructing a framework of moral responsibilities for individual leaders is a central purpose of this book. However, as various moral philosophers have observed over the centuries, this depends on human beings being capable of making some degree of free choice in the first place. Chapter 3 will consider, briefly, the question of "free will" – the capacity of individuals to make their own choices – versus "determinism" – the extent to which any notion of individual choice is illusory and instead influenced by external pressures such as social expectations.

This discussion will form the intellectual foundation for a review of how social scientists since the latter part of the 20th century have sought to explain the problems of organisational malfeasance and individuals' roles in such situations. These studies tend towards those that blame the individual – "bad people" – and those that blame the environment – "bad systems". In doing so these studies echo that older debate between free will and determinism, without fully understanding the interplay between systemic and individual factors.

Hence, in Chapter 4 I draw together two of the key theories on choice-making – human agency – to obtain greater clarity on that interplay of situational and individual factors in the taking of decisions. This chapter then proposes a new model – the *Cruciform of Agency* – that more fully reflects the dynamic interplay of the individual and the social in human decision-making.

The Cruciform of Agency recognises that decision-makers have on one hand to contend with external factors – such as, in a business context, pressure from superiors or markets. But the model also recognises that in decision-making these external factors need not be wholly deterministic but rather can be evaluated in relation to much more personal factors, including the leader's personal moral values and hopes, and other relationships. Therefore, some leaders can plot a more independent moral course when pressures are to the contrary. Understanding this helps empower individual professionals to become more ethical leaders.

It is easy to do the right thing when everyone else is at it, when it is popular and rewarded. Therefore, the focus in Chapter 5 is on application of the Cruciform of Agency where choices have not been popular or easy, and where the decision-maker has had to risk unpopularity and sometimes their lives to assert human dignity by *dissenting* from immoral systems. This chapter uses the Cruciform of Agency to provide insight into seven different examples of ethical leadership in different social and geographic contexts. The examples chosen seek to avoid an excessive Northern hemisphere bias: leadership, ethics and moral responsibility are universal human matters and so affect us all within the web of national and international political, economic, professional and personal relationships in which we are enmeshed.

Chapter 5 shows that the Cruciform of Agency does indeed represent how leaders think when confronting the challenges that they face. It shows that while circumstances may shape leaders' choices they do not determine them. Rather moral responsibility is core to ethical leadership – the choice of life-affirming paths as citizens or in professional environments – and that such choices are motivated by personal moral values and hopes.

The examples explored in Chapter 5 may be of individuals in exceptional circumstances. But ethical choice-making matters in all leadership environments because what leaders do matter for the lives and livelihoods of those who are affected by their decision. This is true even when, as is so often the case, decisions must be made with insufficient information or inadequate resources. In such circumstances the right course of action may not *resonate* clearly. Neither might the incorrect choice cause the moral *dissonance* of something that is sharply wrong. Instead, many choices may have a degree of uncertainty or moral *assonance* to them.

Chapter 6 explores this aspect of leadership more closely by focussing on how a certain group of professionals, doctors, respond to morally complex questions. These include choices in relation to questions such as end of life and child protection.

This chapter highlights how, when these matters are contemplated by professionals in the Cruciform of Agency, moral *assonance* – doubt or uncertainty regarding the correct course of action – is shown to be a valuable tool in ethical leadership, because it can stimulate learning and, with moral responsibility, lead individuals to mature as leaders.

Chapter 7 then discusses the implications of the insights gained from empirical research for professional practice and ethical leadership more generally. This includes identification of the importance of appreciation of moral complexity and depth of understanding in ethical leadership. Drawing on international human rights and environmental standards, the chapter also posits a code of conduct for ethical leadership. The application of this is considered in relation to some of the ethical challenges posited by the 2021 military coup in Myanmar.

Chapter 8 begins the exploration of how a movement of consciously ethical leaders may begin the process of disrupting unjust political economic systems, by asserting new ideals of environmental restoration and human rights.

Chapter 9 continues this theme by exploring in greater detail two issues – contemporary slavery and climate change – which lie at the core of planetary jeopardy. These issues are crying out for greater ethical leadership, both in individuals' professional roles and in their roles as citizens. In exploring the interrelationship between these issues, the chapter aims to demonstrate the importance of obtaining depth and breadth of understanding these issues to be able to better respond to the challenges these issues pose.

Given the nature of the globalising political economy, these are pervasive and urgent issues, both in domestic politics and in international business. These issues frequently bear directly on our lives whether we are aware of them or not. Hence, these matters must become foundational to every ethical leader's thinking and decision-making. As the 2021 Intergovernmental Panel on Climate Change (IPCC) report makes clear, these are matters that, if we do not address them urgently, as citizens and as professionals, are likely to spell the end of much of human civilisation. Hence, the chapter offers some suggestions for the reader to consider on actions that ethical leaders could take to mitigate some of these crises.

Finally, Chapter 10 summarises and considers some of the further implications of ethical leadership and offers some final reflections on the challenges ahead.

Points for reflection

- Who has inspired you in your career and how have they inspired you?
- When you lead others do you consciously consider how this should include guiding their ethical choice-making?
- Do you think that human rights standards and environmental restoration should be matters of central concern to you as a citizen or as a professional?
- Think of an ethical dilemma you have been confronted with in work or elsewhere in your life: how did you go about dealing with this issue?

Chapter 2
The intellectual terrain of ethical leadership

> Those are my principles and if you don't like them, well I have others.   – Groucho Marx

In which . . . the author surveys the predominant ethical guidances available to leaders finding that offered by Milton Friedman an excuse for moral evasion, but also discerning an unfortunate gap – the lack of a moral core – in the much more sophisticated stakeholder theory, which rightly recognises leadership obligations to diverse communities.

Evasions of responsibility

I never saw, let alone met, Jonas Savimbi. All the years I was in Angola he was in the bush, plotting war or waging it. Once or twice I saw the Angolan president's motorcade pass in the streets of Luanda, but I never saw or met him either. The leadership of the warring factions seemed almost like mythic figures, so far removed from my day-to-day experience.

However, in the bars and on the beaches of the capital, Luanda, I did regularly bump into the urbane Western women and men who managed the Angolan operations of the international oil and diamond businesses. These were institutions I had come to regard as morally culpable for financing the bloodshed and corruption in the country.

Stress of working in Angola with the constant fear of violence, particularly for my subordinates working on the sharp end of humanitarian response in the cities of the Angolan interior, made me a rather angry person. And, in part because I could not relate my life experience in any substantive way to the murderous choices of the warlords, the focus of my particular frustrations tended towards those I felt should be more interested in the abject bleakness that the war was rendering on the ordinary people of Angola. This included colleagues in the United Kingdom whose focus seemed only on the humanitarian consequences of wars that got on British television – a category of disaster that did not extend to Lusophone Angola. It also happened upon those seemingly decent people I met in Angola whose business dealings with the warlords kept them in riches and the Angolan civil war machines in arms.

If asked about the potentially devastating consequences of their or their companies' business dealings with such unsavoury characters, their general response was, "It's not my problem".

Of course, on reflection, evasions of his sort are hardly rare.

In the last year of my primary university degree in 1988 I found myself shocked by people I had known for years, from my own nationalist community in the north of Ireland. Despite their own direct personal experience of petty and serious discrimination, they talked excitedly about the job opportunities they were considering taking up in apartheid South Africa, attracted by the standard of living promised to them as whites.

On another occasion, attending a lecture in London one night in early 2009 I fell into conversation with a lawyer. On hearing that I was at the time director of Anti-Slavery International, which had just produced a new report on the use of slavery as a weapon of war in Darfur, he mentioned that he and his company represented the government of Sudan in the United Kingdom. This was the very government that we had identified as ultimately culpable for the widespread use of this policy against their own people.

Even criminals, of course, are entitled to a defence. But this choice to represent such a reprehensible government reminded me not of that principle but rather of an anecdote shared by a business lecturer in Strathclyde University when I was studying for my MBA. He told the class how he had once argued to an oil company that their key strategic competence was their *amorality* and hence their preparedness to do business anywhere in the world with anyone irrespective of the consequences.

The notion of *amorality* in business dealings has pedigree. Milton Friedman (1970) argued that the appropriate social goal of a corporate executive was "to make as much money as possible while conforming with the basic rules of society, both those embodied in law and those embodied in ethical custom". This approach seizes upon Adam Smith's idea that it is the role of governments to regulate businesses and see to the welfare of society, and suggests that, by extension, such concerns are beyond the professional purview of business leaders.

There was a de facto endorsement of this attitude in 2021 when the UK's foreign secretary, Dominic Raab, stated to colleagues in the Foreign, Commonwealth and Development Office (FCDO), "If we restrict [trade] to countries with [European Convention on Human Rights]-level standards of human rights, we're not going to do many trade deals with the growth markets of the future" (Singh, 2021).

In other words, not only did Raab think that it is not business' problem what the "basic rules of society" say, he does not even appear to believe that it is an important consideration for a senior member of the government of a democracy. It is just business' job to make money within those rules. So if the law or custom in a country allows, say, forced labour of migrants or particular castes, then that is not the problem of business even though business might benefit from those rules, through reduced costs, for example.

This is not an abstract point. While international law is unequivocal in its prohibitions of slavery, forced and child labour, for many countries the "basic rules of society . . . embodied in law and . . . ethical custom" not only overlook such abuses, but often enable them.

The political economies of exploitation

The laws, policies and customs that are created to govern employment, business and trade are the *political economy*. Many countries seem to have established political economies that, to obtain a competitive advantage against other countries, allow forced and child labour to flourish in the production of internationally traded goods and commodities. In other words, in many countries domestic law, policy and practice ignore the extensive body of international law that prohibits forced and child labour and other contemporary slavery-like practices.

For example in 2020 state-sponsored forced labour was still being practiced in China in cotton production for international markets (Sudworth, 2020)

The state can also facilitate private actors to practice forced labour. Across the Middle East a system of "sponsorship" for visas (Robinson, 2021) known as the *kafalah* system ties migrant workers to their employers to such an extent that even in the most abusive employment relationships, up to and including forced labour, the workers cannot leave the country or even change jobs.

The impact of this system was described in 2018 in the Global Slavery Index, which reported that

> Among the estimated six million Indian migrants living in the six Gulf countries of Bahrain, Kuwait, Qatar, Saudi Arabia, United Arab Emirates, and Oman . . . exploitation is reportedly widespread, especially among those Indian migrants who come to work in unskilled sectors, such as construction, agriculture, and domestic work. Many of these violations also occur as a result of limited protections for migrant workers under labour law in these Gulf countries.
>
> (Global Slavery Index, 2018a)

The abuses associated with tied visas are not confined to the Middle East. In 2019 the International Transport Workers Federation (ITF) won a commitment from the government of Ireland to introduce new protections for migrant workers in the country's fishing industry. Investigations by the ITF had shown that these workers had been subject to forced labour and trafficking[1] as a consequence of a tied visa system (International Transport Workers Federation, 2019).

Human trafficking at sea is generally practiced with impunity because labour inspection is negligible, particularly on fishing boats. As shipping companies register vessels under flags of convenience (International Transport Workers Federation, n.d.) captains can get away with keeping discipline amongst their deceptively recruited and debt bonded crews with extreme violence, including murder (Urbina, 2019).

Similar problems pertain in Export Processing Zones (EPZs) (International Labour Organization, 2017a) in which states may facilitate exploitation of workers by knowingly failing to protect their rights in these economic areas.

---

[1] "Trafficking" is the process of rendering a person into forced labour or sexual exploitation.

In other parts of the world state passivity in the enforcement of the law enables worker exploitation and forced labour. For example, in large parts of India, Dalits – the community previously known as "Untouchables" – enslaved in brick kilns or agricultural labour (Shahinian, 2009) find it next to impossible to obtain legal remedy for the situations in which they find themselves. There is simply too much corruption, and caste-based prejudice, and too few honest police, labour inspectors and judges to administer the law. South Asia has the largest number of slaves in the world (Global Slavery Index, 2018b) in significant part because for almost one-third of the population, over 300 million Dalits, Adivasi and others from "lower" and "scheduled" castes, the most basic ideals of rule of law are completely meaningless, and successive south Asian governments have never made it a political priority to remedy this.

Reporting on contemporary forms of slavery in India in 2018 the Global Slavery Index observed that the slavery-like practice, bonded labour,

> is still prevalent in India. A 2016 report found that in the state of Tamil Nadu, 351 of 743 spinning mills use bonded labour schemes . . . Fraudulent recruiters reportedly target families in economically disadvantaged rural areas of India and persuade the parents to send their daughters to spinning mills with promises of good working conditions and the payment of a lump sum at the end of their three-year contracts that might help contribute to dowry costs. In these mills, young women are subject to exploitative labour practices, including restriction of movement, removal of mobile phones, and withholding wages and other payments. . . . They work 60 hours per week year-round and cannot refuse overtime. Workers are therefore bound to their employer as changing employers would mean losing their promised lump sum. However, many women under those schemes never receive the lump sum payment they are promised because they leave early, often due to illness.

The reduced production costs that such slavery-like practices ensure means improved profits for the factory owners and provides them with a competitive advantage. Hence, the thread that these young women spin ends up in fabric that is turned into garments that end up in the markets of every corner of the globe.

This is by no means a comprehensive survey of contemporary forms of slavery. But neither are these rare or isolated examples. In the contemporary world there are many countries that don't come up to what Raab called "ECHR-level standards of human rights". In 2017 the International Labour Organization (ILO) estimated that there were 152 million in child labour, of which 73 million were in hazardous work (2017b). In 2017 the ILO (2017c) also estimated that there that there were approximately 40 million people enslaved across the world, approximately 25 million of them in forced labour and the rest in forced marriage. In 2020 the US Department of Labour gave further insight into how those millions of forced and child labourers are exploited in the international economy by listing 155 goods from 77 countries that were produced by forced or child labour (Department of Labour, 2020). Many of these goods, such as cotton from Turkmenistan, garments and shrimp from Thailand, or cobalt and coltan from the Democratic Republic of Congo, find their ways into international markets. So, the taint of slavery may pollute the computer on which this book was written, the cotton underwear of the book's reader, the mobile phones in our pockets and the nice risotto we may be planning for dinner.

These examples indicate how, despite international, and sometimes national law, the "basic rules of society" can still allow forced labour and other slavery-like practices to impinge on international supply chains and by extension into our professional and personal lives.

One could write a similar survey on how ecologically damaging business practices within the "basic rules of society" contribute to the destruction of the earth's environment and the threatening of human survival. In *The Outlaw Ocean*, Ian Urbina (2019) has written extensively on the environmental devastation arising from the routine practices of diverse contemporary businesses that work at sea. These include the continuing butchery of the planet's whales, the environmental devastation caused by bottom trawling, the damage caused by the oil and gas industries, the risks arising from the destruction, "bleaching", of the world's corals, as well as the routine and brutal enslavement of seafarers, particularly fishermen, on the world's ships and trawlers.

Urbina traces many of these abuses to the "tragedy of the commons": because the world's oceans are the responsibility of all nations, no nations take responsibility. Similarly, because all nations are responsible for global warming, few nations, until now at least, have been prepared to lead even as has become clear that the world is heading towards a planet threatening increase in temperature with time running out to halt the devastation.

Given these, Friedman's assertion that the only moral responsibility for business executives is to maximise profits within these "basic rules" sounds woefully glib. In effect he urges business leaders not to bother themselves about abuses that may be going on around them and be beneficial to their profit margins. If society wanted this to be otherwise, then governments should have written and implemented better laws to make it so. That some businesses may be actively advocating to governments that they should refrain from more robust legislation does not seem to have entered into Friedman's simplistic world view.

Rather than moral guidance Friedman only offers a template for moral cowardice, and a very weak template at that. For example, if an international business executive encounters a clash between the requirements of international conventions on child labour, and the prospect of cheap production costs in a garment facility that adheres to local law that does not recognise these international standards and gleefully employs and exploits child labourers, which laws should they stay within? Friedman's banal advice to maximise shareholder value within the law provides little moral guidance in circumstances such as these.

Ruminating further on the prospect of future trade deals for "Global Britain" with countries with poor human rights standards Dominic Raab suggested, "We don't junk whole relationships because we've got issues – we have a conversation because we want to change the behaviour". Perhaps. But business undertaken with those who are exploiting or abusing others as a central function of their enterprises or economies provide incentive that such practices should continue and helps embed such practices deeper in the political economy.

Further, recall the epigram, sometimes attributed to the 19th century theorist of war, Clausewitz, that to wage war, one needs only three things: money, money and money. Business undertaken with undemocratic and violent regimes or factions, such as UNITA in the late 20th century, or Saudi Arabia in the early 2020s, provides those regimes with the means to kill and repress, as the horrifying realities of the war in Yemen demonstrate (Human Rights Watch, 2020) So a bland denial of moral responsibility when contemplating such trading relationships can lead directly to the financing of the sinews of war and repression.

Rule of law and ethical practice

Similar to the idea of "basic rules of society" John Rawls (1993) posited the idea of the "basic structure" of society – the institutional arrangements of politics, law, economics and the family that provide the "background conditions against which the actions of individuals and associations take place". Rawls' idea is similar to that of political economy. But whatever way you put it, it is clear that the diverse basic structures of the world's societies and nations are variable in how well they empower and protect individuals within those basic structures.

Tom Bingham (2010), a former Master of the Rolls, Lord Chief Justice, and Law Lord in the United Kingdom, demonstrated in his book of the same name that rule of law is a concept fundamental to the basic structure of any tolerably functioning society.

Bingham noted that legal scholars trace the concept of rule of law back to Aristotle, who said, "It is better for the law to rule than one of the citizens". However, I would argue that the concept is apparent, at least in nascent form, in Sophocles' *Oedipus the King* written a century earlier. In this the king realises, as his own investigation finds that it is he himself who is responsible for the plague on Thebes, that he must be held accountable, just as anyone else would have been, even though he is still the king.

This ideal of accountability is fundamental to the concept of rule of law, even if a diverse array of some 21st-century leaders of ostensible democracies, from the United States, to the United Kingdom, to Hungary, Turkey, India and Brazil have sought to act as though the rules are only for those without their power.

So, given the centrality of accountability to the concept of rule of law, it is plain to see that Friedman's ethical guidance particularly in the contemporary world, is anathema to the concept of rule of law. It repudiates accountability for many of the consequences of the choices managers make in the name of profit maximisation.

Bingham's principles of rule of law resonate further with Rawls' principles of justice. For example, Rawls' first principle states that "Each person is to have an equal right to the most extensive total system of equal basic liberties compatible with a similar system of liberty for all". This is echoed in Bingham's third principle, "The laws of the land should apply equally to all, save to the extent that objective differences justify differentiation".

Rawls second principle states that "Social and economic inequalities are to be arranged so that they are . . . to the greatest benefits of the least advantaged . . . "; Bingham's fifth principle, that the law must protect fundamental human rights, provides a measure of guidance on how this may be advanced.

So, if business dealings are based, for example as discussed earlier,[2] on slavery, in contravention of article 4 of the Universal Declaration of Human Rights, as the trade in blood diamonds was, or as significant parts of contemporary garment manufacture are, then it cannot be said that the economic inequalities are arranged to the greatest benefit of the least advantaged. Quite the contrary in fact. Business and political leaders who are availing of what economic opportunities may exist in the inequalities and injustices that such systems offer may therefore be identified as undermining fundamental principles of rule of law.

This setting out by Bingham of principles underpinning rule of law was aimed at bringing up to date the Victorian era formulation of the concept, which he summarises as: all persons and authorities within the state, whether public or private, should be bound by and entitled to the benefit of laws publicly made, taking effect (generally) in the future and publicly administered in the courts.

Unfortunately, Bingham's more comprehensive and updated formulation of the concept is still not comprehensive. In particular it fails to consider the challenges posed by the reality of deterritorialising transnational corporations, or international businesses with extensive supply chains beyond the business' national base and into a globalised political economy.

For example, transnational corporations can change their country of incorporation to more favourable legal and regulatory environments. This is often done for reasonable business purposes, such as obtaining better access to financing. But this phenomenon is indicative of the capacity of transnational businesses to operate beyond the control of any given state. In other words, the classical economic belief that individual states should regulate business activities is becoming increasingly impractical.

Further it is a simple step to consider how such practices could be used to evade independent arbitration of disputes, another of Bingham's fundamental principles. For example, this could be achieved by a business changing country of

---

2 See the section "The political economies of exploitation" in this chapter.

incorporation to countries where simply the cost or delay associated with bringing a dispute to court might render it less likely to be brought.

Bingham noted various impediments to the application of law in general and international law in particular. For example, the impediment of delay is particularly accentuated in international law regarding the holding of states to account because of the overwork of otherwise effective courts, such as the European Court of Human Rights. However, I would argue impediments on access to justice as it relates to international corporations is further exacerbated. In addition to a laissez-faire ideology towards business regulation among many national politicians, consideration of how to hold deterritorialising transnational corporations to international legal account is a major lacuna in jurisprudence. This is demonstrated by Bingham's limited treatment of the question, in an otherwise admirably thorough and accessible consideration of the meaning of rule of law.

So the simplistic notion that business executives, particularly those working in international business, have only to consider profits and "the law" as their sole ethical guide is nonsense: for transnational business, operating beyond much current international legal thinking, between states and in countries where rule of law is absent, it can be said in a very real way both satisfactory legislative guidance and the rule of law itself simply does not exist.

Moral exemplars in business

Yet it is unquestionably the case that many, if not enough, business leaders do much more than the minimum that Friedman desires of them. In the United Kingdom the inclusion in the 2015 Modern Slavery Act of a Transparency in Supply Chain Clause, requiring by law that businesses set out publicly what they are doing to eliminate slavery from their supply chains, was directly consequent of British business lobbying government for this legislation. Those of us from a nongovernmental background who had been seeking the same from government had, until that point, been routinely dismissed.

Also in response to contemporary slavery, in 2020 a group of London insurers introduced "a new marine cargo clause for the London Market that is designed to keep the products of modern slavery out of the export supply chain" (Sheehan, 2020). And the garment retailer, ASOS, working with the international trade union, IndustriALL, the Mauritius trade union Confédération des Travailleurs des Secteurs Publique et Privé (CTSP) and Anti-Slavery International, helped establish a Migrant Resource Centre, "through which workers are able to file complaints and grievances about their working conditions in a way that doesn't put them at risk of repercussions from their employers" (ASOS, 2021). This is a significant human rights initiative in a country where the exploitation of migrant workers is facilitated by a tied visa system similar to *kafalah*.

By taking such measures, these businesses can legitimately be said to be advancing rule of law through the upholding of human rights standards.

Elsewhere, Ray Anderson[3] demonstrated how a business can lead on environmental restoration. And in the course of writing this book[4] I had direct experience of working with a group of garment retail business members of the UK Ethical Trading Initiative, as we struggled to find ways to uphold ethical standards in the face of the crackdown of Myanmar's military dictatorship on its own people.

The actions of business executives who lead in such ways are, intrinsically, repudiations of Friedman. It is also clear that their efforts to act morally when faced with such challenges draws upon a more sophisticated ethical code than the sophistry offered by Friedman. This begins with a conception of responsibilities to a much wider group of stakeholders in addition to shareholders.

Responsibilities to stakeholders

The stakeholder view of the firm emerged in the 1960s at Stanford Research Institute (Stoney and Winstanley, 2001) where academics argued that, in addition to shareholders, businesses depended on, and hence needed to be responsible to, a range of stakeholders without whom the organisation would cease to exist.

The stakeholder perspective on business has the advantage of providing an altogether more realistic description of the environment in which leaders operate than Friedman's rather blinkered focus on money. Stakeholder theory recognises that leadership is in significant part about exercising judgement between competing groups and priorities. It is not a mechanistic process of generating cash, but rather about, for example, negotiating with suppliers, organising workers, engaging with customers, attending to regulations. The stakeholder approach is also fundamental to leadership in the not-for-profit and public sectors, whose purposes are, generally, spending money to obtain the well-being of others or transformation of society rather than the generation of profits.

The term stakeholder theory was popularised by Freeman (2000), who went on to distinguish between a wide and narrow definition of stakeholders: "The 'narrow definition' includes those groups who are vital to the survival and success of the corporation. The 'wide definition' includes any group or individual who can affect or is affected by the corporation" (Freeman and Liedtka, 1991). One key departure that this introduced, compared with classical economics, was the idea of the "triple bottom line". That is the idea that businesses must satisfy environmental and social objectives as well as economic ones, and that those environmental and social

---

3 See Chapter 5.
4 See Chapter 7.

objectives are important in their own right and need not be justified in economic terms (Stormer, 2003).

As Stoney and Winstanley (2001) put it, "Thus a clear and fundamental juxtaposition was made between serving the needs of shareholders through dividend maximisation and servicing the needs of a wider constituency of stakeholders: as Hirschman (1970) put it, between the economic and political view of the firm" (p. 604).

Post (2003) contrasts impacts of the Friedmanite shareholder, and stakeholder views of the firm as follows:

> Shareholder theory allows management to ignore the interests of other constituencies while pursuing its own narrow self-interest under the guise (the ethical façade) of promoting the interests of the shareholder owners. The Shareholder Theory does not provide any realistic counterweight against management abuse. The Enron example strengthens the arguments for the use of Stakeholder theory and exposes the utter failure of Shareholder Theory. (p. 57)

This is perhaps putting the potential for good inherent in stakeholder theory a bit too strongly. Stoney and Winstanley note that stakeholder theory can be used simply for analysis without necessarily prescribing a course of action. Indeed, stakeholder theory, as Humber (2002) points out, lacks any explicit moral core. So, two firms sincerely using stakeholder theory when considering the same set of stakeholders can come to completely different decisions depending on the "normative" moral basis these use in conjunction with the stakeholder approach. For example, two stakeholder-oriented firms may be contracted to build two factories on the edge of the same city. On discovering that the construction would threaten a species of endangered frog, firm X, using Kantianism as its moral basis, which judges the breaking of promises as always wrong, and regarding frogs as outside the moral community, fulfils its contract. Firm Y, using ecological principles as its normative core break their contract rather than breaking what they regard as their moral duty to care for the earth.

Further this logic suggests that, shorn of any imperative to fulfil a specific moral core, the insight provided to an unscrupulous agent by knowledge of stakeholder theory could be used to manipulate the perceptions and expectations of various stakeholder groups towards the agent's selfish interest. Indeed, one might regard Machiavelli's *The Prince* as a handbook for such selfish stakeholder manipulation.

More neutrally, Kapelus (2002) notes that there are sometimes positive business benefits from socially responsible stakeholder management: otherwise the stakeholders can impose costs on the business. For example, ill-treated workers may strike. If they cannot impose costs, for whatever reason, there is no economic case for being socially responsible.

This clear-sighted observation is worth bearing in mind because it indicates the limits of benign self-interest and acknowledges that sometimes firms may be starkly faced with the opportunity for doing well by doing bad as so many of the examples cited, of contemporary slavery and environmental devastation, demonstrate.

Adopting a stakeholder perspective on leadership usefully complicates the question of what managers' ethical responsibilities towards the diverse stakeholders are. From the perspective of "economics-based" business ethics Friedman argues that managers should not refrain from profitable investments that satisfy all legal constraints but do not conform to managers' own personal social agenda. In other words, just because a manager might be personally troubled by the thought of making handsome profits by sourcing goods from a factory that uses abused child labour and environmentally damaging work practices, does not mean that they should refrain from doing so: their responsibility to shareholders are, after all, in Friedman's view, paramount.

However, with an approach to ethics that emerges from a stakeholder perspective a leader must be concerned with appropriate behaviour regarding the totality of the complex web of relationships, between both individuals and collectives that interweave their organisation and society. In other words, a stakeholder perspective on management responsibilities at least recognises that in business decision-making there should be some discussion of the interests of child labourers and questions of ecological sustainability.

So, for example, it may have been perfectly legal, and profitable, for De Beers to have purchased UNITA sourced diamonds in Zambia (Global Witness, 1998) and indeed imperative under Friedman's articulation of the economic view of the firm. However, with a political view of the firm insisting on consideration of the impact on those stakeholders who are affected by corporate decisions, and knowing that revenues paid by the company would be used to finance war and terrorism against civilian populations, the question of what the manager's responsibilities are becomes much more complex. Which stakeholder interests should they privilege and why? Certainly, they have responsibility towards shareholders for profit maximisation, but is this a greater moral obligation than one to attempt to deny terrorists the means to murder?

This is the "polycentric character" of business ethics decision-making (Jackson, 2000), which highlights the diverse and often divergent demands of different stakeholder groups of the business. Resolving one set of issues regarding one set of stakeholders may have unpredictable consequences for the rest of the groups. And, as Gonzalez (2002) notes, while stakeholder theory indicates to whom the corporation is responsible it does not indicate what the corporation is responsible for, or to what extent.

Some moral guidance for international business

The UN Guiding Principles on Business and Human Rights go some way to try to address this lack of a moral core in stakeholder theory. Broadly, these principles assert that states have the responsibility to *protect* the human rights of workers, businesses have the responsibility to *respect* the human rights of workers, and both have the responsibility to ensure remedy and remediation of any rights violations. John Ruggie, the author of the principles, argued that international businesses should then be held to legal account by increasing national extraterritorial law. So ideally it should be possible for a European business engaged in slavery-like practices in Saudi Arabia to be held accountable in a European Court.

Unfortunately, legislation lags behind this ideal, and international businesses will often operate in countries where rule of law is at best an aspiration. For example, Wrong (2009) describes in some detail a business environment in Kenya where corruption was not only tolerated by the nation's elected political leadership but required by them. The worldwide financial near collapse of 2008 was the result in large part of the unsustainable business practices that grew up in a deliberately unregulated financial sector. In both these instances adherence to the spirit and letter of Friedman's rule alone can be argued as having had devastating consequences for many ordinary people, ranging from increased unemployment to, as Wrong points out in the case of Kenya, increased levels of infant mortality.

Given these realities, leaders in business or other organisations adopting a position which says, in effect, this is not my problem, threatens disaster for everyone on the planet as opportunities for environmental restoration or protection of human rights are foresworn because they fall outside of the blinkered perspective on moral responsibility encouraged by Friedman's morally bankrupt approach.

Put another way, in a world in which there is such limited rule of law and so many corporate entities operate beyond what limits do actually exist, then the implementation of basic principles, such as respect for the Universal Declaration of Human Rights becomes a matter of personal conscience and moral courage.

Conclusion

As noted in Chapter 1, a central purpose of this book is to outline elements of a moral code for leaders. Such a code, drawing on principles of human rights and rule of law, could then be used in conjunction with stakeholder theory to better guide ethical leadership in the face of complex challenges by indicating what leaders should be responsible for as well as towards whom.

Friedman, of course, suggests leaders should not trouble themselves with such questions. The truth of the matter is that if one wants to evade the responsibilities implicit in the admonishments to uphold human rights or environmental standards, then it is unlikely that there will be many personal consequences, at least in the short term.

So, again in the short term – and there is only short term left if ecological collapse is to be avoided – if standards of human rights and environmental restoration are to be advanced, then this will depend on professionals and citizens of conscience taking leadership in the recasting of the planet's political economies.

Such leadership will be, of necessity, in response to, and in the context of the existing political economies within which individuals live and work. This begs the question as to what is the extent of an individual's capacity to make a difference to the social world.

There is a long debate in the realms of moral philosophy as to whether individuals can even make real choices in the first place or whether what we do is determined by forces more powerful than ourselves and beyond either our control or our full understanding.

Some capacity for free moral choice is a prerequisite for an individual to become an ethical leader. So, in the next chapter we will explore this philosophical debate around free will in some more detail and consider how it has shaped understanding of social scientific studies of business malpractices.

Points for reflection
- Which of the various ethical guidances described in this chapter have you encountered?
- What is your opinion of each of these: Friedman's exclusive focus on the shareholder; the stakeholder view of the firm; the UN Guiding Principles on Business and Human Rights?
- How would you describe the moral code that you used to guide your professional choices?
- Can you describe any tensions you have felt between your personal moral values and some of the choices you are required to make at work?

Chapter 3
Philosophers: What do they know?

> No such thing as innocent bystanding.
> – from "Mycenae Lookout: Cassandra", by Seamus Heaney

> In which . . . the author takes the reader on a gentle excursion into the realms of moral philosophy, in particular the "free will versus determinism" debate, which is at the heart of moral decision-making, and explores how that echoes in social science studies which try to explain organisational malfeasance and other unethical behaviour. He finds this literature somewhat unsatisfactory in its tendency to blame either systems or individuals for malfeasance without fully understanding how the two actually interact.

Introduction

Why "good" people do "bad" things is a question that has particularly vexed researchers since the Second World War. The question of how ordinary people could be induced to atrocity under the Nazis remains a particularly troubling one. Milgram (1992) with his "electric shock experiments" explored individuals' tendencies to carry out harmful activities at the behest of perceived "legitimate" authority. Lantane and Darley (1968) explored the bystander effect and diffusion of moral responsibility in large or anonymising groups. Haney, Banks and Zimbardo (1973) with the infamous "Stanford prison experiment" explored the effects of situational influences on individuals' destructive behaviour (Zimbardo, 2007).

The work of these social psychology researchers has echoed in more recent works of history, for example, Michael Bilton and Kevin Sim on My Lai (1992), and particularly illuminatingly Christopher Browning (2001) on a SS murder squad in Eastern Poland during the Second World War. Both these bodies of social science and historical research pose a haunting question to their reader, specifically, "What would you do if you found yourself in the same circumstances?"

Browning, explicitly drawing on the prior social psychological research of Milgram and Zimbardo, notes starkly that anyone who has not experienced such situations and says that they certainly would not behave in the murderous ways he describes simply does not know what they are talking about. Browning argues that while there is a minority who will happily indulge in sadistic behaviour and another minority who will refuse to collaborate with anything harmful to other human beings, the majority will follow the instructions of authority figures and conform to the group.

Browning's, Bilton and Sim's, Milgram's, and Zimbardo's work, among others, indicates that a variety of social processes including *diffusion of responsibility*, *peer pressure* and *obedience to legitimate authority* will influence the majority of any group in any given social situation to behave in certain, sometimes deeply distressing and evil, ways.

However, we know, also from Browning, Bilton and Sim, Milgram and Zimbardo, that against the vast majority who succumb to the social pressures bearing on them in the situations they describe there is an enduring minority who refuses to follow immoral orders or to comply with group norms towards atrocity.

This begs one of the questions that is at the core of this book: What is it that distinguishes the decision-making of these dissenting minorities from the complying majorities? Or put another way: *How do some people resist the social pressures and instead chart their own moral course?* Why does one person become a Stauffenberg[1] or a Schindler,[2] for example, and another becomes a Speer?[3]

Even the smallest of organisations is a complex social phenomenon, rife with relationships and politics. Such complexity expands with size and is overlaid with yet more complexity as organisations engage with markets and political economies. Hence, the social processes identified by the social psychologists briefly discussed above will be at play in the decision-making of senior and junior executives in the way they pursue their enterprises, be they private sector businesses, public sector, civil society or military.

However, it is a core assumption of this book that even if so much of what we do in groups is determined by social processes that this does not absolve us of the moral responsibility for externally influenced actions, irrespective of what Friedman suggests. But this begs a further question: *What are the moral responsibilities of professional leaders towards other human beings and the environment?* Or, put another way, what should be the moral core that guides our engagement with our various stakeholders?

Warnock and Magee (1987) have noted that for morality to have any meaning it presumes that, "There must be some area, some space, however narrow, in which we can exercise our own discretion. For if there is not – if it is never true to say that we could have acted otherwise than we did – any attempt at moral evaluation is empty and meaningless."

So, before getting to the question of what the moral obligations of professional leaders are, it is first necessary to understand the nature of this "narrow space" in which we can exercise our discretion to chart our own moral course.

---

[1] Claus von Stauffenberg was the military leader of the attempted coup against Adolf Hitler in July 1944.
[2] Oskar Schindler was a German industrialist whose rescuing efforts saved the lives of over 4,000 Jews during the Second World War.
[3] Albert Speer was Hitler's armaments minister.

Freedom versus determinism

Generally, we experience our own daily existences as a sequence of decisions, both trivial and significant, which we believe we make freely. However Browning's argument is that we cannot know the extent and nature of our own personal free will when we encounter particular social pressures in unfamiliar social situations, and that it is probably less than we expect.

That lay people cannot know this perhaps should not be surprising as philosophers have been arguing this question for hundreds of years. Edwards (1965) notes that philosophers have proposed three possible answers to the question: Which is true, determinism – the idea that all events, including human actions are ultimately the result of causes external to free will – or freedom?

There are philosophers such as Holbach who accept determinism and reject freedom, reasoning that all the objective, scientific evidence favours determinism, and that human intuition of freedom is merely illusory. This was a conclusion which Tolstoy famously favoured, regaling the readers of *War and Peace* with what he regarded as incontrovertible evidence as to why this is so: Bonaparte, for example, may have believed that he commanded an army at Borodino. But by the time any of his orders reached their intended destinations the circumstances that prompted them would have changed to the extent as rendering his orders obsolete. So, the battle was fought, as far as Tolstoy is concerned, without the slightest influence of Bonaparte on its course.

Second there are those philosophers who believe that determinism is not compatible with freedom and moral responsibility, and hence reject determinism. They argue that immediate experience, such as the experience of freedom, is more certain than a complicated theory such as determinism.

Finally, there are those philosophers who argue that both freedom and determinism are true and that the appearance of conflict between the two is deceptive. Edwards argues that this view is given its classic statement by Hume and Mills, and that their main idea is that when we call an action "free" in ordinary life, we never mean *uncaused*. Rather it is meant that the agent was not coerced and was acting in accordance with their own unimpeded rational desires.

The philosophical perspectives that recognise the interplay between personal choice and social pressure in decision-making seem to me broadly supported by my own personal experience of life, including working professionally as a leader. That is, while individual's actions may be caused by external factors, that individual may have some significant choice on how they respond to those externalities. Irrespective of what Tolstoy reckons about human powerlessness in the face of grand historical and cosmic forces, we often see diverse choices from people faced with the same or similar situations, and differences in choices can lead to different outcomes. For example, when faced with the appalling orders to murder civilians some of the SS unit that Browning studied simply refused to participate despite these orders and pressure from their peers.

This suggests that while the social world may both formulate the moral dilemmas that confront individuals and strongly influence the consequent decisions, *it does not determine* the ways in which individuals in such settings tend to act.

Illuminating moral philosophy with social science

The classical philosophical approach of a lone genius, such as Kant, armed only with a cup of coffee, wrestling with the knottiest of moral problems and then presenting dazzling arguments to the world certainly has helped advance human understanding in significant ways. However, this brings with it a danger of over-reliance on personal reflection for discerning answers to difficult questions of moral philosophy when those questions are themselves rendered infinitely more difficult by the variability and diversity of their manifestation in the social world. Any attempt by me to explore the questions of moral responsibility arising from the extent of human free will based solely on my personal reflections on its practical and theoretical aspects would bring the risk that it will relate only to myself and my limited experiences and maybe to a few people with similar beliefs or going through similar situations.

If we wish to have a deeper understanding of the extent and limit of human freedom in any social context that poses dilemmas about which individuals must make moral choices, then it may be advantageous to consider that issue in relation to a diversity of human beings making a range of ethical choices.

This is a social scientific approach rather than a classical philosophical one. So, if we are going to use this approach to explore the question of the relationship between individual freedom and personal responsibility and their implications for ethical leadership, then it is perhaps worthwhile first exploring what social scientists have been saying about these issues in the environment in which most leaders lead: the world of work and the wider political economy that shapes how work is conducted.

Why do good people do bad things? It's determinism stupid!

Referring to a 1960 scandal in Pennsylvania when seven electrical equipment manufacturers received prison sentences for a "widespread price fixing and bid rigging conspiracy" Waters (1978) discussed the puzzle as to how and why otherwise admirable and moral individuals became involved in such reprehensible activities.

As indicated, the findings of Milgram, Zimbardo, and Lantane and Darley are profoundly important to modern society in providing particular insight into the risks associated in giving individuals power, particularly coercive power, over others with limited constraints on its use.

The experiences that these researchers describe often may seem far removed from the everyday lives of most professional leaders. This remoteness may deceive many into the comforting fallacy that the research insight has nothing to do with the power and decision-making associated with their professional practice. Consequently, with rare exceptions, there has been very little explicit consideration of the insights from social psychology research in the literature on corporate social responsibility.

For this reason the sort of empirical research undertaken by Waters is significant. Consciously or unconsciously he places the uncomfortable questions of Zimbardo, Milgram Lantane and Darley, and Browning – why do ordinary people do harmful things to other people or acquiesce in its happening? – in a context that is immediately more recognisable to an important section of society that has considerable power over others – business executives.

Waters' (1978) conclusion to his own question was that the blame for illegal and unethical practices fell not on individuals, with the exception of CEOs, but on an "atmosphere" in which "ethical considerations take a back seat to profit considerations, and organizational blocks . . . inhibit whistle blowing".

This is, in terms of the philosophy, a rather deterministic perspective on the reasons for corporate malfeasance. Indeed, some might feel that this is letting individual managers off the hook. As noted, Zimbardo, Milgram, and Browning all showed that some refuse to indulge in harmful behaviour irrespective of the organisational "atmosphere".

Jones (1991) argues that the degree *of moral intensity* of an issue is itself a feature in the decision of individuals to engage in unethical practice. So, stealing a paper clip from work is unlikely to have the same moral implications as purloining food intended for a grey-haired little old lady and her starving grandchildren.

Jones, echoing Zimbardo et al., also recognises that there are organisational factors, such as group dynamics, authority factors and socialisation processes that affect individual moral decision making, as well as questions of the individual's own moral development.

However, as Milgram, for example, demonstrates the relative ease with which individuals can be pushed by authority figures into the most atrocious of actions against other human beings suggests that the moral intensity of an action need not prove an insurmountable obstacle to determined leaders intent on achieving organisational malfeasance. Indeed Milgram's work along with Zimbardo's suggests, very worryingly, that abuse of power, and the acquiescence in such abuse by those subject to it, may be the natural tendency of the vast majority of individuals. This means that any sort of leadership in the opposite direction may be something of an uphill struggle, particularly when the work of Darley and Lantane (1968) is considered, which demonstrates the dislike of humans to stand out in a crowd.

Why do good people do bad things? Maybe it's just bad people?

VanSandt and Neck (2003) are more inclined to place the responsibility for corporate behaviour with individuals. They start from the observation that a review of literature indicates that, "the most generally accepted concept is that the individual within the organisation is the moral agent, but the firm exerts 'significant influence' on ethical behaviour within its boundaries" (p. 366). VanSandt and Neck use Jones' (1991) definition of "moral agents" as "a person who makes a moral decision, even though he or she may not recognize that moral issues are at stake" (p. 367).

As you will recall from the discussion of philosophical ideas earlier,[4] this perspective very much echoes what Edwards argues is the classic statement by Hume and Mills, that when we call an action "free" we do not mean uncaused. Rather it is meant that the agent was not coerced and was acting in accordance with their own unimpeded rational desires in response to the external environment.

VanSandt and Neck outline a number of reasons why there might be ethical gaps – "defined . . . as the lack of moral guidance from the organization to the individual, resulting in unethical behaviour" (p. 365) in businesses. Firstly the "combination of individualistic ideologies and lack of group cohesion . . . indicate that there is a potentially large divergence between a corporate ethical climate . . . and employees personal moral codes . . . both Lewin and Durkheim noted the need for group cohesion to bring about value change and to build morality" (p. 367). Which is of course all well and good if the group pressure is towards moral behaviour, but as Haney, Banks and Zimbardo (1973), Chikudate (2002), Waters (1978), and indeed Maas' (1974) account of the New York City Police Department of the 1960s in *Serpico*, indicate group pressure can also lead to erosion of individual moral positions.

"The second possible cause of ethical gaps is a result of the wording, often deliberately ambiguous, of the code of ethics" (p. 367) – allowing for different interpretations across an organisation. They also note that codes of ethics tend to be focused on protection of the business from the illegal or unethical behaviours of employees rather than the community from the corporation; that the size of some corporations may lead to communication breakdowns on standards of ethical conduct; and there may be a significant discrepancy between what is conveyed in ethics codes and what is communicated in norms values and rewards.

VanSandt and Neck's list has the advantage of being thorough, but the disadvantage of not being thoroughly empirically tested to determine the relative importance of the causal factors. They do seem to intuit that the issue of leadership is important, but their solution is rather glib, suggesting that "self-leadership" should bridge the gap. In the final analysis they come down on the side of this as the principal cause and potential solution to corporate malpractice.

---

4 See the section "Freedom versus determinism" in this chapter.

VanSandt and Neck miss important insights from Milgram, Zimbardo and Browning – that while a few individuals have a capacity to conceive alternative courses of action for themselves, despite overwhelming social pressures to the contrary, most seem to lack this capacity in many circumstances. As Trevino and Brown (2004), drawing on the work of Lawrence Kohlberg and others, have argued, the majority of adults are not fully formed when it comes to ethics and are not autonomous moral agents, but rather reside in an earlier stage of moral development some way short of making their ethical decisions based on principles of justice and rights.[5]

However, if "self-leadership" – in other words "human agency" – is the presumed answer, are we all actually clear on what that actually is? This is a question we will focus on in the next chapter.

In the meantime, Cragg and Greenbaum's (2002) empirically based discussion of one aspect of an organisation's approach to a fundamental social performance issue – identifying responsibility to stakeholders – begins to hint at how individuals justify to themselves their moral inertia even when faced with quite contentious issues.

Cragg and Greenbaum note that in analysing interviews with individuals in a mining company "we found instrumental reasoning about responsibilities, values and the interests of other stakeholders built around a single core value 'getting on with the job', to be pervasive" (p. 326).

Cragg and Greenbaum note that this focus on "'getting on with the job' is an instrumentality without content – pure means without an end" (p. 330). It allowed managers interviewed to represent themselves

> not as making ethical decisions but acting in pursuit of organizational objectives in an environment of impersonal constraints. By arguing not in terms of what the company ought to do but rather what it had to do in order to get on with the job, the management team was able to articulate value positions while avoiding an overt choice between ethical values marked by social, environmental or economic consideration on the one hand and business considerations conventionally construed on the other. (pp. 332–333)

In other words, the managers they interviewed were adept at identifying difficult ethical issues to be "not their problems" because their "problem" was "getting the job done", presumably maximising profits for shareholders within the law: the classical Friedmanite excuse for evading moral responsibility. Put another way, this

---

5 Kohlberg outlines five stages of moral development, from childhood: 1) preconventionally aimed principally at punishment avoidance; 2) getting a fair deal in exchange relationships; 3) conformity to the expectations of significant others; 4) conformity to the expectations of society's rules and laws as key influences, along with significant others, on deciding what is right; and 5) ethical decisions guided by principles of justice and rights.

perspective provided them with a narrative that allowed them to evade moral responsibility for the very decisions they themselves were making.

Darley and Lantane's work on "diffusion of responsibility" suggests another reason for the sort of evasions of moral responsibility that Cragg and Greenbaum describe. The awareness that they are acting as a collective allows the managers they interviewed to reassure themselves that their causal responsibility for anything that was happening was lessened, and indeed, to a certain extent they were mere participants in an inevitable process.

Mellema (2003) introduces the idea of "ethical distance". This suggests that there is less moral responsibility, and perhaps more importantly *felt* moral responsibility, if the causal involvement that an individual has in an unethical situation is obscured. This is a particularly pertinent point in a globalising political economy, where leaders in Dublin or Berlin could conceivably make devastating decisions for the lives and livelihoods of workers in supply chains that stretch into Yangon or Dhaka. Yet their actual physical distance from the consequences of their choices would help lessen the burden to their consciences: it would forever be unlikely that they would be confronted with the moral consequences of their choices.

Why can't everybody just be nice?

As demonstrated, notably by Milgram and Zimbardo, it is clear that individuals look to leaders and peers to determine standards of behaviour. So, it is not inevitable that the powers they describe should be used only to advance the approach of maximising profits for shareholders within the law, or beyond it if the temptation grabs them. If leaders make more life-affirming choices in their organisations, attempting to uphold human rights standards and environmental sustainability, for example, then they have the potential of reshaping a whole or a part of an organisation in a way that becomes more self-sustaining as peers within communities of practice begin to influence each other in the same direction.

Jones (1999) hypothesises a mechanism that may help reverse the glib dismissal of moral responsibility that Cragg and Greenbaum's mine managers describe. Jones suggests that if the discourse of social responsibility is prominent in the "sociocultural system" in which an enterprise is occurring then the incidence of stakeholder management – direct engagement, for example, with the workers or communities affected by the enterprise – will be higher. The opposite is therefore also possible: that if the "sociocultural system" privileges negative stereotypes of particular groups – migrants, for example, or disadvantaged groups such as Dalits in South Asia – then one may expect less constructive or benign engagement with them. This echoes with Zimbardo's discussions of social pressures to conform.

In other words, the nature of what Jones calls the "discursive space" will influence the choices of leaders. Again, this idea echoes with those of philosophers such as Hume and Mills, that posit an interaction between the personal and the social in decision making. This may be positive, encouraging more environmentally sustainable and socially conscious decision-making if everyone in an organisation is discussing the importance of these ideas. Or it may be highly negative, for example, prioritising profits from pesticide sales in the developing world rather than incur the costs of safety measures irrespective of the evidence of the needless and widespread loss of life that the pesticide is causing (Gillam, 2021). If, the carnage is occurring in the global South, thousands of miles away from where the manufacturers have their homes and jobs, then the "ethical distance" would help ensure that ideas of moral responsibility for any harm do not encroach on the "discursive space".

Jones notes how, with time, the discursive space can shift, noting how rights initially restricted to white men on the adoption of the US constitution in 1789 have been expanded to include women and blacks over the subsequent 200 years. As even the most cursory student of history will be aware this was the result of long and bloody struggle requiring a lot of people to stand up, stick out and often be cut down in the process of asserting their rights.

So, if part of ethical leadership is changing the discursive space towards one that prioritises life-affirming values over exploitative ones, then protest must be recognised explicitly as an act of leadership. In other words, even when a leader does not hold all the levers of power their assertion of different values, of dissent from the prevailing wisdom or *taken-for-grantedness* of a situation, can help to transform the situation.

All of this brings us back to VanSandt and Neck's idea that "self-leadership" matters in organisations and other social situations. This allows individuals to plot approaches towards more life-affirming choices towards those affected by their decisions by recognising that they have a role in the way the world is structured, and they can use this role to reduce environmental destruction and social injustice.

So, why would an individual act in this, more life-affirming way to demonstrate ethical leadership when all the other pressures may be to the contrary? This is a critical question as the urgency to find solutions to saving the planet from ecological collapse mounts.

Conclusion

The public and academic debates that have been provoked by recurrent business scandals, which seek to obtain explanations for and insights into corporate malfeasance, tend to fall towards two polarities of explanation. There are those, such as Waters (1978), who emphasise the primacy of institutions in their explanations of what drives corporate malfeasance: these can be classed as the ones that tend towards deterministic explanations. On the other hand, there are those who emphasise the primacy of individual responsibility.

Whittington (1989) argues that each of these positions presumes to explain the nature of "agency" – the human capacity for free choice – either by extending or restricting its conception. Hence neither approach can provide a satisfactory explanatory basis for human choice. Social psychological experiments suggest that deterministic explanations may have a particular cogency in predicting *tendencies* in groups towards particular types of behaviour in given circumstances, including under the influence of particular leadership approaches. However, such experiments do not predict who will behave in a given way, nor do they explain why the dissenting minority behaved differently to those who acquiesce in the will of the majority.

So rather than gravitate to either of these polarities it is important to recognise, as Whittington argues, that there is an interplay of individual and institutional factors that result in any given set of choices. Taken as a whole, that is what the literature surveyed in this chapter also suggests.

So, if leaders or policy makers wish to encourage particular ethical practices by their organisations and their staff, it is important to understand just how these individual and institutional factors interplay when individuals resist social pressures towards the negative, and instead chart their own independent moral courses, particularly when they follow a life-affirming path rather than a more exploitative or destructive one.

Indeed, given that changing the world starts with changing ourselves, it is perhaps most important for leaders to understand how these individual and social factors interplay in themselves if they wish to better understand the factors that will affect their own choice-making when they finally encounter that "moment of truth" in their career.

In other words, we must understand more clearly what exactly we mean by "human agency" – our own individual capacity to make free choices when confronted by challenges from our professional environments or the rest of the social world. This is the heart of the matter that we will turn to in the next chapter.

Points for reflection
- What constrains or enables your freedom of choice in your professional environment?
- Have you ever done something you thought was wrong, or failed to do something you thought was right, because of instructions from superiors or social pressures from colleagues?
- How do you feel about that now?
- Have you done anything different in your life or work because of such experiences?

Chapter 4
The Cruciform of Agency

> We do not display greatness by going to one extreme, but in touching both at once, and filling all the intervening space.
> – Blaise Pascal

> In which . . . to lead ethically professionals must understand the scope and basis of their discretion to choose. This understanding is not obtained from the extremes of free will or deterministic explanations, but rather from a synthesis of the two that more realistically describes how individuals actually interact with the social world in their decision-making. This more realistic description is set out in the "Cruciform of Agency", which emphasises the importance of personal moral values in human agency.

Introduction

In her extraordinary book on the South African Truth Commission, *Country of My Skull* (1999), the South African poet and journalist Antjie Krog recounts a moment of respite from the daily grind of reporting atrocities, at a poetry conference at the old slave fort of Goree in Senegal. She describes asking a question of a panel of Senegalese poets: "In my culture you are a good poet if you can say old things in a new way. We have been saying 'I love you but you don't notice me' for centuries. The 'newer' the way you say it the better poet you are. In the culture of Senegal, what makes you a good poet?" (p. 336).

One poet, from a nomadic community replied, "In my culture the task of the poet is to remember the watering places . . . the day you betray the position of the waterholes to someone else, that is they day they will leave the poet behind in the dunes" (p. 336).

In other words, the particular social milieu in which we find ourselves constrains the nature of our choices in quite radical ways. But it does not define them. There is always at least some human agency available, that narrow space for our own discretion, as Warnock and Magee put it. So, for example, a nomadic poet leading his community to a rare Sahelian spring, might also choose to compose a sonnet for their lover as they walk. Or a South African writer might learn to be a wilderness guide while they wait for greater recognition of their crime novel.

However, in search of an agreed meaning of the term "human agency" it is, perhaps, as easy to get lost in the literature on the subject as it is if seeking water in the Senegalese desert. This is because the meaning of "human agency" is a contested one, with arguments on the subject tracing their roots into both the debates on free will and determinism, and in allied questions relating to the nature of reality and consciousness.[1]

In other words, this is where things get a bit complicated for a while. But we've got this far so stick with it.

Human agency is a complex subject so it is not at all unreasonable that there are different perspectives on it. However, some write of "agency" meaning quite different things to others who use the same term, often not acknowledging that different perspectives exist. So let me be clear: it is the human capacity for choice-making in the social world that I am concerned with when I use the term "agency". That is not quite what others mean when they use the term "agency", but this is *my* book.

The previous chapters have described that various writers in philosophy and the social sciences have emphasised individual and social factors at play in choice-making. In this chapter I will focus on two contributions to the literature on human agency that deal with these aspects and then go on to discuss how these ideas themselves may interact.

First though, recognising these social and individual aspects of agency, it will be useful to distinguish between *ideas* and *thoughts* (Archer, 2003). Thoughts are those things that float around our heads, capable of being known only to the thinker. Ideas however have an objectivity to them: they are animated through word or deed in the material world. This book, for example, translates my thoughts into ideas which others can then think about. Or, we can see that various historians have presented ideas about why Hannibal did not storm Rome when he had the opportunity (e.g., Goldsworthy, 2006), but Hannibal's own thoughts on the subject remain an enduring historical mystery.

So, ideas are available to others to think about and discuss, but thoughts are wholly private. However, in giving voice to a personal *thought* a human being creates a social *idea*. Consequently, it becomes open to interpretation, misinterpretation and reinterpretation by others.

The social world is created by a mixture of ideas and things: Hannibal's Italian campaign, for example, had a strategy to overthrow Rome and a load of elephants. In the case of Cragg and Greenbaum's mines the idea of "getting the job" done and the extractive machinery for doing it formed central aspects of their corner of the social world.

It is into such social worlds that we as individual humans enter, with our own thoughts on life the universe and everything. Some of these thoughts may be at odds with other prevailing ideas – Roman commanders, such as Fabius, thought

---

[1] As a point of information, the core ontological assumption of this book, that is the idea regarding the nature of reality that is foundational to this book, is that of a "subjective reality of thought". That is, one's own personal thoughts are real things, composed in your own head and knowable only to the thinker. This might seem obvious to the reader, but it is a contested idea that gives rise to some of the divergent opinions on what agency actually is.

the overthrow of Rome not a good idea – and it is in these competing thoughts and the ideas that emerge from them that the seeds of change can lurk.

Got that?

Okay. Over the next three sections of this chapter I will construct a new model of human agency – the Cruciform of Agency – that recognises explicitly its social and individual aspects. I will do this by drawing on the work of Emirbayer and Mische (1998) who focussed on the social aspects of human agency, and on the work of Margaret Archer (2003) who focussed on its individual aspects. These two sets of ideas provide important insights. However, neither are complete.

A more complete model arises when these two sets of ideas are recognised as complementary. This recognition produces the model of the "Cruciform of Agency" and with that sets out a clearer understanding of the interplay of free will and determinism. In other words, the Cruciform of Agency provides a fuller description of that narrow space of our own discretion. This helps us better understand how some individuals plot their own moral courses while so many others are merely following the mob into some very dark places.

Social aspects of human agency

Emirbayer and Mische (1998) define agency as "the temporally constructed engagement by actors . . . which, through the interplay of habit, imagination, and judgement, both reproduces and transforms . . . in interactive response to the problems posed by the changing historical situations" (p. 970). More succinctly, the social aspects of agency relate to *ideas* about *the past, present and future* that influence the choices of those individuals caught up in them.

Generally, Emirbayer and Mische indicate, this past aspect of agency, "the routinised reproduction of past habits and practices" may gain primacy. Therefore, the things that make up traditions, cultures, customs and accepted ways or behaviours tend to endure relatively unchanging with time. Part of the reason for this is individuals' *selective attention,* or ability to only focus on a very small part of the social world at any one time. For example, in a given office environment in which we have our own demanding work goals to achieve, we may choose not to expend precious time and energy on changing practices that would otherwise irk us, such as formal dress codes, meeting protocols or somewhat inefficient organisational arrangements.

This human tendency towards continuity of the past into the present is accentuated by what Emirbayer and Mische call *categorical location,* that is the interpretation of experiences in terms of relationships between people and contexts defined by identities and values. So, the *ideas* relating to the roles of poets, for example, that Antjie Krog discovered in Senegal are deeply rooted in cultural contexts and individuals' identities.

However, things never quite remain static and that is because the social aspects of agency also include a "projective element", which, simply put, relates to ideas about the future. Sitting by a desert oasis, a West African poet, for example, may be inspired by the great Senegalese singer Youssou N'Dour so perhaps begin to experiment with his compositions beyond the traditional.

Strategy processes in organisations are formal ways for thinking about the future and these can lead to government departments, businesses, armies and non-governmental organisations alike forming new approaches for themselves and different ways of working. Individuals can also transform their lives through imagining different futures for themselves. Paul McGrath, for example, described how, as a black child in Irish social care, he imagined if he played more football he would become bigger and so get beaten up less often.[2]

However, bear in mind that the discursive space, that opportunity for new social ideas and personal thoughts to take root, mentioned earlier,[3] is shaped itself by existing ideas that form the culture and context in which new thoughts are formed and different ideas allowed to take root. So, if the membership of a leadership group all come from a similar social and economic background with shared cultural frameworks and assumptions this can constrain different ideas from emerging in that community unless they also recognise their lack of diversity as a weakness that they act to remedy.

Sometimes limiting the range of ideas of the future under consideration may be useful – a publisher's business model may be undermined if all its lyric poets decamp to the Sahara to be wilderness guides. But it can also have less happy outcomes. Communities that tell their kids to know their place and not dream of a better future for themselves crush not just individual hopes but also huge quantities of social potential. Or, in an era of rapid global warming, a continued reliance by an industrialised nation on fossil fuels, because that is what has always been done and they're comfortable with it, may well spell doom, quite literally, for people living precarious lives and much more vulnerable to the negative effects of global warming.

In other words, belief in determinism can become a self-fulfilling prophesy: if you think there is no point in imagining a different future for yourself or your organisation because of the external environment in which you find yourself then you remove your free will from the process and your future will be determined by that external environment.

In the end, both for individuals in their personal lives and leaders in their social roles, it is the "practical-evaluative element" – their exercise of judgement in the present-oriented aspect of agency – that decides how past practices and future strategies will be synthesised. Leaders will know from experience that judgement

---

[2] See the film, *Finding Jack Charlton*, 2020.
[3] See Chapter 3.

between competing ideas and stakeholder groups is a central part of their function. Here Emirbayer and Mische state it is central to their conception of agency as well.

As Emirbayer and Mische describe it, this aspect of agency "entails the capacity of actors to make practical and normative judgements among alternative possible trajectories of action in response to the emerging demands, dilemmas and ambiguities of presently evolving situations" (p. 971). For example, in setting strategy for an organisation a leader must consider the resources and competences that it has gathered from its past experiences against where the organisation imagines it may like to go in the future and make decisions in the present based on their best judgement of what will achieve that envisioned future.

This echoes individual choice-making in personal life: For example, Paul McGrath, having become a good footballer, realised at some point that it was possible for him to imagine a professional career and success beyond social care, even if the *thought* that this could lead him to becoming a national hero may still have seemed implausible to him.

Clearly the "emerging demands, dilemma and ambiguities of presently evolving situations" increase exponentially as social structural complexity increases. The social world is not a homogeneous one. Rather it is a mosaic of different instances of organisation, community, tradition and society, with which individuals interact, occasionally conflicting and competing with each other, for example, over scarce resources or competing visions of the future. Choices made in response to these situations of conflict or complexity can consciously or unconsciously change the ideas which animate different aspects of the social world.

Giddens (1984) used the term "penetration" to describe the depth of understanding that an individual may have of the social circumstances in which they find themselves. He suggests the greater degree of "penetration" the greater manoeuvrability of choice that individual may have, personally or as a leader. Greater "penetration" enables individuals to identify a wider range of options arising from a larger pool of ideas and resources that make up the social world around them.

But Emirbayer and Mische's conceptualisation of past, present and future aspects of agency and their observations on the human tendency towards continuity of the past means that efforts towards change are often likely to be met with less than whole-hearted enthusiasm. This is again something that leaders will naturally understand from their experience: Change can be hard, particularly when it conflicts with cherished traditions and comfortable practices.

The private self

Emirbayer and Mische raise the idea that "the point of origin of agentic possibilities . . . must reside one level down (so to speak), at the level of self-dynamics" (p. 974).

In other words, the point of origin for individual choice-making in any given social context lies in the thoughts of the individuals who participate in that social context.

Archer (2003) argues that "the self-dynamic aspects of agency are exercised through the 'internal conversation' . . . the modality through which reflexivity towards self, society and the relationship between them is exercised" (p. 9).

Let us pause for a moment to consider the word "reflexivity": this is the process of thinking about our own thoughts and the social ideas we encounter. Remember that. It comes in useful.

So, what Archer is saying is, in essence, reflexive deliberation is when we talk to ourselves about ourselves, the society we find ourselves in, and the relationship between the two.

Archer argues that there are two main topics of reflexive deliberation – planning for the future and evaluating the past. So, she describes the internal conversation as a process by which an individual reflexively considers herself in the present ("I") with reference to her past "me" and the possibility of the future "you" – who she may become or how she may change depending on decisions taken by the present "I". Archer describes the "me" as " . . . a summation of the past, which provides us with an orientation to the future, from its deposition in the present" (p. 72). She associates the "me", or the *critical self*, with the individual's conscience.

She notes that, " . . . through inner dialogue we prioritise our 'ultimate concerns', with which we identify ourselves. Simultaneously, we accommodate other, ineluctable concerns to a subordinate status with an overall modus vivendi, which we deem worthy of living out and also one with which we think we can live" (p. 32). So, in talking to ourselves we decide what we believe and how we engage with the world.

As an individual lives the accumulation of memories and experiences increases and influences the present internal conversation accordingly. Archer conceptualises the process as shown in Figure 4.1.

Figure 4.1 illustrates Archer's "internal conversation" with the present "I" always the dialogical self, mediating between the past "me" (M) which develops with time and experience, and the future "you" (Y). As Archer puts it, "I am my own and only interlocutor" (p. 111), alternating as subject and object, reflecting upon utterances we know to be our own.

The Cruciform of Agency

In consideration of temporal concerns Archer echoes Emirbayer and Mische. Clearly, as both Archer's and Emirbayer and Mische's discussions of agency demonstrate, contemplation of both the personal and social – *thoughts* and *ideas* – are fundamental in individuals deciding the way they are going to act: Plainly for any particular period of time, it is highly improbable that the present "I" will conduct an internal dialogue in complete isolation from the social world – what would there be to talk to

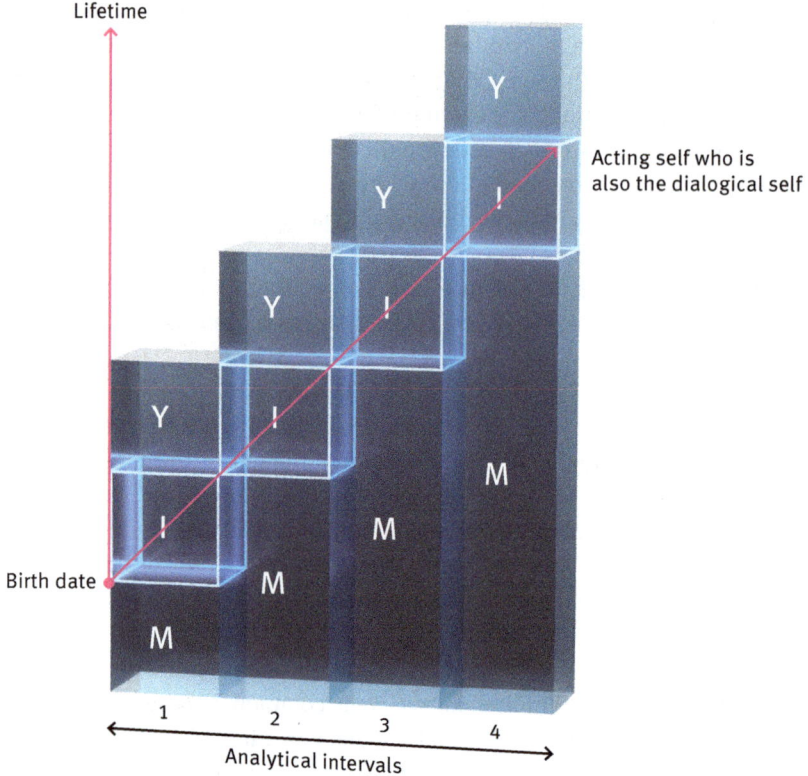

Figure 4.1: Archer's "internal conversation".

yourself about? Explicitly recognising this point adds further insight into the nature of agency.

So, if a social phenomenon is considered as being composed of a set of ideas relating to the past, present and future of that phenomenon, as described by Emirbayer and Mische, then this may be graphically represented as shown in Figure 4.2.

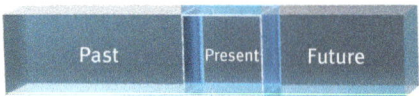

Figure 4.2: The ideas that compose a social phenomenon.

One moment of agentic reflexivity relates, as Emirbayer and Mische point out, to an individual forming their thoughts relating to these aspects of the social world which is the constraining and enabling context of human action and individual choice.

On the other hand, a domain of personal thought at any given instant in an individual's life may be graphically represented in Figure 4.3.

Figure 4.3: Thinking: The wholly subjective, reflexive self.

This second moment of reflexivity may be thought of as the consideration by the present self ("I") of the beliefs and values that an individual has accrued through life (me, "M") along with the resulting hopes and ambitions for the future (you, "Y") arising from her personal biography up to that point in time.

Combining these two moments of reflexivity we can see an individual's reflexive deliberation on choices arises from their contemplation of wholly personal thoughts, of substantially social ideas and of the interaction between the two. This may be represented graphically in Figure 4.4.

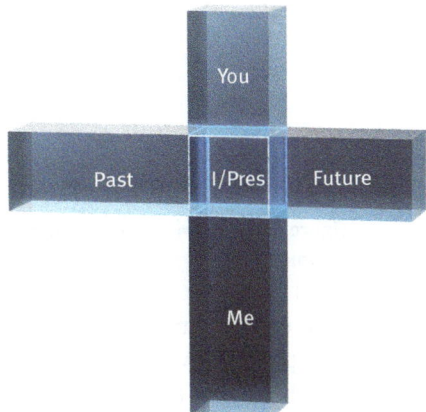

Figure 4.4: The "Cruciform of Agency": The reflexive individual in the social world.

In this model the reflexive individual considers her own life in relation to the exigencies of the social phenomenon encountered and, vice versa, considers the social phenomenon in relation to her life. It is by considering both personal thoughts and the social ideas encountered that an individual – the "I" in the "Present" – makes her judgements and choices, both in personal life and as a leader.

At any given instant in time an individual will be engaged in a plurality of social situations, and hence social conversations. These would include social conversations relating to ideas of work, family life, sports, politics and other interests. Consequently, there would also be internal conversations regarding personal thoughts on each of these social phenomena as well as social conversations regarding the ideas pertaining to other social phenomena, for example, the pillow talk of two lovers – Rick and Ilse maybe – may sometimes relate to their worries and concerns about their professional lives; Rick may also discuss the tumult of his love life with his chess partner Louis who he meets weekly for a game.

So, a more complete model of agency should be three dimensional, with the social portion of the model occupied by a range of social engagements intersecting with the present experience of the "I". A simplified version of this, considering only two contemporaneous social engagements is presented in Figure 4.5.

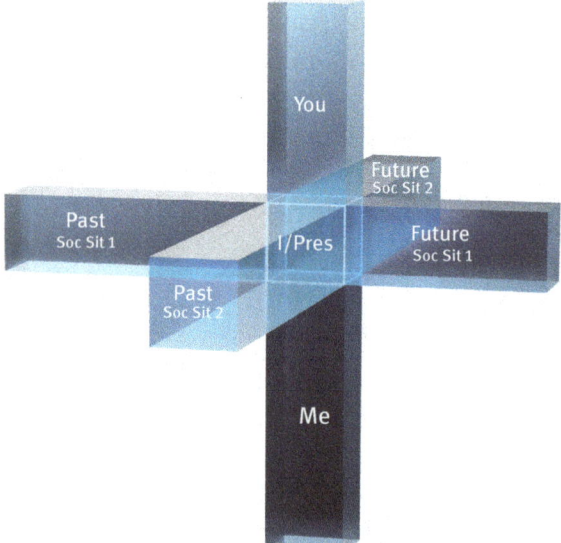

Figure 4.5: Human agency in social complexity.

Already it can be seen from this diagram how choice can expand and be facilitated with social complexity. For example, in a work situation, suppose Rick is feeling social pressure, to conform to corrupt practices in his business, betraying the professional trust of Victor, a former colleague. He could decide to acquiesce, taking the path of least resistance and harmonise himself to that social situation, privileging perpetuation of the past by conforming to the taken for granted practices of corruption. That is what everyone else seems to be doing after all. Milgram, and Darley and Lantane suggest this to be the most common occurrence. As Emirbayer and Mische point out people have selective attention and rarely consider multiple wider issues leading to a tendency to ensure continuity of the past into the future.

Alternatively, Rick may assess the situation against a personal code of morality, remembering the things he once fought for, and find the situation unacceptable and refuse to conform. Again, he may imagine his future "you" in jail if he conforms and is caught, or, more hopefully maybe, living in Mediterranean luxury off the proceeds of that corruption. However, while he may find this work situation personally and socially acceptable, he may then assess it against an alternative social framework: "What would that nice woman, Ilse, who I've just started seeing again, say if she knew I was engaging in these corrupt practices at work, so at odds with who I once was?" This may lead him to accept disharmonious relationships professionally, or maybe go off looking for another job like the one his pal Louis suggested, to preserve the integrity of his relationship with his lover.

In this instance of a conflicted individual, then the conversations that Rick privileges, whether social or personal/internal, will be decisive in resolving which choices he makes, and the moral course he charts. This in turn is dependent on the values he has determined for himself in his conscience up to that point during his life: does he value the esteem of a woman and his past business ideals more than the gratitude of corrupt colleagues and the material wealth this would bring. In this instance the problemisation of the situation itself is a product of the individual's beliefs, values and hopes for the future.

Implications of the Cruciform of Agency

The literature regarding human choice highlights that there are individual aspects to it, and social ones. The "degree of penetration" (Giddens, 1984) – the depth of understanding of their social context – that an individual obtains may increase their agency by making them aware of a wider range of possible choices from the social circumstances in which they find themselves. Hence, it is good to be informed. However social scientific research, particularly Milgram, Zimbardo and Lantane and Darley, indicates that most people will conform with what everyone else is doing in a particular context, whether that context is personal or professional.

Nevertheless, it is also clear that some do not just go with the flow, particularly if a situation causes a particular dissonance with a person's private thoughts and values. This leads to an evolution of Hume and Mills view that free action means that an agent was not coerced and was acting in accordance with their own unimpeded rational desires. "Free action" also means that, even if coerced or otherwise pressured, individuals can choose in accordance with their deepest personal values different moral courses to those upon which others are embarking. Some individuals pay a high price for such choices. Others change the world.

In other words, individuals who conceive of different or dissenting choices in a particular situation will demonstrate that they are considering the choices posed to them in both personal and social terms. It is this assessment of choices against cherished values, rather than because they are solely possessed of some penetrative insight regarding their material "best interests" in a particular context, that guides them to chart alternative moral courses.

This choice-making process must occur in the "present/I" portion of the Cruciform – the practical-evaluative element of agency. So, for greater clarity we should recognise that the exercise of judgement relating to choosing a course of action at the core of the Cruciform of Agency, should follow the generic structure of: Reflexive deliberation on the social and the personal in interaction → Reflexive conclusion on options in that situation →Choice of course of action. This is represented in Figure 4.6.

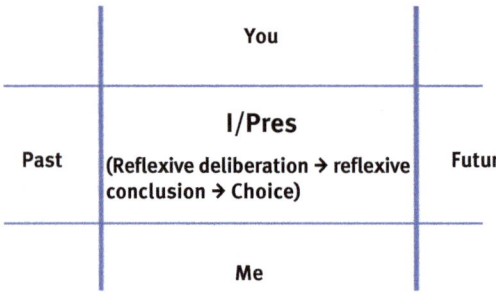

Figure 4.6: Exercising judgement at the heart of the Cruciform of Agency.

The Cruciform of Agency recognises that there are individual and social aspects of agency and indicates how they interact. So, individuals may account for dissenting from a community, professional or personal, by reference to a wholly personal set of values or hopes or with reference to other social relationships.

If the Cruciform of Agency reflects the way that individuals think about making choices, then we should anticipate this would be reflected in the ways in which individuals describe their choice-making.

For example, an individual may express the personal reasons for a particular choice in terms of a deliberation on the current situation against a more valued set of beliefs, or of *hypothetical resolution* (Emirbayer and Mische, 1998) where the individual expresses distaste for the *future* social or personal situation that would arise if a particular course of action were followed.

Alternatively, dissent might arise because an individual is privileging one social relationship over another, maintaining a relationship with an idealistic lover, for example, rather than acquiescing with corrupt practices in a toxic workplace. Perhaps we could term this phenomenon of "redemption through love" as the "*Casablanca* effect"? But just because it's a powerful romantic archetype doesn't necessarily mean that it is not true.

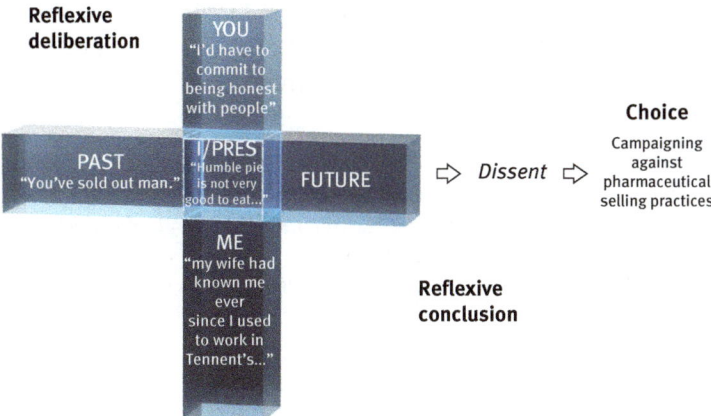

Figure 4.7: Dr Lynam faces the error of his ways.

For example, during my PhD research I met Dr Lynam,[4] a prominent campaigner against pharmaceutical companies' selling practices. He had previously worked with, and enjoyed working with such companies, savouring the travel and the luxuries that this work brought.

But he described having a conversation one afternoon with his wife which was key to him changing his position (see Figure 4.7):

> I've been married for a long time and my wife had known me ever since I used to work in Tennent's [pub] across the way and I was some sort of radical young member of the Labour party, stupid hair-cut and you know . . . and she looks at me and says "look how you've become, you've sold out man, you're just a pawn", and that's – Humble pie's not very good to eat but it does you some good and I suppose it made me realise it's true and it tends to reconnect you with what you actually think's important. Because you do get kind of lost don't you, in the pressure, it's very easy to lose your sense of perspective and so as part of my penance I think I decided I'd have to commit to being honest with people, telling what I've experienced and what I know is going on and use it to try and change the situation.

The next chapter will explore some further accounts of choice-making for such evidence. If we were to focus on accounts of people who have done what everyone else is doing, then we may see evidence in those accounts of strong *resonance* between their beliefs and the practices with which they were involved. Or we may see little thought about social practices and their bearing on personal values or hopes: their social context may simply be taken for granted.

However, the focus of this book is on ethical leadership: the assertion of life-affirming choices even when the social pressures are to the contrary. This is one of the greatest challenges in any leadership situation. So, the next chapter will look at

---

4 This and all names of doctors in this chapter are pseudonyms.

some specific examples of individuals who have endeavoured to do this at the "moment of truth" and explore, from the perspective of the Cruciform of Agency what we can learn of the principles of ethical leadership from these cases.

> **Points for reflection**
> - Do you recognise the interplay of social and personal factors in your decision-making?
> - Between social pressures and personal moral values, which tend to dominate when you make professional choices or choices as a private citizen?
> - Are there some circumstances when your personal values would trump social factors in decision-making or vice-versa?

Chapter 5
Exploring some narratives of moral choice

> Coming in sight of Wades Mill in Hertfordshire, I sat down disconsolate on the turf by the roadside and held my horse. Here a thought came into my mind, that if the contents of [my] Essay [on slavery] were true, it was time some person should set these calamities to their end.
> – Thomas Clarkson, quoted in *Bury the Chains*, by Adam Hotschild

In which . . . the author shows that the Cruciform of Agency describes how real leaders from diverse backgrounds made some fundamental moral choices in their careers. These show that ethical leadership is not only about how rules are made and resources allocated. It is also about dissent and protesting to create discursive space within which new ideas can be broached and fostered.

Introduction

The Cruciform of Agency indicates that *reflexive deliberations* in individual accounts of conscious choices should show consideration of both social ideas (past, present and future-oriented ones composing the situation that confronts the individual with a choice) and personal thoughts, particularly those relating to moral values and hopes.

As the preceding chapters indicate, leaders will often encounter difficult and complex ethical issues that can have major impacts on the lives and livelihoods of others. While a majority may simply conform with what everyone else is doing, a few *dissent* from the majority and assert different moral ideals.

Sometimes these dissidents reshape a situation to such an extent that their initial marginalised or minority position becomes a majority one or at least more mainstream. For example, the ideals of human rights, democracy and rule of law that are now at the core of the concept of the European Union were bloodily suppressed across much of the continent for large parts of the 20th century.

While the ideals of the *dissidents* to European totalitarianism may be mainstream now, they are still anathema amongst some strands of European thought. Moral courage is undoubtedly required of those with whom these ideals still *resonate* to enable them to assert these life-affirming ideals in the face of more cynical challenge. However, for the purpose of this chapter we will focus on some initially minority *dissident* accounts and examine them for evidence of reflexive deliberation in line with the Cruciform of Agency, and choice-making in relation to personal hopes and values. These will then be considered for more general lessons regarding ethical leadership.

Executive on a mission: Saving the planet

In a 2007 *New York Times* profile (Dean, 2007), Ray Anderson describes a "conversion experience" occurring in the summer of 1994, "when he was asked to give the sales force at Interface, the carpet tile company he founded, some talking points about the company's approach to the environment".

"That's simple", the *New York Times* quoted Anderson as thinking: "We comply with the law".

But, as the *New York Times* went on to note, "as a sales tool, 'compliance' lacked inspirational verve". So, he started reading about environmental issues, and thinking about them, until pretty soon it hit him: "I was running a company that was plundering the earth . . . . I thought, 'Damn, some day people like me will be put in jail!'" . . . "It was a spear in the chest."

The *New York Times* describes that,

> instead of environmental regulation, he devoted his speech to his newfound vision of polluted air, overflowing landfills, depleted aquifers and used-up resources. Only one institution was powerful enough and pervasive enough to turn these problems around, he told his colleagues, and it was the institution that was causing them in the first place: "Business. Industry. People like us. Us!"
>
> He challenged his colleagues to set a deadline for Interface to become a "restorative enterprise", a sustainable operation that takes nothing out of the earth that cannot be recycled or quickly regenerated, and that does no harm to the biosphere.

Considering Anderson's decision-making against the Cruciform of Agency we can see that his deliberative processes engaged with both social ideas and personal thoughts (see Figure 5.1).

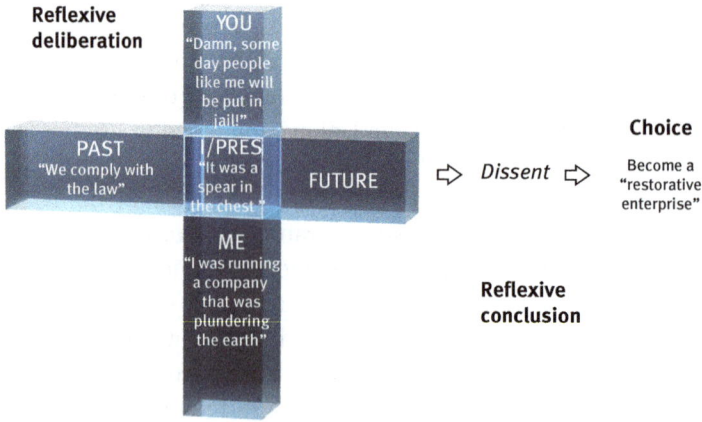

Figure 5.1: Mr Anderson decides to try to save the world.

The deadline they ultimately set to become a "restorative enterprise" was 2020.

In describing the moment of realisation of what his business was doing to the environment as a "spear in the chest" Anderson described an emotional reaction that prompted his subsequent strategic choices. Again, we see how a leadership choice emerged not from a coolly rational appraisal of interests but from a much more visceral impulse arising from personal values.

By 2007 the *New York Times* profile observed that Anderson's idea had "taken hold throughout the company . . . in the process, Mr Anderson has turned into perhaps the leading corporate evangelist for sustainability". In other words, Anderson had created the discursive space in his company for others to participate in developing new responses to the environmental challenges he had raised.

But in addition to the changes Anderson made in his own enterprise he also endeavoured to change the wider political economy by creating greater discursive space around the imperatives of environmental restoration in the wider manufacturing sector. He did this by raising his own voice in protest against industry damage to the environment.

In 2009 he announced (Mason, 2011) that

> his company was 60% of the way to achieving the target. InterfaceFLOR had reduced its water use by 75% since 1996, cut greenhouse gas emissions by 44%, and dropped energy use by 43%. It also switched to using 100% renewable electricity at its sites in Europe and made 36% of its products from recycled content, up from 0.5% in 1996. And it managed to eradicate any petroleum from the fabrication of its products.

Speaking to the *New York Times* in 2007 Anderson acknowledged that he had certain advantages in getting his ideas transformed into company action. He was, after all, CEO and controlled most of the business' voting stock. He was also able to demonstrate that for his business "sustainability 'doesn't cost, it pays' – in customer loyalty, employee spirit and hard cash".

In these points Anderson was referencing the social processes that underpin the direction of organisation: legitimate authority of the leader; the opening of discursive space for subordinates to develop new ideas to advance the environmental objectives that the leader was setting; and then validation of this new approach by the commercial benefits it brought.

So, paradoxically, ethical leadership means transforming into a life-affirming direction the same social processes that once led to atrocities in Eastern Poland during the Second World War described by Browning, or those at My Lai described by Bilton and Sim.

The conscience of the Colonel

The 2021 film, *The Mauritanian*, tells the story of Mohamedou Ould Slahi, a Mauritanian national captured by the United States and imprisoned in Guantanamo Bay on suspicion of involvement in the September 11, 2001 attacks on the United States.

Lt Col V. Stuart Couch, a US Marine Corps pilot and lawyer was assigned to prosecute Slahi, in a case that he anticipated would seek the death penalty. Couch was personally motivated: his friend, Michael Horrocks, was co-pilot on United 175, the second plane to strike the World Trade Centre.

In a 2007 *Wall Street Journal* article, The Conscience of the Colonel (Bravin, 2007), Couch was quoted as saying that he wanted "to get a crack at the guys who attacked the United States. I wanted to do what I could do with the skill set that I had."

Slahi had been identified as a key figure in the September 11 attacks by Ramzi Binalshibh, an al Qaeda operative captured in Pakistan. According to the *Wall Street Journal*, "He [Binalshibh] told the CIA that in 1999, Mr. Slahi sent him and three future 9/11 [attackers] . . . from Germany to Pakistan, and then to al Qaeda headquarters in Afghanistan. There, according to the 9/11 Commission, Mr. bin Laden assigned them to the 9/11 operation."

After initial interrogations in Mauritania and Jordan, Slahi was moved to Guantanamo Bay in Cuba where his interrogations continued. He consistently denied involvement in the attacks on the United States until late 2003 when Slahi suddenly started corroborating Binalshibh's allegations. Couch described Slahi's confessions as "like a 'Who's Who' of al Qaeda in Germany and all of Europe".

Initially Couch had no idea why Slahi had changed his story. But then he began to hear of the "varsity program", "an informal name for the Special Interrogation Plan authorized by the then defence secretary Donald Rumsfeld". Investigating this further Couch concluded that what had prompted Slahi's confessions was that he had been subjected to a sustained process of torture including isolation, extreme temperatures, beatings, sexual humiliation and simulated drownings. According to the *Wall Street Journal* "On Aug. 2, an interrogation chief visited [Slahi and gave him] . . . a forged memorandum indicating that Mr Slahi's mother was being shipped to Guantanamo and that officials had concerns about her safety as the only woman amid hundreds of male prisoners . . .".

The *Wall Street Journal* reported the climax of Couch's moral crisis:

> By May 2004, Col Couch had most of the picture relating to Mr. Slahi's treatment, and faced a painful dilemma: Could he seek a conviction based on statements he thought were taken through torture, as permitted by President Bush's November 2001 military commission order citing a "state of emergency?" Or was he nonetheless bound by the Torture Convention, which bars using statements taken "as a result of torture . . . as evidence in any proceedings".

Mary Lowth (2017) writing in the *British Journal of General Practice* notes that, "Interrogation by torture relies on an assumption that fear, stress, and pain 'break' suspects into delivering useful information", and asks the question, "Yet, aside from the overpowering moral, ethical, and legal arguments against it, does torture work?"

Citing research by Shane O'Mara, professor of experimental brain research at Trinity College, Dublin, Lowth noted, "that there is probably no technique for creating pain that will induce a well-prepared individual to reveal information before going into shock or a dissociative state. Torture makes confession more likely, but such confessions are unreliable: false confessions are easy to elicit."

Doubtless with these concerns in mind, "In May 2004, attending a baptism at Virginia's Falls Church, Col Couch joined the congregation in reciting the liturgy. The reading concluded, as is typical, with the priest asking if congregants will 'respect the dignity of every human being'."

> "When I heard that, I knew I gotta get off the fence", Col Couch says. "Here was somebody I felt was connected to 9/11, but in our zeal to get information, we had compromised our ability to prosecute him". He says, in retrospect, the tipping point came with the forged letter about Mr. Slahi's mother. "For me, that was just, enough is enough. I had seen enough, I had heard enough, I had read enough. I said: That's it."
>
> In May 2004, at a meeting with the then-chief prosecutor, Army Col Bob Swann, Col Couch dropped his bombshell. He told Col Swann that in addition to legal reasons, he was "morally opposed" to the interrogation techniques "and for that reason alone refused to participate in [the Slahi] prosecution in any manner".

From the perspective of the Cruciform of Agency, with Col Couch as the individual at the centre of a social process relating to the capture, interrogation and prosecution of suspects in the course of a war: In this case the past weighs heavily on all the US individuals concerns, particularly, perhaps, Couch himself remembering the loss of his friend in the September 11 atrocities.

The patterns of action and behaviour that had been established in response to those events provide the context of his decision. This context is a process aimed at obtaining in the immediate future retribution on supposed perpetrators of the attacks, something Couch himself admits that he favoured. Nevertheless, in his own personal conscience Couch maintained a belief in rule of law and, with that, the implicit need both for dependable evidence and to uphold treaty obligations under the Torture Convention. In addition, his Christian faith led him to a belief in the need to maintain "respect for the dignity of every human being". These beliefs required Couch to take the morally courageous position of *dissenting* from the processes seeking to prosecute Slahi based on tainted evidence (see Figure 5.2).

From Couch's account it is clear that he was less acting in accordance with his own "unimpeded rational desires" as philosophers such as Hume and Mills have theorised human agency, and much more in accordance with his own profoundly held values. This led him to take the morally courageous path of protesting an immoral prosecution.

As noted earlier, protest is also leadership. It is protest that ultimately extends the discursive space for others to think new and different thoughts, to claim their rights and dignity as human beings, and to give voice to different ideas. Couch's articulation of a conviction that justice is not co-equivalent to random retribution was a powerful assertion of the ideals of rule of law, most particularly the upholding of the

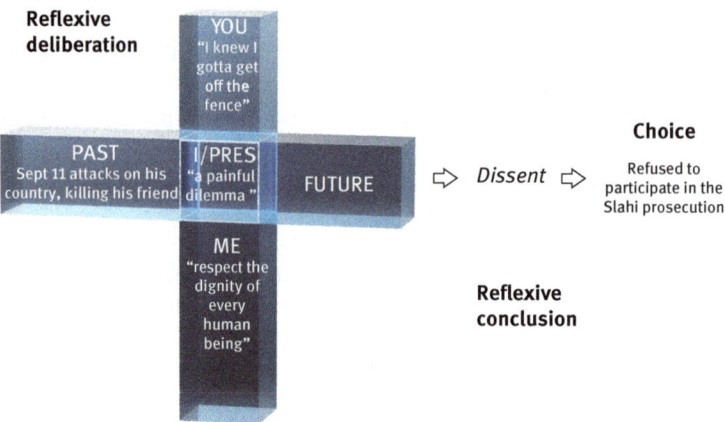

Figure 5.2: The cruciform of Col Couch's deliberation.

dignity of human life. In essence he repudiated Cicero's aphorism that "In times of war the laws fall silent".

"You can't eat a flag"

One of my earliest memories is watching a neighbour being shot. Another was of almost being caught, while on my way to primary school, in a culvert bomb attack launched by the IRA on the British Army. The brother of a classmate was "shot trying to escape" by a unit of the British Army's Special Air Service (SAS). A few years ago, I discovered that a bunch of "Loyalist" paramilitaries had planned to massacre the children and staff of my Belleeks primary school. Fortunately for all of us, this was called off. Some war crimes were even too much for the war criminals of the North of Ireland.

I repeat these brushes with violence not to suggest that I am special in any way, but because these were typical life experiences for people living in the North of Ireland during the 1970s and 1980s. Indeed, I was very lucky: my family was notably unscathed by the squalid little war that engulfed the North.

At the height of the bloody "Troubles", as this conflict from 1969 to 1998 in the North of Ireland was known, the political scientist Richard Rose wrote, "Many talk about a solutions to Ulster's political problem but few are prepared to say what the problem is. The reason is simple. The problem is that there is no solution" (O'Malley, 1983).

It is true that much of the intractability of the conflict in the North of Ireland arose from the deeply entrenched nature of political and religious sectarianism in the very structure of the state. But John Hume didn't agree that there was no solution. Over a political career that spanned four decades, Hume became famous for his "single transferrable speech". A former teacher he knew the value of repetition to instil the rules of French grammar or elements of the history curriculum into even the most obdurate of skulls. So, in politics he decided to keep repeating his beliefs on what was needed to obtain peace until enough got the message to make it happen.

One anecdote that he often told got to the heart of what motivated him:

> I never forget my first political lesson when I was 10 years old. The Nationalist Party were holding an election meeting at the top of the street and waving their flags. And my father who was unemployed saw that I was getting emotional too. He put his hand on my shoulder. He says: don't get involved in that stuff, son. I said why not, da? He says, "You can't eat a flag". Think of the wisdom of that, that real politics shouldn't be about waving flags. It should be about developing the standard of living of all sections of your people. And that's common ground because both sections need that. And now our people have started working together through their representatives, spilling their sweat not their blood. And I look forward. That is what I call the healing process, as they work together, break down the barriers of the past, the distrust of the past. And a new society in Ireland, north and south, will evolve. But it will not give victory to either side It will be based on agreement and respect for difference.

Considering this statement, just one in a long life devoted to nonviolent political struggle, we can again see the interplay of personal beliefs and values with the social ideas that formed the conflict in the society that he grew up in.

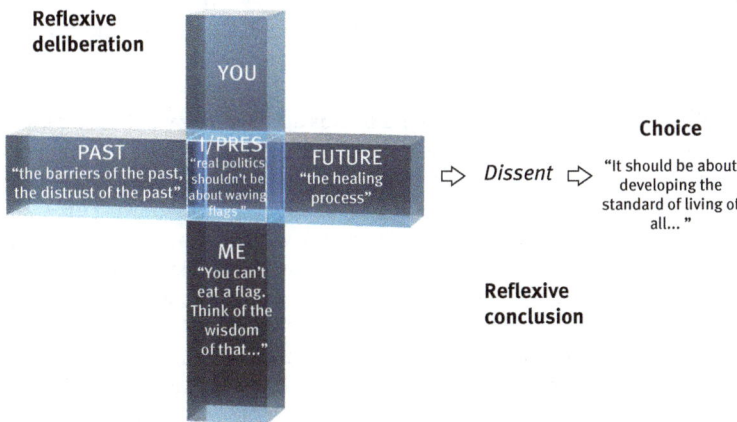

Figure 5.3: John Hume gets sick of flags.

In this statement Hume describes his initially positive emotional reaction to the flag waving and sloganeering (see Figure 5.3). But this was put into perspective by his father's clear-sighted observation. That this resonated with him to such an extent that he spoke of it until the end of his life indicates not just that he was impressed by the rational logic of his father's comments and how they spoke to their direct experience of poverty, but that he valued it because of the love he held for his father. Again, this demonstrates that much agency, particularly the plotting of a divergent moral course from those surrounding an individual emerges from personal values born of hard experience not simply cerebral calculation.

Hume's commitment to practical responses to developing the standard of living of all the people led to his fundamental dissension from the tribal politics that had dominated the first half century of the existence of Northern Ireland. Instead, he first focussed on helping to found credit unions, to break the hold of usurious money lenders on the poor of his native Derry. He then started working on community housing, to help obtain decent homes for impoverished neighbours.

Hume's involvement in politics increased when he realised that the gerrymandered nature of the electoral boundaries in his city meant that the Derry Corporation, which controlled housing, was never going to build more houses for poor Catholics in case it upset the balance of political power in the city's electoral representation. This led him into first the civil rights movement and then, as violence erupted, to become a founding member of the Social Democratic and Labour Party (SDLP) committed to non-violence in the struggle to obtain social and political justice for all.

Writing in his 1984 biography of Hume the journalist Barry White noted, " . . . while there are some unexplored avenues, defeat is inconceivable for someone who sees his destiny in showing the Irish, North and South, how much they could achieve together once their political ambitions were reconciled" (p. 284).

It was not an easy path. Speaking to the *Irish Times* in 2021 Hume's daughter, Mo, remembered that,

> When he challenged the IRA throughout the Troubles he was attacked by republicans. "There were a few really bad attacks, and then there were lots of small attacks." The "small attacks" constituted daubings on the house with local republicans branding her father a "traitor" or other such comments, much of it in the late 1970s and 1980s when she was growing up. . . In one of the bad attacks Mo was at the window at West End Park when it was smashed with ball bearings, then came the petrol bombs exploding across the window. Luckily a second inner window, there as a protection, was not penetrated. "You heard the smash, and then the window went up [in flames]. And they would have seen a kid, like a 12-year-old, sitting in the window. There was intent behind that one. And the irony was, if they'd been clever, they could have just opened the front door because the door was unlocked. Our door was never locked."
>
> (Moriarty, 2021)

In his search for peace Hume began talks with Gerry Adams, the leader of the very violent "republicans" who had put him and his family under such sustained attack. When this became public knowledge in the early 1990s, "he was attacked and vilified from all sides", including the media (O'Callaghan, 2020). One Dublin newspaper in particular, the *Sunday Independent*, led a protracted and vitriolic personalised campaign against Hume (Archer, 2020).

It is easy to be glib about war when it is not something that is likely to cut short your life or that of someone you love. That is something that the relatives of some of the innocent civilians butchered in another attack, this time by pro-British

Loyalist gunmen in the small village of Greysteel, understood. At the funeral of the victims the daughter of one murdered man told Hume that they had prayed over her father's coffin that he would be successful in his efforts with Adams so that other families would not have to suffer as they had (McClements, 2018).

Towards the end of 1993, Hume was hospitalised for stress and his wife, Pat, an extraordinarily brave and committed leader in her own right, was so concerned for his health that she wondered for a moment if he should step back for a while from his involvement in politics. But he did not.

When Hume died in 2020 the *Irish Times* noted, that, "the only framework convincingly proposed for a lasting settlement [in the North], centred on equality for Irish and British identities through power-sharing with a formal involvement of Britain and the Republic [of Ireland], was substantially Hume's prescription" (O'Connor, 2020).

Shortly before he died Pat was interviewed by Irish television. What, she was asked, did John think of the current political situation? Tensions were rising as the foundations of the peace process, particularly the United Kingdom and Ireland's common membership of the European Union, came under threat from British government blundering around Brexit.

Ach, said Pat, dementia meant that John didn't even know that he was involved in the peace process himself once.

But the peace process that eventually took hold in the North of Ireland emerged from Hume's conviction, born on a Derry street when he was a child, that politics had to be about something more constructive and life-affirming than waving flags. It was a conviction that drove him for decades to help build a discursive space that recognised and accommodated the different political identities on the island of Ireland such that bloody conflict could be replaced by ill-tempered disputation – just like most other places.

Malawi's fearsome chief, terminator of child marriages

In a profile for Al Jazeera, Theresa Kachindamoto stated that she could not ever have conceived of leaving her job of twenty-seven years as a secretary at a city college in Zomba in Southern Malawi (McNeish, 2016).

However, somewhat unexpectedly, as a daughter of a senior Malawian chief, "Malawi's traditional authority figures", following her elder brother's death, she was chosen to be senior chief to more than 900,000 people in her home district, Monkey Bay, in Dedza District on Lake Malawi.

Kachindamoto stated to Al Jazeera that when she started touring the district to meet her people, she was shocked when she saw girls as young as twelve years old with babies and teenaged husbands.

Unicef (2018) notes that "child marriage is a serious problem in Malawi", estimating that about 46 percent of girls there were married before the age of eighteen, and

9 percent before the age of fifteen. The main drivers of child marriage, they note, are poverty, cultural and religious practices and peer pressure. "Child marriage is often associated with limited education and employment opportunities." Furthermore, it often occurs in the context of more widespread sexual exploitation of children, and many instances of child marriage correspond to slavery-like practices (McQuade, 2015).

In another profile for *inews* in 2019, Kachindamoto stated that "I had to act – I could not allow mistreated and uneducated girls under my rule" (Flanagan, 2019).

So Kachindamoto gathered her fifty-one subchiefs, including eleven women, and made them sign an agreement banning child marriage in their areas.

Kachindamoto stated, in the *inews* article, that she believed that her own upbringing was the driver behind her championing of young women: her father insisted that she complete her education and in her job at the college in Zomba she "delighted in seeing young women whose studies allowed them to pursue careers and gain financial independence".

She began to visit villages to annul existing marriages. According to *inews*, "When she discovered that four male subchiefs had ignored the agreement – local chiefs usually receive gifts of money or cows from parents for authorising weddings – she fired them" (Flanagan, 2019) (see Figure 5.4).

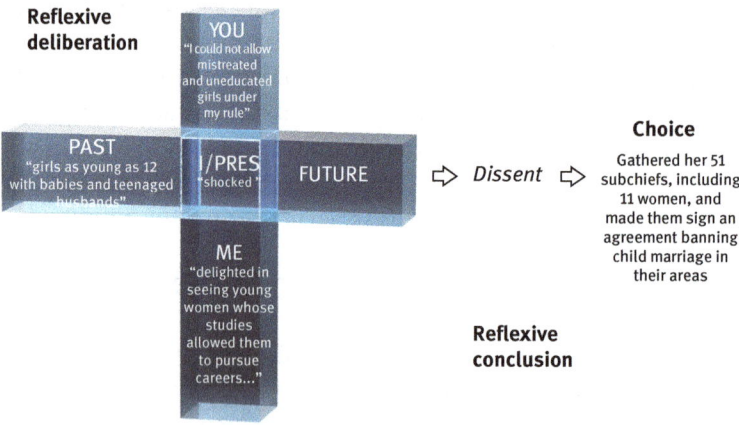

Figure 5.4: Chief Kachindamoto uses her power to end some child slavery.

According to Al Jazeera in the three years up to 2016 Kachindamoto broke up more than 850 marriages and sent all the children involved back to school. She had received death threats and criticism for disrupting "cultural traditions". But by 2016 she stated "now people are understanding" her campaign to end child marriage (McNeish, 2016).

Like Ray Anderson, Kachindamoto, motivated by her "delight" in girls' potential and her "shock" at witnessing so many child marriages in her district, has used her legitimate authority as senior chief of her district to change the practices of her subchiefs and wider community around the issue of child marriage.

In other words, she has used her traditional authority to dissent from practices justified through tradition, and she has changed the rules accordingly. In doing so she has begun to increase the discursive space within her community to such an extent that the political economy of the community has also changed. Consequently, the community increasingly recognises girls' rights to a childhood, schooling, and freedom of choice over their own lives.

"The Whistleblower"

In a 2001 interview for the *Guardian*, Kathryn Bolkovac, a former American police officer, "described how she was hired by DynCorp Aerospace in Aldershot for a UN post aimed at cracking down on sexual abuse and forced prostitution in Bosnia" (Barnett and Hughes, 2001).

Her first case of human trafficking, she told the *Independent* in 2012,

> was in [the city of] Zenica. I was working with a woman who had escaped, and she tipped me off about the Florida bar. I went there and found it empty. Behind the bar I discovered all kinds of passports of women from Eastern Europe, along with a lot of US dollars. On a second floor there was a locked room. I found seven women trapped inside. There were used condoms all over two mattresses on the floor, as if they'd been gang-raped there. . . . I didn't do too many more raids where I found conditions like that, but other monitors in the mission did. And many women described those same conditions when they escaped. (Applebaum, 2012)

To make matters worse, however, Bolkovac told the *Guardian*,

> When I started collecting evidence from the victims of sex trafficking it was clear that a number of UN officers were involved from several countries, including quite a few from Britain. I was shocked, appalled and disgusted. They were supposed to be over there to help, but they were committing crimes themselves. When I told the supervisors they didn't want to know. (Barnett and Hughes, 2001)

She told the *Independent*,

> To me, one of the worst examples of involvement by someone in the mission was a police officer from the US who told me how he'd purchased a young woman outside Sarajevo. How could anybody think it was OK to buy another human being when he had the power and authority to do something about it? That kind of mentality was appalling and made me think, "OK, how do we change this?" (Applebaum, 2012)

The *Guardian* report (Barnett and Hughes, 2001) explained that

> Many of the hundreds of women working in Bosnia's sex industry are lured from countries such as Romania and Ukraine with promises of jobs as waitresses but then delivered to brothel owners who confiscate their passports. Bolkovac claims that Dyncorp officers forged documents for trafficked women, aided their illegal transport through border checkpoints into Bosnia and tipped off sex club owners about raids.

When her supervisors failed to act, Bolkovac sent an email to more than fifty people – including Jacques Klein, the UN Secretary-General's special representative in Bosnia. The email was headed "DO NOT READ THIS IF YOU HAVE A WEAK STOMACH OR A GUILTY CONSCIENCE" (Applebaum, 2012) and "described the plight of trafficked women and noted that UN police, Nato troops and international humanitarian employees were regular customers. It was shortly after this email went out that Bolkovac was reassigned" (Barnett and Hughes, 2001). Dyncorp claimed that Bolkovac had filed erroneous timesheets, but this was overturned by a British employment tribunal in 2002 (Vulliamy, 2012). Speaking to the *Independent* in 2012, Bolkovac reflected (see Figure 5.5),

> People ask me where I got my strength from to do this, and I don't know. Maybe I'm stupid to try to push issues like I do. But I guess I do have a line that I don't want to cross and when I see others crossing it – especially law enforcement officers or politicians or diplomats – that really bothers me. What can I say? Right's right and wrong's wrong. (Applebaum, 2012)

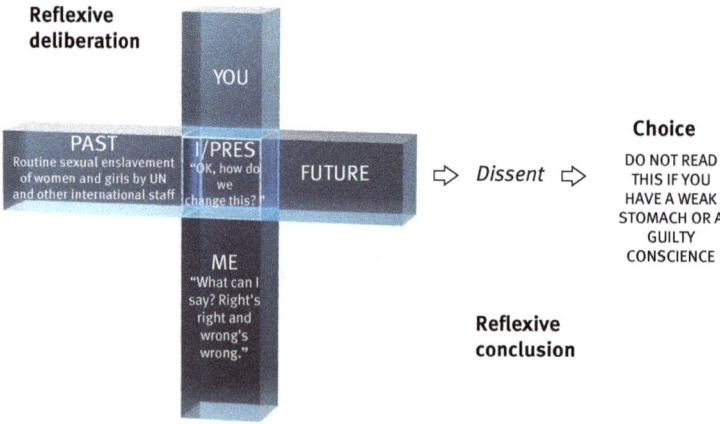

Figure 5.5: Kathryn Bolkovac blows the whistle.

Bolkovac is a stark example of an individual plotting her own moral course when so many others in her professional community are acquiescing in, and collaborating with, a system of appalling exploitation and cruelty towards other human beings. Furthermore, "Right's right and wrong's wrong", is as concise a statement of values driving this choice to dissent from their actions as one could wish for.

Speaking to the *Observer* in 2012, Bolkovac said:

> The thing that stood out about these cases in Bosnia, and cases that have been reported in other [UN] mission areas, is . . . that police and humanitarian workers were frequently involved in not only the facilitation of forced sexual abuse, and the use of children and young women in brothels, but in many instances became involved in the trade by racketeering, bribery and outright falsifying of documents as part of a broader criminal syndicate. (Vulliamy, 2012)

Like Stuart Couch, Bolkovac refused to acquiesce in what she regarded as a corrupt system, and, even though more junior in the system than Couch, she sought to protest the injustice she encountered rather than acquiesce in it.

Speaking in 2014 to the Women's International League for Peace and Freedom (WILPF) after a screening of the movie, *The Whistleblower*, about her experiences in Bosnia, Bolkovac was reported as reflecting that

> the last 15 years have not exactly been fun. She [Bolkovac] has suffered emotional, financial, familial and professional turmoil since she decided to do the right thing, and still struggles to give the fight for justice a place in her daily life. "People ask me continually if I regret what I did or if I would do it again, and, as time has progressed, I would now really need to think about my answer" . . . being a whistleblower really is such a difficult thing to do. . . . The system is still incredibly stacked against any victim of sexual violence in the context of peacekeeping, and there are close to no records of peacekeeper prosecutions for these crimes. Meanwhile, there are now more peacekeeping missions than ever and still no whistleblower protections, vetting systems or victim-centred procedures in place. (WILPF, 2014)

Bolkovac's agency did not arise from rational consideration of what actions would best serve her interests, but from a commitment to certain ideals and values. The results of her choices may not have been easy for her. But they did help end the enslavement of some vulnerable people that had been brought about by the venial and corrupt practices of a group of people who betrayed their most fundamental responsibilities.

"This is a fight for human rights"

In 2012 the *New Yorker* magazine called Alice Nkom one of the "eight most fascinating Africans of 2012" (Okeowo, 2012). The list also included the war criminal Paul Kagame of Rwanda (Wrong, 2021), so her inclusion meant that Nkom found herself in some dubious company.

What had drawn international attention to her was not that she had been the first woman called to the bar in Cameroon at the age of twenty-four. It was her vocal gay-rights advocacy. In 2003 she founded the Association for the Defence of Homosexuals to represent people being persecuted under Cameroon's homophobic laws that make homosexual acts illegal.

Speaking to the *Guardian* in 2011 however, Nkom noted that it is laws such as these, not the [homosexual] acts themselves that are illegal:

> the declaration of human rights is part of our constitution – but the judges still apply [the homophobic laws]. It's very difficult to prove you have had sex. Under the procedural code you cannot be put in jail unless caught *in delicto flagrante*. But they always put people accused of homosexuality in jail straight away. People are targeted because they wear makeup or looked effeminate.... It's a very corrupt environment and people get paid for informing on others.
>
> (Bowcott, 2011)

Detainees, Nkom asserted to the *Guardian*, are sometimes tortured in police stations until they confess, being beaten on the soles of their feet – a form of torture known as *bastinado* that, perhaps, saw its heyday in the Middle Ages.

Nkom told the *Guardian* in 2011 that her decision to establish her organisation originated after she met four young men who had returned from Paris. "I knew they were gay. I told them that homosexuality was a crime and to be careful. They were shocked. When they left I felt so guilty so I decided to try and do something about it. I founded the Association for the Defence of Homosexuals and tried to register the organisation at the prefecture. I knew it was a bit provocative. I wanted everyone to know that [gay] people also have rights. The prefecture officer told me I should be sacked" (Bowcott, 2011).

"Some Cameroon lawyers say that I should be killed because I'm 'spoiling the youth'", she told the *Guardian*. "One went on TV with a Bible to urge that I should be put to death. The minister of justice took me to the bar council. He said I was promoting homosexuality and should be struck off. I know there's a risk but when you are doing something that is right, you just do it and take care.... Someone has to do this."

One of Nkom's cases involved Roger Jean-Claude Mbédé, who was convicted in 2011 of suspected homosexual conduct after he sent a text message to another man that read "I am very much in love with you". His conviction was upheld by the court of appeal but Nkom appealed to the supreme court. Mbédé died in 2014, his appeal still pending. He died one month after his family removed him from the hospital where he had been seeking treatment for a hernia. "His family said he was a curse for them and that we should let him die", Nkom said (Associated Press, 2014).

"Even in Europe, when we look at the countries that penalise homosexuality today, and I am thinking of Russia, we see that the problem is an absence of democracy. The two are linked", she said in 2015 (Ní Chonghaile, 2015).

"This is a fight for human rights. It does not pit African traditions against western traditions or the colonised against colonisers. Africa has the same universal values and belongs to humanity. It is not separate, and neither is Cameroon," she said (see Figure 5.6).

There are some positive signs of change, the *Guardian* reported in 2015. "Pope Francis' reference to gays – 'who am I to judge' – helped Nkom redefine her

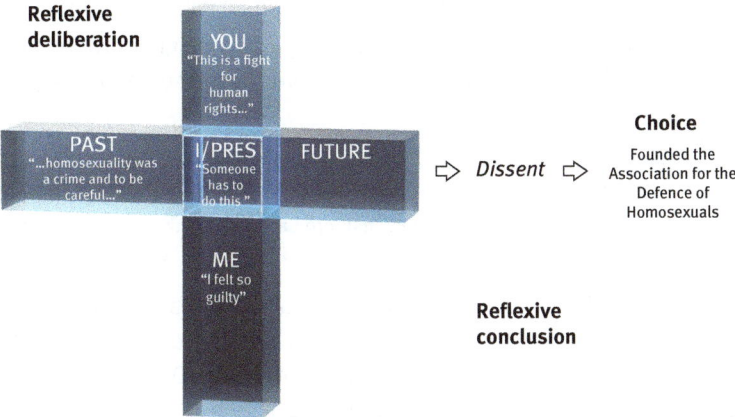

Figure 5.6: Alice Nkom holds her country to its human rights ideals.

discussions with the Catholic church in Cameroon. Some members of the judiciary occasionally send her discreet messages of support, grateful for her willingness to say what they feel they cannot" (Ní Chonghaile, 2015).

But while Francis' intervention may have assisted with the opening of space in Cameroon for discussion of gay rights, this good fortune is the residue of the painstaking work that Nkom and others across the globe have undertaken in asserting the human rights of gay people in the face of medieval prejudice. Once again, Nkom shows that protest and advocacy are leadership, and that the moral courage to undertake these arises from her fundamental values of what is right and wrong.

"I have a duty to serve my community"

> There cannot be a more degrading system of social organisation than the caste system.
> – B. R Ambedkar

The American writer, Isabel Wilkinson (2020a), defines casteism as "the granting or withholding of respect, status, honour, attention, privileges, resources, benefit of the doubt, and human kindness to someone on the basis of their perceived rank or standing in" a hierarchy. The Indian writer, Sujatha Gidla (2017), herself from the Dalit or "Untouchable" community, describes casteism in India as akin to racism in the United States, and Wilkinson identifies India and the United States, along with Nazi Germany as exemplars of caste societies (Wilkinson, 2020b).

The role of the "Untouchables" in the hierarchy, their "hereditary duty", as Gidla puts it, is "to labour in the fields of others or to do other work that Hindu society considers filthy" (p. 4). Because of this association with community sanitation, Dalits are regarded by the "higher" castes as "ritually unclean" and shunned by them.

Kiruba Munusamy, an Indian human rights lawyer from the Dalit community, describes an experience growing up. Her family had moved to a new neighbourhood and tried to disguise the fact that they were Dalits. However, word got out somehow. So,

> when it was time to collect water from the public tap, Kiruba was refused a spot in the queue. One time, another girl left her pot under the tap, and Kiruba moved it to stop it from overflowing. When the girl returned, she poured out her pot and cleaned it thoroughly, because Kiruba had touched it. This must be what it feels like to be considered a Dalit, Kiruba thought. This is how higher castes perceive us: as unclean, as untouchables. (van Wersch, 2018)

Munusamy is not the only Dalit lawyer in the Supreme Court, but, according to the nonprofit organisation, Justice and Peace Netherlands, she is unique in openly identifying as one, and she is a vocal advocate for the rights of the Dalits.

Casteism underpins slavery across South Asia, and it is at the root of other forms of discrimination and violence throughout Indian society. Justice and Peace Netherlands describes how Munusamy once

> represented a husband whose pregnant wife was murdered soon after they got married. The wife's family allegedly poisoned her because the husband belonged to a lower caste. . . . According to Kiruba, the Hindu nationalists oppose inter-caste relationships and marriages in order to protect caste purity . . . they see inter-caste marriage as a serious threat to their ideology. Violent attacks on inter-caste couples, especially by their family members, are quite prevalent in Indian society. The family members of the high-caste boy or girl often end up carrying out honour killings. They kill either their own children or their low-caste lovers.

In addition, "The upper caste groups use sexual violence as a tool, to reinforce their caste hegemony, and their caste supremacy", Munusamy told *Time* magazine in 2020. More than 3,500 Dalits were raped in India in 2019, she added, an increase of 18.6 percent compared to 2018 (Perrigo, 2020) (see Figure 5.7).

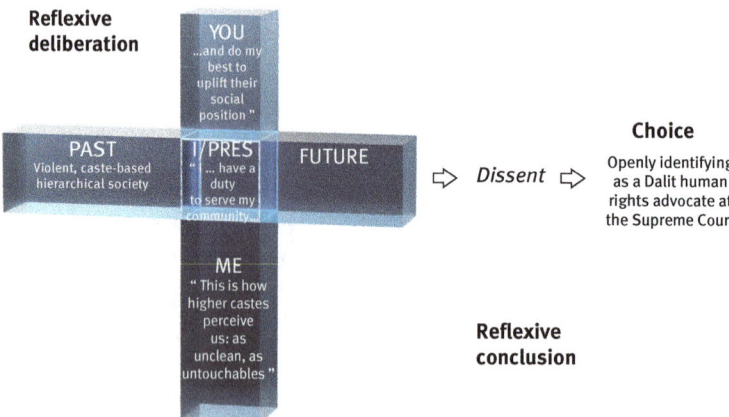

Figure 5.7: Kiruba Munusamy has enough of people trying to wash their hands of her community.

According to Justice and Peace Netherlands, Munusamy has on numerous occasions given legal help to inter-caste couples,

> to the grave dislike of some. . . . One day, as she was returning from court, unidentified ruffians stabbed her on the left side of her body. . . . Having lost a lot of blood, Kiruba says her condition was "very serious". She still has a long vertical scar from her chest to her abdomen. . . . When she came through, her mother pressured her. . . to give up human rights work altogether, and start a "normal family life", as she called it. "Because I didn't oblige, my family temporarily excommunicated me", says Kiruba. "For a few years, I only spoke to one of my elder sisters."

Following the attack that almost cost her life, Munusamy still receives abuse, including rape and death threats, both online and offline. In 2019 Meenakshi Ganguly, the South Asia director at Human Rights Watch, described that, "The room for dissent in India is getting ever smaller, and anyone who critici[s]es government actions can become a target . . . . Authorities seem more interested in silencing activists and journalists than in addressing the problems they bring to light" (Human Rights Watch, 2019).

Ethical leadership, such as Munusamy provides, is in the long tradition of protest and action to expand the "discursive space" available for people to obtain their rights and dignity irrespective of who they are or which community they come from. As her story illustrates, such leadership is not without risk. Many other people, perhaps more "rational" ones, might seek to avoid such risks, particularly, as Justice and Peace Netherlands notes, as Indian society currently "constitutes a hostile environment" for Munusamy's work. But, she says, "I . . . have a duty to serve my community and do my best to uplift their social position . . . . Wherever I go, my message will always serve that purpose."

Ethical choice: Acting in accordance with (even impeded) values

We all like to think that at the "moment of truth" we will meet the challenge with courage and wisdom and show the sort of ethical leadership that others will appreciate and talk about with admiration. But the lessons of history and of social psychology are that most of us fail most such tests.

Nevertheless, these disparate examples of ethical leadership show that such leadership is possible by all sorts of people in diverse contexts. Despite the diversity, it is worth highlighting that there are a number of common factors across these cases.

First each individual when describing their choices shows the reflexive deliberation on social and personal issues suggested by the Cruciform of Agency. Some of the examples privilege a distaste with the ideas of the past. Others emphasise the hopes and possibilities of the future. But all reflect an assessment of these social ideas against personal hopes and values, the "Me" or the individual's conscience. It is this emotional engagement of values in the thinking process that enables individuals to plot moral courses independent of the masses.

In other words, when reviewing the Cruciform of Agency against narratives of ethical choices such as these, we see that these narratives do indeed confirm that, as Emirbayer and Mische put it, the motivations for choices made in the social world occur "one level down", in the realm of an individual's reflexive deliberations on their values in interaction with the social world. By being aware that every situation we encounter can engage with the Cruciform of Agency allows us to think about that situation more thoroughly. Even if we are unfamiliar with the social context, we can seek bases of choice within our own values as well as within the social situation: we don't have to do what everyone else is doing if we are uncomfortable with it.

As noted, review of each of these cases shows that it is in an individual's personal hopes and values that the motivation for making the life-affirming choice resides. It is also striking that Munusamy's reflection, "I have a duty to serve my community", Couch's "I knew I gotta get off the fence", Nkom's "Someone has to do this", Bolkovac's "OK – how do we change this?" all echo each other and Thomas Clarkson's thoughts that, "it was time some person should set these calamities to their end". These are the words of individuals, prompted by their moral values, taking personal responsibility for undertaking dissenting action to the unjust situations that they have encountered.

It is worth bearing in mind that an alternative course, of an individual ignoring "these calamities" because they think their single voice will have no impact is a self-fulfilling prophecy.

The values that each of these cases represent come from different sources: Hume from his background growing up poor and discriminated against in 20th century Derry; Anderson from an emotional reaction to learning more about the environmental crisis faced by the world; Couch from a religious faith that emphasised human dignity; Kachindamoto from a delight in the potential of Malawi's girls and an empathy with their plights; Bolkovac from a decent cop's plain view of what is right and wrong; Nkom from a fundamental commitment to human rights and empathy for the plight of her gay friends; Munusamy from a personal experience of casteism. But despite the diversity of their origins, the sense of moral responsibility that emerged from these disparate values compelled them to make the choices they did to emphasise human rights and dignity.

Reviewing these examples we can also see that while power can facilitate change, as shown in particular by Anderson and Kachindamoto, it is the nature of one's personal thoughts, hopes and values and how these interact with the challenges posed by the social world, that facilitate the choice for ethical leadership. Without their values, on environmental protection and girls' rights, neither Anderson nor Kachindamoto, for example, would have shown the leadership that they offered and used their power as they did.

Likewise, Couch, Hume, Bolkovac, Nkom and Munusamy, while hardly at the apex of power within their given societies, made choices to assert different values to those social contexts in which they found themselves and volubly express their dissent from that which they found immoral. Consequently, they painfully sought change in communities and societies when hope may have seemed forlorn otherwise.

It is worth reemphasising that all of these cases are examples of how protest and dissent are ethical leadership by expanding the discursive space for new ideas to be considered and for the human dignity of the marginalised to be asserted.

In his book *War* (2011), Sebastian Junger reflects that the physical courage he saw amongst American troops fighting in Afghanistan was a manifestation of love: comrades risked their lives in order to try to save those they fought alongside. It could be instantaneous with little pause to consider the consequences to self that might emerge from a selfless act in battle.

The examples of Couch, Hume, Anderson, Kachindamoto, Bolkovac, Nkom and Munusamy show that moral courage is somewhat different from the physical variety. It emerges, as the name suggests, from the compulsion that individuals feel arising from their most deeply held values and beliefs about what is right and wrong. Its deliberative nature means that often an individual must act with moral courage beset by some painful imaginings of the negative future consequences such action may hold for them personally: Hume spent almost his entire public career in the shadow of death. Nkom and Munusamy live to this day under threat of violence.

So, given all this, we should be reminded that cases such as these show, as with so many other things, just show how wrong and wrong-headed Hamlet was: conscience does not "make cowards of us all". Rather conscience can be the source of, if not the greatest heroism, at least of the most vital ethical leadership.

Points for reflection

- Do any of the cases discussed in this chapter remind you of challenges that you have faced in work or as a citizen? If yes, what and why?
- Are there other particular leaders whose example of moral courage you admire? Why?
- Do you think you have displayed moral courage as a citizen or in your professional career? If yes, describe some examples.
- For which of your own personal values, if any, do you think you would break with your wider community and risk public embarrassment or professional disadvantage?

Chapter 6
Just what the doctor ordered

> FRANK: Do you know Yeats?
>
> RITA: The wine lodge?
>
> FRANK: No, WB Yeats, the poet.
>
> RITA: No.
>
> FRANK: Well, in his poem 'The Wild Swans At Coole', Yeats rhymes the word "swan" with the word "stone". You see? That's an example of assonance.
>
> RITA: Yeah, means getting the rhyme wrong.
>
> – from *Educating Rita*, by Willy Russell

> In which . . . the author explores some doctors' accounts of how they deal with weighty ethical dilemmas in their day-to-day work. These introduce the concept of "assonance" – moral uncertainty – and show the value of doubt and regret in professional leadership. These can facilitate learning in moral decision-making and contribute towards professional maturation. These cases also show the usefulness of codifying a hierarchy of moral responsibilities to help make the most appropriate choices in complex ethical environments.

Introduction

The examples discussed in the previous chapter are important because they show how, at a "moment of truth" when confronted with major, even overwhelming, injustice, individuals of moral courage can assert their *dissidence* from the prevailing situation and assert a different moral course for themselves and others.

Not all of us will ever be in a position to become a Stuart Couch or a Kathryn Bolkovac, the sort of exemplars that they make movies about. Instead, it falls to us to carry out some of the numberless acts of courage and belief of which Robert Kennedy spoke.[1] These can indeed build to a mighty current that can change the world, perhaps through greater environmental restoration and human rights protections being enacted by leaders across the globe. But even before that, the choices that leaders make will have direct impacts on the lives and livelihoods of those who are most immediately affected by them.

What leaders do matters. There will always be things, great and small, from petty unkindness to bullying to systemic discrimination and violence, which leaders can affect and that present "moments of truth" that test their true nature and the depth of

---

[1] See Chapter 1.

their moral courage. By exercising their power or raising their voices in protest they can directly bring change or help to create the discursive space within which more tolerant attitudes can grow. Even if these choices do not become more widely known they can contribute to vital social movements that "can sweep down the mightiest walls of oppression".

However, in the routine of professional leadership, choices are often not clear cut in any way. Anyone who has led even for a short period discovers that they are frequently confronted with a need to make decisions, including ones that can have long-term impacts on the lives of affected stakeholders, with limited information and less than ideal levels of resources. Managing humanitarian operations during the Angolan civil war, for example, would have been much easier if I had at my disposal more engineering staff and well-drilling equipment, and, more than anything else, perfect knowledge of UNITA's military intentions and how that might affect the security and well-being of my team, and population displacements across the country.

In other words, doubt and uncertainty are central aspects of leadership. This also applies to moral decision-making. In many cases the options available to a leader do not *resonate* as clearly right, or cause a moral *dissonance* because they are felt so sharply to be wrong. Rather there is a certain *assonance*, a sort of moral half-rhyme in which the most life-affirming option is not easily apparent.

To explore this aspect of ethical leadership let us focus in this chapter on one profession, the medical profession. Doctors must regularly deal with a high volume of complex ethical challenges, ranging from end of life to child protection. This chapter will focus through the prism of the Cruciform of Agency on how some doctors have dealt with such issues and then seek to draw some more general guidance from these examples.

All in a day's work

End of life

As a general practitioner (GP) Dr Rosamund has to deal with a lot of end-of-life issues:

> I did a talk on it once and I was talking about the difference in attitude and recognising the individual's response to the approach of death and I think I quoted someone saying they want to just die in peace and want to die in their own home, they want to die pain free, quiet death with some nice Mozart in the background, something like that. That's fine for some people but I hope I'm not misquoting Dylan Thomas who said "rage, rage against the dying light". So, for some people it's really important to fight it and so you have to deal with that on an individual basis, you can't presume. . . . Some people might want AC/DC blasting in the background and be smoking their last spliff. Whatever that person needs at the end of their life is important to recognise and so it's not always what you think it's going to be.

In describing this choice Dr Rosamund describes a strong *resonance* with the idea of supporting the patient's wishes on how they meet death. This principle of supporting patient choice was an important one for the doctors I spoke to in this research.

However, while such an approach may be common and generally appropriate doctors dealing with trauma raise some different issues in dealing with end-of-life issues. Dr Clooney, a surgeon, notes that (see Figure 6.1),

> the ethical decisions [relating to end of life] come about if the patient then develops complications and problems after [surgery], it's how far you pursue doing something about that. And how you deal with relatives – as someone who has an unrealistic expectation of what should be done, and what the next stage is . . . a 90 year old who has dementia and multiple problems and ulcers, and bed bound and so on . . . and I say "Well, we'll do lots to this patient and we could keep him going for another week or two and another month, or we don't". I would tend to think, well why prolong this poor person's agony? They've had a good, long, fruitful life, but then how do you deal with family and relatives who may think differently, and that's one of the ethical problems that I would face.

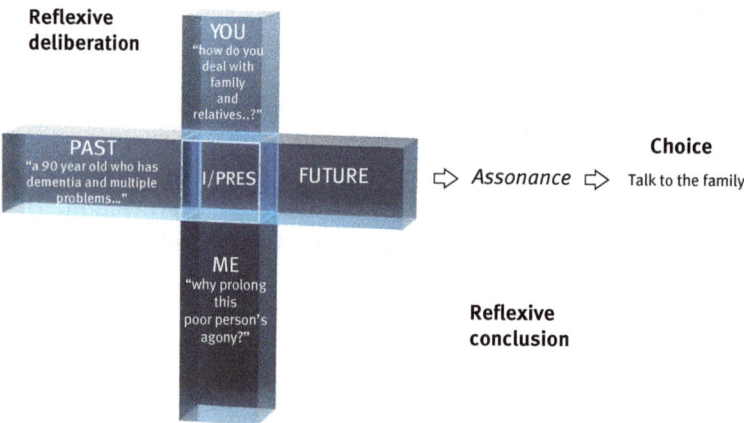

Figure 6.1: Dr Clooney ponders patient treatment options.

Dr Marilyn, who is an anaesthetist, describes similar dilemmas, where the judgement of the doctor as to what is in the best interests of the patient may come into conflict with the wishes of the family. She describes a typical trauma situation that she attends:

> So you're at the point where obviously somebody is critically ill, so I need to start doing something otherwise the patient dies . . . very often at that point you will say, "Right I institute emergency treatment" because that's the only thing I can do. So you start to ventilate somebody, you will give them appropriate support to improve their blood pressure. . . . Then we get a little bit more history through [and] realise that this isn't a well patient, it's somebody who has been going downhill and their seizure it's a pre-terminal event. . . . Recently we had an elderly gentleman who was admitted to intensive care. He was very, very unwell. We knew the

chances of him surviving to leave intensive care, let alone hospital, were very, very slim. . . . His family couldn't accept that, so we ended up going through the motions for about two months, which was really cruel, until the family could accept they were going nowhere and would allow us not to escalate and to withdraw treatment. Those are difficult decisions. They are huge decisions to make.

Both Drs Clooney and Marilyn describe situations where what they perceive to be in the best interests of the patient is complicated by the desires of the patients' families on how they should be treated. Their response then is an effort at a gentle but clearly put *protest* – to transform the understanding and expectations of the families towards an approach that they feel to be more in the patients' interests. But their overwhelming appreciation is that with so many "stakeholders" involved they are confronted with a much more complex decision than the ones Dr Rosamund describes in which just the final wishes of the patient are involved.

Abortion

Many of the doctors I interviewed for this research, including Dr Rosamund,[2] were clear that they had no principled objections to abortion. All these doctors recognised it as a highly sensitive issue and felt that their role should be to support their patients to make their own decisions, not to impose their views one way or the other.

However, other doctors find that this issue can bring them into conflict to some extent with their own personal beliefs.

Dr Audrey, a general practitioner, describes how she works to the principle of the best interests of patients even when the issue under discussion is abortion, a matter that she finds morally problematic:

> I think I can support the patient regardless of whatever decision they make and I think it's more important that they feel there's somebody who's non-judgmental, who's a support to them, as opposed to somebody – and again, my position truly I can't think very black and white in it. I remember at school we all learned about abortion and things, but you're sitting in a position [as a doctor] and a lot of them it's tragic because the decision is not necessarily being made for them, it's been made for their family . . . maybe somebody has got pregnant by some guy and they end up getting married, settling down, they're not going to stay together, and that, the pregnancy has accelerated that relationship into a situation that it would probably have never gone into . . . but . . . I truly don't see it as my position to be judgmental. And [unwanted pregnancy] is a problem [that] we see an awful lot, you know.

These moral complexities are one of the matters that led Dr Clooney away from an initial interest in obstetrics:

---

2 See section "End of life" in this chapter.

> I can see it is easy if you're well removed from it to be absolute on your views on abortion. I'm removed from it, it's easy for me to say I'm against abortion, and take that stand, but if you're close to it, it's much more difficult to be that absolute. . . . Let's say for example, [my wife] was pregnant and the scan showed there was encephalic, so a child with no brain, who is going to die, the child will be born and will die, this is an extreme example, is it right or fair to make her carry a pregnancy for 40 weeks, deliver a child that is going to die? And that it is going to die, there's no question about it. So that's the absolute. Then you start to bring it back a little bit and say well let's say it's not encephalic, let's say it's micro cephalic. . . . So . . . . they're not going to die, they're going to be extremely, severely handicapped, they're going to need lifelong care. Then you say do I want the child to go through that? Some of these children suffer terribly. Some of them do, and some of them don't, and do I know enough about it, do I want a child to go through that? So faced with that situation I don't know . . . Where's the next line? Where would it go? . . . where do I stand? . . . it's exceptionally grey, and I know that . . .

Here Dr Clooney resolved this issue by removing himself from that discipline of his profession, obstetrics, where he would have been confronted daily with ethical issues that he recognises are of considerable complexity. Nevertheless, he displays considerable sympathy with those who disagree with him and respect for their position. He had simply decided that this was not something he wished to be involved in.

Introducing the concept of "assonance"

Assonance is moral doubt or uncertainty about what, in a given situation, is the most life-affirming option (see Figure 6.2).

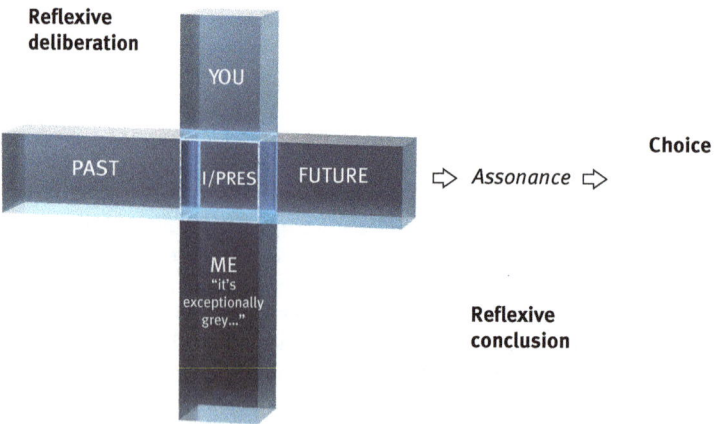

Figure 6.2: Origins of assonance.

Whatever the issue, such assonance is likely to emerge when the decision-maker perceives the issue requiring a choice to be "shades of grey" rather than simply "black and white". This is what Drs Audrey and Clooney describe in relation to the issue of abortion and what other doctors also describe in relation to end of life issues. In relation to abortion Drs Audrey and Clooney describe a morally complex landscape in which they feel it is appropriate to set aside, albeit with some discomfort, personal values to privilege a deeper ideal regarding the role of the doctor and the doctor's relationship with the patient.

The greying of moral certainty, and hence assonance, tends to arise when there are a conflict of rights and responsibilities around the stakeholders involved in an issue. It echoes Martha Nussbaum's (2001) observation that life often presents individuals with a choice between competing systems of "good" rather than explicitly about a choice between good and evil. For example, in the cases of Drs Clooney and Audrey we see a personal view that it is "good" to be anti-abortion and a professional view that it is "good" to uphold the wishes of a patient. Alternatively, in relation to the end of life situation that Dr Marilyn described, she thought it a "good" to avoid prolonging a patient's suffering while also recognising that it was also "good" to take cognisance of a patient's family's wishes.

In other words, the Cruciform of Agency is still in play in their thinking, considering professional and social issues in the context of personal values, and other social relationships, particularly those of the patient. However, the result is not *dissonance* leading to a dissenting course of action, but rather a much more uncomfortable *assonance* or awareness of moral uncertainty guiding subsequent professional choices.

Assonance – doubt – is important in ethical leadership in that it can ensure that a professional carries an awareness that they might be wrong in the choices arising from their deliberations. This uncertainty increases the potential for leaders to be open to new information, aware of their fallibility and prepared to rectify any errors they come to discern.

But is should also be remembered that Nussbaum showed, in her book, *The Fragility of Goodness*, how the desire to uphold one moral system over another can lead to the justification of immoral conduct. So, care must be taken in moral decision making to ensure proper weighting of moral rights and responsibilities. It may, for example, be inappropriate for a doctor to withhold treatment from a patient because they think the quality of the patient's life is poor if that patient actually and vocally values that life and wishes it to continue. Or it may be inappropriate for a doctor to continue treatment for research reasons if such treatment is hopeless and merely drags out false hope and prolongs pain for a patient.

These are issues that doctors have to deal with in their professional routine and which highlight the value of a framework of moral guidance to help make ethical choices. In the next sections we shall look more closely at elements of doctors' ethical principles.

Treatment of patients against their will

When discussing decisions regarding end of life and abortion, the doctors I interviewed, irrespective of their personal views on the matters, tended towards principles of facilitating the choices of the patient and upholding their best interests. But, as consideration of some of the end-of-life issues faced by doctors shows, this is not always straightforwardly applicable. Consider a portion of a narrative from Dr Zola, a consultant psychiatrist, discussing a process that led him to section a patient:

The patient, Dr Zola recounted,

> somehow got unwell, left her job . . . [no] benefits . . . she did have savings . . . had been buying food but very meagre things, biscuits and basic narrow range of food but at the same time [she] was ok, her flat was in reasonable order, didn't want very much help from us and wasn't at risk of death, wasn't in any kind of danger, wasn't going to harm anybody else . . . she just gradually lost a bit more weight, the flat was a bit bare, there was less in the cupboards . . . so it wasn't the kind of life threatening crisis, it just had gone on a long time and was many months. It just felt sad to leave her in that way . . .

Dr Zola was faced with a difficult ethical issue that required him to come to a choice regarding the best interests of the patient when the patient herself, as a result of the very condition that was giving rise to Dr Zola's concern, had different wishes that Dr Zola felt were not really in her best interests (see Figure 6.3).

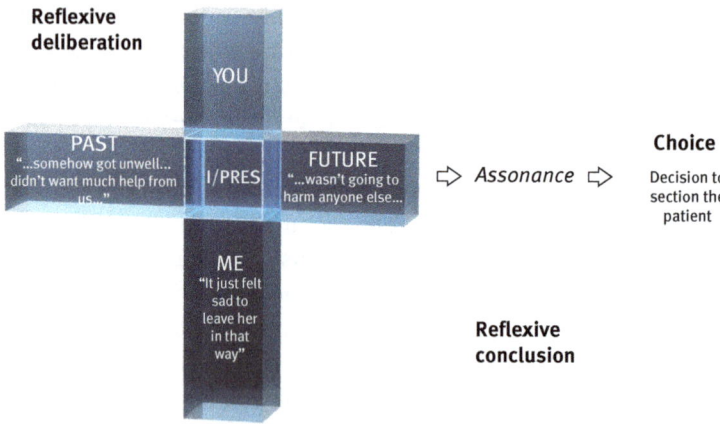

Figure 6.3: Dr Zola considers sectioning an ill patient.

In the terms of the Cruciform of Agency Dr Zola's reflexive deliberation on the case regarding the ill patient led to a reflexive conclusion that may again be termed *assonance*: part of him felt that he should treat the patient but part of him felt that to do this against the patient's wishes would be ethically and clinically problematic. This *assonant* conclusion remained up to and including the point at which he chose to section the patient and treat her against her will. What had changed was the increased likelihood of a more negative future transpiring if an interventionist approach was not taken. This led to a choice to use his power to section and to extend psychiatric treatment to a person who had previously refused this. This choice seems to have been a result of some quite solitary reflexive deliberation as well as social conversations about the case that Dr Zola had with his team.

Child protection

At the time of my conversation with Dr Rosamund, a GP, she was dealing with a particular issue of child protection that she was finding difficult, in part because of the importance of confidentiality and trust in treatment of patients:

> Child protection on the surface seems a very simple thing: If there's a child you think is at threat you need to contact social services immediately . . . however, you may, for example, . . . have built up a relationship with a patient. . . . You may have been dealing with their alcohol abuse and getting them to a stage where they are recovering but then they regress and start drinking again and they have access to their child, and you are responsible, as is any adult who knows that child, in ensuring their safety. As a GP you know this person . . . had no history of violence, history of a good relationship with his son, a very fine balance to try and get this man to stop drinking and only one episode of drinking around his son but confronting him with the need to actually speak to somebody about this, ending up in threats and all sorts of things and a total breakdown of the relationship with him, means that . . . although it's obvious you need to act on it, you do have to think it through quite carefully: are you actually causing him to go deeper into this drinking? In which case is he going to be more of a danger to his son? He's not living with his son but he has access to his son – are you going to push him to do something spontaneous and damaging like abducting his son? All these things go through your mind. . . . But you have to just be influenced by the law . . . however uncomfortable it is with the other person it's still an obvious decision you need to do something about.

Again, Dr Rosamund describes a sense of *assonance* arising from the tension between what the law says, rightly she believes, is her duty towards the child in the case, and her sense of responsibility for the best interests of her patient. Here she describes that law as a guide to her responsibilities, not, as is the case of Friedman's ethical formulation, a guide to which responsibilities she should abrogate.

Dr Keira, a community paediatrician, is regularly confronted with child protection issues:

> You know, the worst one I had was, it was a Friday night and I was the last one in the department. I'd seen this little kid, a little boy with a bruise to his balls and I had to work out whether this was possible that he'd got it accidentally and I felt it wasn't. I felt he'd been hurt on purpose. I had the social worker there, parents were there, and brothers, three brothers. So I had to make my decision and say to the social worker I think this is non-accidental. The parents called in all their friends, who started getting menacing, in the end we had to call the police to come and protect us and the children were taken into care. I think . . . it was an horrendous situation, very frightening, but I had to make a judgment call . . . it has been decided

> they were in a dangerous environment and so it eventually came to light that judgment call that night was right, but we don't know, we can't know [when making the decision]. We're being told one story. . . but you just have to use your judgement. And it proved that one was right but I didn't know it at the time and it was horrible, very distressing.

Dr Keira's reference to "using your judgement" gets to a fundamental truth about leadership. It is so often about the exercise of judgement in difficult environments with less-than-ideal information. Despite these uncertainties Dr Keira's *assonant* reflexive conclusion requires her decision, because even while she worried that she might be mistaken, she was clear on her responsibility to the child who was her patient.

The courage to face down the threats of the children's family in the case of Dr Keira, and the resolution to sacrifice the trust of a patient in the case of Dr Rosamund both appear to originate with a clarity of purpose on the part of both doctors regarding their responsibilities towards the protection of children. In the instance of Dr Rosamund she understands this responsibility as superseding her responsibility towards what her own patient might have thought was in his own best interest.

Is the system more important than the patient?

The principle focus of Dr Robert's work is the treatment of drug addicts. This sometimes brings with it echoes of the concerns voiced by Dr Audrey to not let her personal values interfere in ensuring the best treatment of the patients.

Dr Robert describes how:

> it's really difficult to keep my own sense of disgust, it's not quite as strong as that, but really my own personal distress or whatever it is, about a situation. . . . I need the concentration for the patient's view. I've got to be firstly, what is best for them, and put my own issues out of that and find ways of trying to help what their want is, not necessarily what I'm wanting. And it's not putting moral ideas onto whether they should be sex working or shouldn't be sex working. It's how can you do that safely? . . . It's how can I help somebody do something safely? So with injecting heroin how can I help somebody inject and teach somebody how to inject safely? . . . If I'd said, "Oh you mustn't do it" he would have just stuck two fingers at me and walked out, it would have been a dead loss. . . . [So] It was how do you do this better, safer and in a more controlled way so that you're not going to kill yourself, or lose your leg or whatever?

But while the issue of best interest of patient was a strong guiding principle for Dr Robert, as for so many doctors, Dr Robert's practice showed how it was not necessarily the pre-eminent one. He described a situation,

> Somebody who came in that said they'd lost their prescription, that's sort of common . . . your cat steals it, somebody steals it, it's got lost, it's gone down the drain, all sorts of places. It's just to get another prescription so they can get the drugs and we generally have a policy that we don't do and I talked to this lass and said, "No, I'm sorry I won't". She was very distressed. . . and I think she genuinely had lost it. I saw her the next week and she'd had a terrible week, she

didn't have any medication, and. . . . I don't think I made the right decision. Maybe a decision for the whole system so that it didn't get out into the streets, you just tell the doctor you've lost it and get another one, and there's an important message but for that individual she had gone and done things that weren't good for her.

But if someone walks in tomorrow saying "I've lost my prescription . . . "?

"I'll probably go back to saying 'try and work it out' and probably it would come down to then saying, 'No, I'm sorry I can't'".

So, for Dr Robert, the maintenance of the integrity of the service that he works in must, on occasion, take precedence over what he believes to be the best interests of the patient. This led him to a choice which he had clearly found personally distressing, to maintain the rules of the service over the needs of the patient. While he regrets the distress his choice caused he recognises that he would probably follow the same course of action again if the situation presented itself.

The professional value of doubt

> Doubt is not a pleasant condition, but certainty is absurd. — Voltaire

Ambiguity and uncertainty in relation to moral decision-making seem to pervade the medical profession. Doctors consistently express their awareness of the diversity and complexity of the issues they are dealing with and are often prepared to *thinkingly* put to one side some of their personal values in order to privilege others such as their ideals of being a doctor. A core element of this is treating patients without passing judgement on their choices. Above[3] Dr Robert notes setting aside his occasional sense of "disgust" at some of the actions of his patients.

Dr Marilyn notes that:

> in my working life I think when I started working there was a little bit of black, a little bit of white and a bit of grey. Now . . . The more I see the more I experience life, the more I become grey. . . . I'm not very judgmental now at all. I accept most things, or I try to see round them. . . . It changes how you approach, and how you talk to people, and how you deal with people.

Reviewing the interviews with doctors one of the most striking issues across all the conversations is the centrality of doubt as an aspect of their work. Drs Marilyn and Audrey describe moving from a "black and white" view of the world to one composed of shades of "grey". Dr Clooney describes seeing issues in terms of "grey". All three describe how this has evolved across the course of their professional career. Implicit is a description of their evolving values and the increasing *assonance* of their reflexive conclusions.

---

[3] See section "Is the system more important than the patient?" in this chapter.

Confronted with this web of ethical complexity, law and professional principles provide guidance. Dr Keira, working in the stressful area of community paediatrics, has a clearly articulated purpose in her role:

> Working with child protection and there are a lot of difficulties, it's very hard to make them generic actually because they tend to be case based. The biggest difficulty we sometimes face is looking at the rights of the child in the context, the rights of that family, and their parents. Particularly when it comes to confidentiality, but as a guiding rule in our department we tend to only really see the rights of the child . . . when push comes to shove it's what's best for that child even if it contravenes their parents' wishes.

But even clear principles and explicit regulation do not necessarily assuage the conscience when it comes to difficult choices. Dr Robert remains troubled by denying a patient her medication when she lost her prescription, even though he feels it was the right course of action for the preservation of the integrity of the service he works in. Dr Rosamund worries about damaging trust with her alcoholic patient when she was concerned that his son was being endangered.

This residual worry and doubt seem important in facilitation of learning. That doctors review and reflect upon their choices and follow up on their consequences allows them the opportunity to question their own values and to assess future choices in the context of previous ones. Dr Marilyn describes one case:

> So, we had one [old lady] who fell in the geriatric ward. . . . [I thought] this lady is not going to survive. I spoke to the consultant and he said, "No we've got to do something". I thought "well this is not right". . . . So I stayed with her, I took her to the scan, I came back, I looked at the scan, unsurvivable, spoke to the surgeon, unsurvivable, but the radiologist and the doctor on the scanner said "you should be doing more". You do think this isn't the right thing to do, you're not giving her appropriate treatment, and it was very hard to stand back and not just to go through the motions. It wasn't the right thing to do. . . . She had something that was a terminal event, she was going to die, but the pressure from other people around were saying "You've got to go down this route, you've got to get her a bed in intensive care". Totally the wrong thing to do. But it's hard to resist.

The comment "Totally the wrong thing to do" indicates a judgement that Dr Marilyn has made of that choice and carries with her in future encounters as a basis upon which future choices will be judged.

Reviewing all of the ethical choices that doctors described over the course of my interviews with them indicated the predominance of reflexive conclusions that could be termed *assonant* – morally uncertain – when confronting the ethical choices posed to them by their work (25 out of 46 cases).

Functionally, there is greater flexibility in this reflexive conclusion of *assonance* than in other reflexive conclusions of greater certitude, either positive or negative. Franz Fanon, the political philosopher, quoted by Michela Wrong in her 2021 book, *Do Not Disturb*, noted that "Sometimes people hold a core belief that is very strong. When they are presented with evidence that works against that belief the new evidence cannot be accepted . . . And because it is so important to protect the core belief, they will rationalise, ignore or even deny anything that doesn't fit with that core belief" (p. 70).

Jo Berry, founder of the peace-building charity Building Bridges, in an interview for this book, observed that certainty is a problem in human relations. Attitudes of certainty lead to presumptions of betrayal at expressions of doubt and limit the opportunities of learning that admissions of mistakes bring.

However, that sense of *assonance*, that awareness of the tension between different principles is almost the polar opposite of Fanon's observation. It represents an enduring questioning of the rights and wrongs of a situation and a professional's choices within it.

Dr Rosamund, for example, describes a case that shocked her even after many years in medicine and general practice:

> A woman . . . came in with some gynaecological problems and I realised she had her clitoris removed, she's had female circumcision. . . . So to me that is the greatest violation you can ever cause to a female and yet I had to deal with my standards and I had to resolve that very quickly because when I broached the subject to her "Would you like to see somebody about this?" the answer was no. She was showing no signs of low mood, no signs of problems to her self-esteem, she made good eye contact, she was smiling appropriately, she was talking to me. . . . For her the proportion of my discovery, the proportion of the importance of my discovery was far less important in her life than it was in mine. I wanted to say to her, "My God, you've been mutilated", of course I didn't. You run two conversations in your head when you're a GP, this is an outrage, this is a woman that this is happening to. . . . That was interesting because my reaction was so much more extreme than hers . . . but it's just interesting that I have to have these parallel – I want her to come back to me in the future . . . and want her to be able to trust me and me not to have said potentially insulting things, I could have insulted her family and her beliefs and her relations.

Elements of a code of conduct

The value of *assonant* reflexive conclusion is emphasised when considering the multiple levels upon which thinking is necessary to allow doctors to function in this ethically complex environment. Dr Audrey describes a fundamental principle about working for the best interests of the patient, which supersedes some of her own values. Dr Rosamund describes breaking trust with a patient to ensure protection of his child. Drs Robert and Audrey note that they are legally obliged to break confidentiality if it will prevent someone from being endangered. Dr Robert notes that the nature of his role means that he has a professional responsibility to his organisation that sometimes supersedes what the patient may regard as their best interests.

The ability to make the right ethical choices in these situations depends on not only clarity of purpose on the part of the doctors but also on clarity of hierarchy of

purpose. The conversations suggest that doctors operate on the following hierarchy of purposes, with "1" representing the highest imperative:
1. Prevent harm to others
2. Protect the integrity of the service that the doctor is offering
3. Act in the best interests of the patient
4. Support the patient's choices

We will return to this question of hierarchy of ethical principles in the next chapter and explore how a similar system may be constructed to guide moral decision-making in the profession of leadership.

Professional maturation

> On every hand, in a small way, we find that a certain amount of evil is a condition by which a higher form of good is brought.
> – William James

The importance of social pressures in influencing choices of courses of action is well noted in the literature. Milgram and Darley and Lantane in particular show that social pressures may, despite a degree of anguish on the part of the individuals involved, be used to make individuals act in ways that they feel are contrary to their values or even their best interests in particular circumstances.

Dr Keira notes the importance of social pressures on junior doctors:

> I've developed with experience and time and I've a little bit more confidence in my own judgement. I think as a junior doctor you don't have any self-confidence, and you very much have to do as you're told. There are . . . I can give you specific incidents of things I went along with as a junior doctor that now would make me sick.

And Dr Audrey remembers that:

> Certainly . . . there's things in the past I've done that I now know I shouldn't have. You know, I'm not happy to do as I did, a procedure again . . . over the phone with a very sick baby, which as a very, very junior doctor – I mean I'd done no paediatrics, and the consultant told me through the phone with the help of a nurse who'd seen it a few times, but this was a procedure that somebody very qualified in paediatrics would have been trained to do and I didn't really know that I could have said no to that . . . when I [later] went back into hospital medicine for a year I was much more clued into the fact that ultimately the responsibility lay with the consultant and they actually I think were quite lax in letting somebody do something they were clearly not able to do. Especially now as a mother I wouldn't have let me do what I did.

This outcome of conformity with the perceived legitimate authority of more senior doctors that Dr Audrey describes, would not be surprising for anyone familiar with the work of Stanley Milgram. This showed how easily individuals could be compelled to participate in something as extreme as, they were led to believe, torturing other human beings if they were told it was in the interests of science.

However these comments by Drs Audrey and Keira give some insight into some of the thinking processes in the Cruciform of Agency at play in those important studies of Milgram Darley and Lantane, and Zimbardo (2007). Key aspects of the experiments that gave rise to these studies involved placing of individuals in unfamiliar social settings. For individuals, such as junior doctors in new jobs as well as the subjects of those classic social psychological experiments, unfamiliar situations represent a radical curtailing of their Cruciform of Agency (see Figure 6.4).

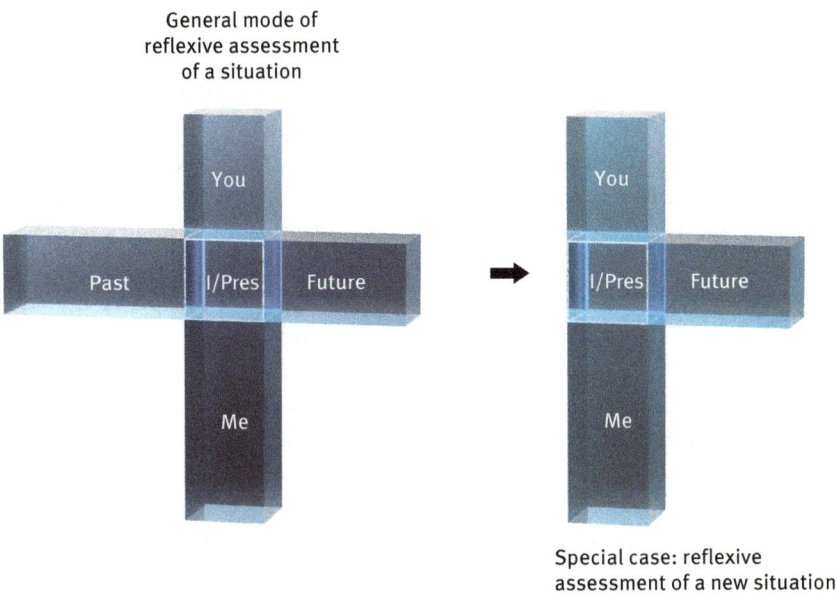

Figure 6.4: Thinking in unfamiliar situations.

In other words, in unfamiliar situations an individual has no personal knowledge of the past rules and resources that have created the present situation. They only have what they can glean from the present situation itself. Likewise, they have a limited store of relevant personal experiences to draw upon to assess the situation and the appropriate course of action to follow. Instead a dominant aspect on which to make choices becomes the "projective element" of agency, which refers "to the imaginative generation by actors of possible future trajectories of action, in which received structures of thought and action may be creatively reconfigured in relation to actors hopes, fears and desires for the future" (Emirbayer and Mische, 1998, p. 971).

Browning's work indicates that, in maintaining the conditions in which transgressions occurred it is possible that groups of people can sustain serious abuses over protracted periods, despite the distress these abuses may cause some of the participating individuals. In such instances the understanding and experience of the participants of the social situation increases over time. However this does not seem to lead to an increased diversity of choice if the conscience remains unengaged, or, perhaps more likely in the atrocities that Browning describes, if the conscience has become so distorted by the trauma of experience to have normalised some dreadful behaviours.

The accounts reviewed in this chapter, particularly of Drs Marilyn, Audrey and Keira, alongside those presented in Chapter 5, indicates that the capacity for agency is less a matter of social penetration – that is deepening understanding of the wider situation – and more a matter of personal values, and that these values can evolve with time. But they can also be stunted by trauma and bullying. So, a further imperative to ethical leaders is to develop more ethical leaders and not, as is certainly possible, destroy their potential by destructive or thoughtless behaviour.

For junior doctors the agentic orientation that often seems dominant at the outset of their career is conforming in the present to the will of more senior doctors or respected colleagues. This is much like the participants in the experiments of Milgram, and Darley and Lantane. However, as this is occurring, their biographies are evolving and they may be constantly interpreting and re-interpreting past actions in the light of present choices, evolving values of professional responsibility and hopes for the future. Furthermore, and perhaps crucially, junior doctors are not kept in the same social settings for the length of their training but rather move across social settings learning from different seniors and peers with different outlooks, values and modes of working. And they may be confronted with the consequences of their choices if a patient or their family is dissatisfied with the results of their treatment.

The imprints of various social engagements are reflected in the accounts of the doctors I interviewed and reflect how their personal values have developed. As noted above,[4] Dr Lynam described how his wife's judgement on his involvement with the pharmaceutical industry had a profound impact on his thinking; Dr Audrey now describes her treatment of that ill child on the instructions of her supervisor as something deeply at odds with her professional values.

From these accounts I would argue (with Archer[5]) that values emerge from personal biography. However, we can also see that the diversity of social complexities that some individuals have experienced can facilitate both broader and deeper reflexivity.

It is not inevitable that experience of social complexity facilitates reflexivity. Social complexity can facilitate, at least in part, a *diffusion of responsibility* (Darley and Lantane, 1968) as well as providing justifying narratives for denying responsibility: everyone else is doing it.

---

4 See Chapter 4.
5 See Chapter 4.

However, the doctors whose experiences are described in this chapter, in common with those cases considered in Chapter 5, have ownership of their decisions even if they are not at complete ease with the consequences. In other words, because of their commitment to ideals of professional responsibility and competence this has led them to take responsibility for what they have done. As a result, these people have chosen to become different professionals to the young people they were when, often bullied and overworked, they made the mistakes they now lament.

For the cases discussed in this chapter, the particular social dynamics of these doctors' roles, the relative sophistication of professional development that they describe, and their commitment to professional responsibility has led to the transgressions and failures that they highlight becoming moral guides for them.[6]

Conclusion

Reviewing the decisions and choices considered in Chapters 4, 5 and 6 suggests that reflexive deliberation in the Cruciform of Agency can lead, broadly, to three types of reflexive conclusions: *resonance*, when the options provided by the social group are right by the lights of the individual's personal values; *dissonance*, when the options provided by the social seem profoundly at odds with the individuals values; and *assonance*, when there remains moral doubt and uncertainty in the choice.

All professionals begin their careers in unfamiliar environments. Hence, they begin their careers with constrained reflexivity, as illustrated in Figure 6.4. Nevertheless, it is a responsibility of professionals in general and leaders in particular to not only obtain familiarity with their professional settings but to achieve a degree of mastery over them. This implies being able to demonstrate responsibility for the decisions they take in their roles no matter how difficult or morally ambiguous these may be. It is from this that authority arises.

Points for reflection

- Do you recognise the experience of assonance – moral uncertainty – in some of the decisions you have made as a professional or as a citizen?
- Have you ever been led into making choices in your professional life or as a citizen that you now regret?
- What would you say you have learned from those experiences? Is there anything you would now do differently?
- How have your values changed over the course of your career? What, if anything, has caused these changes?

---

[6] This phenomenon is discussed at length by Jed Mercurio (2002) in his semi-autobiographical novel, Bodies, on the experiences of a junior doctor in the UK's National Health Service.

Chapter 7
Becoming an ethical leader

> It is not the responsibility of knights errant to discover whether the afflicted, the enchained and the oppressed whom they encounter on the road are reduced to these circumstances and suffer this distress for their vices, or for their virtues: the knight's sole responsibility is to succour them as people in need, having eyes only for their sufferings, not for their misdeeds.[1]
> – from *Don Quixote*, by Miguel de Cervantes

> In which . . . the author, drawing on insights from the Cruciform of Agency, builds on lessons from doctor's professional practice, and international law and policy, to articulate a code of conduct for ethical leadership.

So where have we got to?

Too often ethical choice-making goes by default when the person responsible simply presumes that no choice really exists because things have always been done this way or because social pressures suppress consideration of alternative courses of action.

However, the examples set out in preceding chapters demonstrate that ethical leadership, even in dangerous and complex circumstances, is possible when those involved take moral responsibility for their choices of action. These ethical leaders are united in demonstrating *moral integrity*: they try to do the right thing in relation to their own personal moral values, experiences, hopes and responsibilities towards others, aware of, but not determined by, the social pressures that bear upon them. This is a self-learned and *self-learning* process that is both enabled by and emerges from the taking of personal responsibility for the consequences of an individual's choices and actions.

Occasionally this process can be facilitated by others in learning or mentoring situations but it is fundamentally a personal matter rooted in the processes of human agency described in Chapter 4, particularly in *reflexivity* – the concept of thinking about thought that I said was going to be important in Chapter 4 – and the personal learning and self-awareness that this can bring. Often the values and hopes that guide *moral integrity* may be burnished by the experience of regret or shame over past failures to live up to these values, as described, for example, by both Drs Audrey and Marilyn in Chapter 6. The subsequent desire to do better can

---

[1] In the interests of full disclosure, this is part of Don Quixote's justification to Sancho of his decision to free the galley slaves . . . who then proceeded to rob them.

provide an even more compelling force to personal, ethical choice-making than any of the social pressures that may be exerted.

Ward (2006), in a discussion of Kant's philosophy, suggests that in thinking about morality "we should begin with the certainty that morality *does* apply to us, and then ask ourselves not *whether* it is possible, but *how* it is possible".[2] As noted, Warnock and Magee argue that a fundamental requirement for the possibility of morality is free will.

This book provides some further insight into this question of *how* morality is possible by exploring the nature of free will and how it has been exercised to make moral judgements in different circumstances. It is a fundamental assumption of this book that human beings have the capacity for reflexivity – thinking about thought – and that this at the heart of our free will, which is exercised in response to social challenges in the mode represented by the Cruciform of Agency. The plotting of an independent moral course by individuals in challenging social settings arises then from the privileging of individual's personal moral values over the wishes of superiors or peers, and sometimes over what might otherwise be considered the individual's rational best interests.

Ariely (2008) argues that humans hold predisposition for relative thinking. That is, we are always looking at things in relation to the other things around us. He argues that this can influence us, negatively, into agreeing to bad deals because when presented with a range of options we tend to compare them with each other rather than against questions of utility or original purpose.

However, this tendency for relative thinking also suggests that it is possible, at least in moments of reflection or more systematic learning environments, that past actions can be compared in memory with each other and against more recent choices posed to individuals in the social world. The process of professional maturation discussed in the previous chapter can then be seen to be a result of reflexive conclusions drawn by individuals thinking about their choices and experiences in the Cruciform of Agency.

The evolution of common principles in human morality may then arise in part from a combination of this predisposition to contemplate the world in relative terms in conjunction with a human capacity for reflexivity. That the rules of morality would emerge from these common human deliberations suggest that a predisposition "to do unto others as you would like them to do unto you"[3] may also be in play at some level in many people's thinking. Though, as Zimbardo (2007) discusses, this tendency, if it is there at all, can be suppressed because of stress, embarrassment, the pleasure of exercising power or a host of other factors, particularly in the case of individuals and groups in unfamiliar situations.

---

2 Emphasis in original.
3 The "Golden Rule", from the Gospel according to St Matthew.

If it is these predispositions and capacities that give rise to morality then this also suggests that Kant's Categorical Imperative – "Act only in accordance with a maxim that you can at the same time will to be a universal law" – sits contrary to human tendencies of relative judgements made with consideration of personal values in the Cruciform of Agency, rather than absolute, rational thinking. The humanity and humaneness emergent from doubt and appreciation of human frailty and social complexity exhibited by many of the doctors who participated in my research suggests this may not be a bad thing.

All of this helps us to begin to understand the question posed earlier in this book: *how do some people resist social pressures and instead chart their own moral courses*. They do this because their values compel them to do so. From the cases considered in Chapters 5 and 6 we can see that past regret and the love of another person, can help clarify for them the values that they will not compromise in a professional or any other environment. This then enables individuals to take personal responsibility to do what they believe is right.

Agency and ethical leadership

As noted in Chapter 4 there are a range of understandings of the nature of human agency. In this book I argue that all agency, including the moral variety, is rooted in the social, but has specific personal aspects, particularly as it relates to moral values. These create the capacity for individuals to deviate on occasion from group norms and/or taken-for-granted social structures.

So in this regard Trevino and Brown's (2004) argument, that the majority of adults are not fully formed when it comes to ethics and are not autonomous moral agents, but rather reside in an earlier stage of moral development some way short of making their ethical decisions based on principles of justice and rights, misses the point: No agency is fully autonomous. All are rooted in the social complexity of the situation which presents the ethical dilemma. This is a fundamental insight offered by the idea of the "Cruciform of Agency". However, some individual's moral values provide them sufficient motivation to plot alternative moral courses by making more life-affirming decisions in the face of complex professional or citizenship challenges.

The terrain of ethical choice-making (Chapter 2) presents a considerable challenge to the practice of ethical leadership. It means that if we are to hope for leadership sufficient to twist the moral arc of history back towards both justice and the survival of human civilisation, then we will find ourselves depending to a large extent on people who have been professionally formed by socially irresponsible or unresponsive enterprises. For such professionals to become ethical leaders will require them to break with past patterns to conceive of new thoughts about appropriate human rights and environmental responsibilities. They must then articulate those thoughts socially as ideas that may begin to expand the discursive space sufficiently to allow others to develop their own thinking and ideas that can then change the patterns of future behaviour of organisations.

For example, a manager who has been happily conducting business in accordance with Friedman's principles would require a radical change in their values to decide to implement a "triple bottom line" giving equal, or at least more, weight to the importance of social and environmental impact as well as the economic.

Of course, this can happen as the example of Ray Anderson shows.[4] And, as this book argues, there are a mix of social and personal factors that can aid development of professional capacity to identify fundamental personal values, or to change personal values and stimulate personal intent to act in harmony with these values. How this occurs can be seen in considering how junior doctors move from an agency that is frequently about conforming with the instructions and suggestions of more senior colleagues, to one of *moral integrity*: that self-learned and *self-learning* process that is both enabled by and emerges from the taking of personal responsibility for the consequences of an individual's own choices and actions. This often-difficult choice, to have *moral integrity* in any given situation, facilitates individuals to chart their own moral course through the complex issues that work and life poses.

Because of the operation of aspects of international business beyond the rule of law attainment of *moral integrity* is an imperative for all business leaders: without this too many businesses will continue to cause unrestorable environmental damage and to seek profits from the forced labour of vulnerable workers, including children.

Review of the empirical material gathered for this book in Chapter 6 suggests that the development of *moral integrity* among doctors arises from three key sources:
1. A strong culture of taking personal and professional responsibility for decisions
2. The codification in law and professional ethics of a hierarchy of moral purposes
3. A training regime that ensures experience of a wide variety of professional settings, and hence professional outlooks

If, in contrast, the social system in which professionals are implicated is focussed on facilitating denial of responsibility then the development of personal moral integrity, a difficult endeavour at the best of times, will be further impeded. In other words, Friedman's ethical guidance is a fundamental constraint on ethical leadership.

Some key aspects of leaders' moral purposes, such as health and safety responsibilities, and some labour and environmental standards, are in places codified in

---

4 See Chapter 5.

law. But this is hardly comprehensive. So, leaders may regularly have to make major ethical decisions that have far reaching consequences with no clear legal guidance. For example, if a business is operating internationally, beyond the rule of law, its executives may find it easy to avoid the consequences of their choices. It is unlikely that a business executive making, for example, buying decisions for their garment retailer based only on price will ever meet the young women trafficked to keep costs low. And, as of 2021, there is no criminal penalty in UK law for a London business knowingly sourcing garments from a supplier in southern India that keeps its costs low by enslaving young women involved in the manufacturing process (Kaye, 2016).

More international and extraterritorial law and law enforcement is desirable to protect human rights and environmental standards. Until that happens however, we must lean heavily on encouraging ethical leadership to limit damage and advance human well-being.

Still not my problem!

In 2006 I presented a class of business students I was teaching with a question based on research conducted by a British NGO, Global Witness, in the late 1990s:

> You are a buyer working in Zambia for an international diamond wholesaler. You have the opportunity there to legally buy cheap diamonds from a group of sellers. However, you know that these diamonds must be sourced from Angola, because of their type and that Zambia produces no diamonds. You also know that those who are selling the diamonds are agents of UNITA, the Angolan rebel movement, who will use the profits to finance a terrorist campaign aimed mostly at civilians, often including children. What do you do? Buy and make a considerable profit for your shareholders or refuse to buy?

This question regarding trade of blood diamonds split the class evenly between those who argued the duty to shareholders within the law, and those who felt higher moral obligations may pertain in a case such as this.

The question of moral intensity (Jones, 1991) seems not to have provided a significant issue for at least half of the class in this discussion. The evenness of the split in opinion suggests that organisational factors, suggested by Browning and identified by Zimbardo, Milgram, and Darley and Lantane, such as obedience to legitimate authority, peer conformity, diffusion of responsibility, were not overwhelmingly in play, and certainly not to the extent that they would be in a professional environment discussing a real decision as opposed to a hypothetical one.

Mellema's (2003) idea of "ethical distance", the lesser degree of felt moral responsibility arising from the lesser identifiable causal involvement that an individual has in an unethical situation, may have been a factor in the opinions expressed in the class: To young business students in Glasgow, Africa and the trade in blood diamonds may seem a long way away and difficult to conceive. These limitations, or similar, are likely to be echoed in professional environments where the complexity of the international business environment provides plenty of potential to obscure causal linkage. For example, for the mine managers described by Cragg and Greenbaum, the reified[5] notion of the business they work for provided them with a concept to distance themselves from the consequences of their choices.

As noted, Kohlberg posits the idea that the highest form of ethical decision-making is based on the ideas of justice and rights. Students expressing their opinions on the primacy of responsibility to shareholders in this instance may not have met the standard that Kohlberg would have thought represented ideals of justice and rights. But that begs the question, when Kohlberg is considering justice and rights, whose justice and rights is he talking about? Friedman's view is quite clear regarding managers' responsibilities to prioritise respect for the rights of the shareholder above all other stakeholders. This is an ideal that is perhaps easier to buy into than stakeholder theory because, as discussed in Chapter 2, there is currently no agreed moral core to stakeholder theory to guide how the competing stakeholders should be privileged in leaders' decision-making.

Furthermore, robust arguments can be made that if business executives just focus on delivering value for shareholders, then ultimately everyone benefits. It is arguable that South Africa is better post-Apartheid because of the investments that were made in its industry, despite the protests in favour of sanctions and disinvestment made at the time by millions of other ordinary people, including myself.

From this emerges the question: given that so much is unknowable, about the immediate conduct of markets or wars, for example, and the future unfolding of history, how can one take personal responsibility for one's own actions as they touch upon these matters? Friedman responds to this question essentially that one cannot and should not. Instead, one should only concentrate on that which is within one's area of commercial expertise.

But just because something is hard does not mean that it should not be thought about. Leaders frequently must take responsibility for decisions in uncertain circumstances. Entire schools of strategic thought have been developed to help guide them through such responsibilities.

And, some things are already plain. It is not a sustainable argument to suggest that anyone is left better off by business leaders decisions to neglect environmental restoration in their business and instead pollute water courses with toxic chemicals and pump greenhouse gases into the atmosphere. In an interview for this book Charles Mathias, director of underwriting at Fidelis Insurance, observed that global warming was already making it difficult to price risks properly given unprecedented climate-related disasters that environmental degradation is already prompting. Presumably as the pricing of such risks gets easier that will mean that environmental

---

5 Reification – the process of treating an abstract idea as if it is a concrete thing.

collapse will merely have become more imminent. So, eventually even wealthy shareholders in their Manhattan penthouses will be negatively affected by the pollution and devastation of ecosystems that are currently being enacted thousands of miles from their gilded existences.

Nevertheless, in considering my students' values that their primary responsibilities are to shareholders, it is arguable that individuals voicing these beliefs are indeed fully developed morally. Their choice indicates simply that they have chosen moral values that privilege a narrow community. These values may then shape not only their choices, but also the very way in which they look at the world.

Other individuals' moral values will mean that they think about the world quite differently. This will indicate other stakeholders towards whom they feel responsibility to consider the priority of their interests in professional relationships.

Irrespective of the precise reasons for the class voting pattern it did indicate a significant appreciation for the reductive ethical guidance that Friedman offers to business executives in complex international environments. However, considering the legitimate societal concerns regarding the social and environmental impact of business in the contemporary globalising political economy, the idea that responsibility to shareholders within the law alone is a satisfactory moral purpose must, as Ray Anderson (Chapter 5) recognised, be considered as out of date. At the very least such a perspective is a mere excuse to evade moral responsibility and hence a fundamental repudiation of the ideal of ethical leadership.

Furthermore, the view that such a straightforward rule alone could ever be sufficient to provide moral guidance in the ethical complexity of international business is at best dangerously naïve. Doctors, whose ethical decision making, while complex, generally relates to cases involving only a few people, must rely on an array of moral rules as outlined in Chapter 6. Even the most cursory examination of some of the ethical conflicts that the international business environment can throw up, such as blood diamonds, demonstrates critical limitations on the shareholders-first logic, if minimisation of social or environmental damage is any concern.

As has been explained and demonstrated in earlier chapters of this book, the world is composed of things and of ideas competing. Friedman's moral guidance is one set of ideas that has animated a considerable portion of the world's leaders with a conviction that whatever the problem is, it is not theirs.

Alternative ideas are needed that assert the contrary and articulate a lexically ordered system of principles (Rawls, 1999) that can guide moral decision-making for professionals leading in a world that is under mortal threat.

Personal responsibility

As Martha Nussbaum points out in her book, *The Fragility of Goodness*, sincerely held and well-intentioned moral positions can still have negative consequences.

For example, a government's desire to prevent corporate malfeasance through increased regulation may stifle small business and drive away inward investment leading to increased unemployment and poverty. Alternatively, a desire to increase inward investment and entrepreneurialism could lead to deregulation resulting in falling labour standards and increased environmental damage.

In other words, no legal or policy order is ever going to eliminate ethical challenges completely. So, there will always be a need for ethical leadership identifying where problems are arising and how these may be resolved.

As discussed, ethical leadership requires moral integrity. And moral integrity starts with personal responsibility.

In Chapter 6 I argued, from consideration of doctors' practices in relation to ethical choice-making, that decision-making about complex ethical dilemmas is best undertaken from a reflexive conclusion of *assonance* that explicitly recognises the potentially negative as well as positive outcomes from the choice of a particular course of action. Given the complexity of, for example, the international business environment, and the potential negative consequences that any single regulatory approach might bring, it seems that many of the challenges of conducting business in the globalising economy are also best contemplated from an *assonant* position. This is best achieved in the first instance by dispensing with the comforting fairy tale that the only responsibility of business managers is to maximised profits for shareholders within the law. The recognition that there are legitimate responsibilities to other stakeholders, even if only vaguely defined at this point, immediately complicates the moral landscape.

The importance of *moral integrity* in such a dispensation is therefore accentuated because of this: an *assonant* reflexive conclusion implicitly recognises that some decisions that a person makes will be wrong and, indeed, that some correct decisions will have negative consequences. Hence, it is vital that the individual learns from the experience to enhance the possibility of mitigating any of the negative consequences of the decision and to provide a more sophisticated basis for subsequent decision-making.

John Rawls suggested that the principles for the basic structure of society should be selected as if behind a "veil of ignorance", as if the chooser had no knowledge ahead of time of what position they may have in that society. Of course, those aspiring to be ethical leaders know, broadly, the position that they hold in society. Indeed, they may feel that they have a selfish interest, or considerable social pressure, to maintain the status quo because of the benefits that they obtain from this position.[6]

---

[6] Geoffrey had also been a Special Operations Executive officer in Greece during the Second World War, working with the anti-Nazi resistance. He was rumoured to have been the inspiration for the character of the British officer in the novel, Captain Corelli's Mandolin. Though, as Geoffrey once pointed out to me, unlike that character he could, of course, speak modern Greek.

This suggests we should make a virtue of the necessity and instead strive to practice ethical leadership through a "window of knowledge" rather than from behind a "veil of ignorance". In other words, perhaps the most fundamental personal responsibility of professionals striving to lead ethically in the socially complex contemporary world, is to be as informed as possible and hence increase their appreciation of the complexity in which they live and lead.

This *knowledgeable* approach to ethical decision making suggests three processual elements to any credible ethical leader's professional practice in *assonant* ethical environments if they wish to maintain their *moral integrity*:

1. Appreciate complexity: For the explicit purpose of morally complicating any potential decision, an ethical leader should consider its consequences in relation to the hopes and values of the diverse range of stakeholders who are implicated
2. Take responsibility: An ethical leader must take personal responsibility for the consequences of their professional choices, assessing how it sits with their own moral values not just with the expectations of superiors or peers
3. Reflect and learn: Later, with the benefit of hindsight, an ethical leader must decide if they would make the same decision over again and in the same way

Of course, any useful ethical guidance must include a moral core, that is substantive as well as processual. Consideration of these substantive elements is something that we will now turn to.

Moral guidance for ethical leadership

Stakeholder theory provides no moral guidance while recognising that there are moral responsibilities. In contrast, with Friedman's principle that the *only* responsibility of business is to maximise profits for shareholders within the law there is no moral sophistication. As a moral guide its attractiveness lies in its simplicity. Occam's razor (Fearn, 2001) advocates that, all other things being equal, the simplest solution is usually the best. However, such simplicity is simply not sufficient to provide sound moral guidance in complex and corrupted moral environments that professional leaders cannot avoid encountering in the contemporary world.

The hierarchy of doctors' guiding ethical principles stands in stark contrast to the simple-mindedness of Friedman's ethical guidance. While doctors' most common concern relates to the best interests of the patient this is by no means necessarily their paramount ethical concern: where there is risk to others, particularly to children, then the desires of the patient are of secondary, and sometimes tertiary, concern.

Some of this ethical guidance for doctors comes from law. But, as discussed, business executives sourcing from international supply chains that devastate their local environments with pollution, or exploit and enslave vulnerable workers, may not only be tolerated by the governments and political elites of many countries, but sometimes facilitated by national law. Therefore, South and Southeast Asia have some of the highest incidences of forced labour in the world. It is why the enslavement of migrant workers in the Middle East and parts of Europe, or in the maritime industries the world over, is so endemic.

It is axiomatic that if businesses cannot make a profit then they will cease to be going concerns. Such financial concerns are similarly fundamental for public sector and not-for-profit entities. Charles Dickens' Micawber principle pertains: if expenditure exceeds income the result tends to be misery.

But in all these instances Friedman's rule by itself excuses leaders' behaviour by providing an apparent moral imperative to justify it: they are, at least in theory, maximising profits for shareholders within the de facto law, even if the letter of the legal code suggests matters may be different. This runs contrary to the conception of *moral integrity*, the individual leader's effort to do the right thing in relation to their own personal moral values and sense of responsibility towards others, aware of, but not determined by, the social pressures that bear upon them.

Sir Geoffrey Chandler[6] (2009), a former senior executive at Shell and a founder of Amnesty International's Business Group argued that as a basic principle businesses should endeavour to ensure respect for the Universal Declaration of Human Rights across their supply chains and throughout their operations.

The idealism of this Declaration has been, in part, translated into a body of international law relating to the world of work and the environment. This includes, for example, the International Labour Organization's eight fundamental conventions, which cover collective bargaining, forced labour, child labour and discrimination. Unlike other UN conventions, the ILO conventions are drawn up by representatives of business and trade unions alongside governments. So, they reflect the evolving human rights challenges at work as experienced by those who are directly affected by them.

As the UN Guiding Principles on Business and Human Rights acknowledge it is the responsibility of states to *protect* the human rights of workers through the domestication of international law such as these. It is only states, after all, that have the authority to uphold rights through the enforcement of law. But this is still the body of international law that the UN Guiding Principles implicitly refers to when stating that it is the responsibility of businesses to *respect* and *remedy* the human rights of workers. So, there is an expectation that businesses should be aware of this law and not be acting contrary to it irrespective of how craven or greedy they, or the agents of the state that they are dealing with, may be.

International environmental law is not nearly as well established as that on labour rights. However, there is a Framework Convention on Climate Change, on Protection of the Ozone, and on Biological Diversity which give some guidance on humanity's current priorities. Of course, as Ray Anderson realised several decades ago, mere legal compliance, even to extant international environmental law, is unlikely to be sufficient to transform a business from one that is destructive of environment to one that is restorative.

But it would be a start. And it would be a considerable improvement if Friedman's guidance was modified to state that business leaders responsibilities were: *to sustainably maximise profits for shareholders within the letter and spirit of international human rights and environmental law.*

Such a reformulation would do two things. First it would reflect the ideal of the "triple bottom line": that businesses must satisfy environmental and social objectives as well as economic ones, and that those environmental and social objectives are important in their own right and need not be justified solely in economic terms.

Second a reformulation in this way would begin to clarify the nature of moral responsibilities towards members of stakeholder groups beyond the shareholders, including, most directly, workers and those affected by businesses' environmental consequences.

Placing human rights at the centre of business practice also dovetails with Bingham's conceptualisation of rule of law, which, likewise, placed at the heart of his formulation respect for human rights. This is important because for some time to come, until the rule of law is extended into all of the places where international business currently operates, business leaders are going to encounter a risk of human rights abuses encroaching on their operations and on their supply chains. Increasingly society will expect them to take some responsibility for rectifying these problems.

Kate Raworth's idea of "Doughnut Economics" (2017a) provides an even more clear and robust framework than extant international law to guide leaders' moral responsibilities in the face of contemporary crises in the environment and human rights. She argues that, in the 21st-century humanity must meet the needs of all within the means of the planet. In other words, "ensure that no one falls short on life's essentials (from food and housing to healthcare and political voice), while ensuring that collectively we do not overshoot our pressure on Earth's life-supporting systems, on which we fundamentally depend – such as a stable climate, fertile soils, and a protective ozone layer" (Raworth, 2017b). It is towards this goal that all leadership activities, directly and indirectly, must tend. It is the achievement of this that will finally bend the arc of history back towards justice.

So, irrespective of the knowledge and expectations of society at any given point in time, operating within the "Doughnut Model" to resolve human rights abuses and environmental destruction from any leaders' area of responsibility is perhaps the clearest practical test of a professional's moral integrity.

A code of conduct for ethical leaders

In summary then, from the previous sections I have drawn elements of a professional code of conduct for ethical leaders. This has six elements, three processual and three substantive:
1. **Appreciate complexity:** For the explicit purpose of exploring the moral complexity of any potential decision, an ethical leader should consider its consequences in relation to the hopes and values of the diverse range of stakeholders who are implicated
2. **Take responsibility:** An ethical leader must take personal responsibility for the consequences of their professional and citizenship choices
3. **Reflect and learn:** At a later time, with the benefit of hindsight, an ethical leader must reflect on whether they would make the same decision again and in the same way
4. **Attend to financial sustainability:** Whether a leader works in the private, public or not for profit sector it is unethical to bust their own organisation, or to financially exploit others. Downward pressures on costs can lead to labour exploitation and environmental destruction in supply chains and business operations
5. **Operate within the Doughnut Model, employing a "triple bottom line" to monitor:** This is applicable for non-profit as well as for-profit enterprises. Leaders who ignore the imperatives of human rights standards and the urgent need for environmental restoration are by definition, not leading sustainably and, indeed it is no exaggeration to say they are contributing to the undermining of human civilisation
6. **Choose life:** In situations that are morally complex, where the impact of choices is not clear-cut and information and opinion is conflicting, leaders must attempt to judge which course of action has the most positive benefit to the lives and livelihoods of others

Codes cannot eliminate ethical dilemmas. But they may illuminate that such dilemmas exist where previously some leaders have been in blissful ignorance. Such discomfort is the price of responsibility, which, I would argue, is also the core of professionalism and leadership.

Myanmar: Fumbling towards ethical leadership

In May 2021, as I was writing this very chapter, I was asked by an organisation, the Ethical Trading Initiative (ETI), to draft some ideas on ethical practice by business in response to the February 2021 military coup in Myanmar. It seemed like an opportunity to apply these principles in practice.

ETI is a London based membership organisation composed of businesses, trade unions and nongovernmental organisations working to improve human rights standards in domestic and international business. Hence, in particular, ETI wanted their garment retailing members to consider the question that if they continued to trade with Myanmar following the coup whether this might be of significant benefit to the illegitimate military dictatorship in the state.

It is easy to say, as I probably have on other occasions, that you should not risk having anything to do with such corrupt systems as military dictatorships, and the best way to avoid them is simply to pull out of the country until democracy is restored. The hope of such economic boycotts is that they would add to the general pressure on the ordinary soldiers and junior ranks to surrender their generals to prison and return to barracks. However, the first thought that came into my mind after considering this position was of a group of about twenty textile workers who I met one Sunday morning in a community centre in Yangon in 2019.

All were female. All were young. One of the things they explained to me was that it was very rare for anybody to be employed in garment manufacture past the age of twenty-six: older workers simply could not work at the pace demanded by the contemporary garment assembly line. Most came from rural areas. As a result of prior decades of corrupt military rule most of their families were not only extremely poor but often deeply indebted having been compelled to take money from local loan sharks merely to survive.

The consequence of all of this was that all these young textile workers were working ferociously hard in a desperately difficult industry to earn as much money as they could for their families before they became unemployed.

Before I even picked up the phone to any ETI member business or other stakeholder organisation to discuss their perspectives, I was sharply aware of just how morally complicated was the question that I had been asked to try to answer. Advice to ETI members to cease trading with Myanmar could lead to these young women's lives becoming immeasurably harder. Advice to ETI members to continue trading could also contribute to considerable hardship, as tax and other revenues created by the trade would help the military dictatorship sustain their position.

It should also be recognised that a military dictatorship is antithetical to the concept of ethical trade: not only do the Myanmar generals not protect the human rights of the country's workers, they are in contempt of those rights for all of their citizens. So, again under the UN Guiding Principles of Business and Human Rights, there must be an imperative on businesses to somehow contribute to the democratic movement in Myanmar as the restoration of democracy provides the only prospect for any remedy of the abuses the population is currently enduring.

Most responsible campaigning organisations will only call for comprehensive economic sanctions as a last resort, such is the pain they can inflict on ordinary people. However, it is perhaps important to note that the question of what to do in Myanmar is one to which the ideals of human rights and environmental standards only give very limited guidance. What is the right choice now for the best possible future is obscured by the fog of the war being waged upon the Myanmar people, by the dynamics of SE Asian regional politics, and by other business interests in other industries, such as oil and construction which are much more lucrative to the Myanmar military than the garment sector.

Given all of this, there is little clarity on what is the right course of action. The truth of the matter, of course, is that sometimes no one can be sure what is the right thing to do in a particular circumstance.

As already noted, leaders know this. So often their strategic choices are constrained by insufficient information and resources. So good leaders cease thinking about right answers and instead think in terms of robust arguments and considered judgements. In other words, even in problematic situations, *particularly* in problematic situations, good leaders take personal responsibility to organise a response to the challenges. This means they also take responsibility for the consequences of their actions even in the face of vast unknowns. This is what professionalism requires of us and that we do this in honest accordance with our hopes and values. Time will sort out what was right and why.

In considering all of this it could be suggested that I am trying to discern the lesser evil. But in this instance, I would prefer to categorise my thinking as searching for the more life-affirming choice: that which helped preserve most lives and livelihoods through this period of upheaval. This is something I described in Chapter 1 as the essence of ethical leadership.

In the end in May 2021, amongst other things, I wrote the following:

> The fundamental question that businesses must consider is this: does their continued trade offer more benefits to garment workers and their communities than it does to the military. At the point that this balance tips to the military then businesses must withdraw. Currently stakeholders consulted . . . express deep concern that comprehensive, as opposed to targeted, sanctions will lead to increased hunger and indebtedness amongst Myanmar's poor and expose them to risk of trafficking. So, the preponderance of their views is that garment businesses should endeavour to continue trade, at least in the immediate term.

Perhaps in writing this, I have made more difficult the democratic struggle of the activists and protesters risking their lives on the streets of Yangon and the other cities of Myanmar. Perhaps I have helped sustain the livelihoods of some young women in brutal jobs that offer them little support or respect. Perhaps I will have helped ensure that there is some remaining industry in Myanmar for the day when the Myanmar military dictatorship is finally consigned to the dustbin of history. Perhaps my advice will affect no one.

In any event I will review my thoughts in a couple of months to try to learn what I may have done right, and what I did wrong.

Points for reflection
- Does the code of conduct for ethical leadership seem applicable to you in your professional work or as a citizen? If yes, how?
- If you think the code of conduct is not applicable to you, why do you think so? Are there other ethical guidances that you would draw upon in your work?
- In addition to human rights and environmental standards, are there other priorities that you think are important for ethical leadership in the 21st century?

Chapter 8
Towards a movement for ethical leadership

> Revolutions can, and often have, begun with reading.
> – from *The Doctor and the Saint*, by Arundhati Roy

In which . . . the author identifies the need for a movement of ethical leaders from business, government, trade unions, civil society and the rest of the citizenry, to press for radical change in the political economies of the planet earth, if humanity is to have a future.

Corporate governance: A tragedy

> If you can keep your head when all around are losing theirs and blaming it on you, then you plainly do not fully understand the situation.
> – anon

On 2 September 2004 the *Economist* gave some details of a report by a special committee at Hollinger International, a newspaper firm, which examined how Conrad Black, its majority shareholder, allegedly looted the company. The *Economist* noted how,

> The report alleges that Richard Perle, a former chairman of the Pentagon's Defence Policy Board, is personally liable for his "abject failure to fulfil his fiduciary duties". As head of an executive committee at Hollinger International, it says, he repeatedly failed to "read, evaluate, discuss or attempt to understand' documents that he signed that facilitated Lord Black's wrongdoing. The report says that Mr Perle should return over $5 million he received from the firm."

The *Economist* also noted how Hollinger International's audit committee, which included a former governor of Illinois and a former US ambassador to Germany, was repeatedly condemned in the report for its passivity and inaction in failing to call Black to account for some particularly dubious deals. "In the audit committee's favour, however, the report says that Lord Black often misled the board, and that its members co-operated fully with the company's investigation" (*Economist*, 2004).

In 2007 Black was convicted in a Chicago federal court of fraud and obstruction of justice and cleared of racketeering and wire fraud. In 2010 a federal appeals court reversed two of Black's fraud convictions but upheld one of the fraud convictions and one of his convictions for obstruction of justice (*BBC*, 2011). In 2019 Donald Trump granted Black a presidential pardon (Greene, 2019).

While the ideals and practice of corporate governance may have moved on since this sorry Hollinger scandal some aspects of this story remain relevant to the question of ethical leadership. For example, despite careers that included positions of exceptional power and influence up to that point many of the Hollinger board members appear to exemplify the sort of constrained agency discussed above in relation to junior doctors, As illustrated in Figure 6.4, unfamiliarity with a new situation can lead to a radical curtailment of individuals' reflexivity and hence their agency. In the case of Hollinger International, unfamiliarity appears to have contributed to failure by board members in their governance responsibilities such that senior executives may have been enabled to abuse their positions within the business with greater ease.

Ethical leadership and hence the ethical code of practice presented in the previous chapter should apply to directors undertaking their board responsibilities as much as to leaders undertaking their operational and other responsibilities. Directors must obtain mastery of their governance domain and consider not just whether profits are being generated for shareholders, but how those profits are being generated and how well they meet the triple-bottom line challenges of environmental restoration and human rights protection. Blithely accepting the lies of any manager, no matter how brilliant or charismatic that manager may be, does not fulfill that requirement.

The G20/OECD Principles of Corporate Governance (2015) are meant to help "policy makers evaluate and improve the legal, regulatory, and institutional framework for corporate governance, with a view to supporting economic efficiency, sustainable growth and financial stability". These Principles also "recognise the interests of employees and other stakeholders and their important role in contributing to the long-term success and performance of the company". Further they acknowledge that human rights and environmental laws may be applicable to companies and make explicit reference to the UN Guiding Principles on Business and Human Rights. Such things, the Principles of Corporate Governance note, "may be important for certain investors" (p. 38).

However, the focus of these Principles is on financial matters and responsibilities to shareholders. Acknowledging the existence of core ILO standards is different to close consideration of how these might relate to governance responsibilities. Rather, the Principles note that "the risk of the variety of legal influences may cause unintentional overlap and even conflicts, which may frustrate the ability to pursue key corporate governance objectives. It is important that policy makers are aware of this risk and take measures to limit it."

This is hardly a ringing endorsement of the "triple-bottom line" let alone the Doughnut Model. Instead, the Principles take a position that might be classified as recognising the need for legal compliance, something that Ray Anderson[1] understood decades ago was insufficient to meet the urgent challenges of environmental restoration facing the planet. Neither does this legal compliance idea address the reality that many corporate entities operate beyond the rule of law, as discussed in Chapter 2.

---

[1] See Chapter 5.

The OECD Corporate Governance Factbook (2021) "provides an important and unique tool for monitoring the implementation of the G20/OECD Principles of Corporate Governance". It "supports the implementation of good corporate governance practices by providing easily accessible and up-to-date information about countries' institutional, legal and regulatory frameworks".

However, given the particular focus of the G20/OECD Principles, it should be no surprise that the Factbook contains no references whatsoever to human rights and only three to the environment, one of which is specifically "an environment of market confidence" (p. 3).

Consequently, it is difficult to regard the G20/OECD Principles as something to provide confidence to consumers who wish some modicum of assurance that the goods and services they purchase are not tainted by labour exploitation. It gives little assurance to ordinary people that the boards of companies are aware of, let alone contributing to, the sort of environmental restoration essential to stave off ecological catastrophe.

But there remain question marks over whether it is even sufficient to ensure ethical economic stewardship of businesses. Despite the 2008 financial collapse, corporate malfeasance seems be of enduring popularity. In December 2020 *Fortune* magazine editors wrote,

> In a normal year, the wickedest corporate scandals and worst executive malfeasance are impossible to forget. But in 2020, many of us found ourselves hard-pressed to even recall what evil acts went down over the past 12 months. To that end, *Fortune*'s editors have rounded up the 10 strangest, juiciest, most out-there business scandals of the year.

These included the

> Wirecard saga ... to put the most charitable construction on events; the company collapsed in June and investors lost billions. The parallel scandal is the failure of regulators and auditors to spot the looming disaster despite years of warning signs. Bruce Dorris, a former prosecutor who is president of the Association of Certified Fraud Examiners, says, "When you look at the magnitude of what happened, this is the Enron of Germany".

Fortune also gave special mention to Luckin Coffee, a Chinese company, with

> $310 million in made-up money inflows – a large portion of its reported revenue for 2019. The company acknowledged the inflated figures, saw its stock delisted, reorganized its leadership team, and in December reached a $180 million settlement with the US Securities and Exchange Commission ... Carson Block [founder of US short-seller firm Muddy Waters] tells *Fortune* that he believes Luckin is just the tip of the iceberg when it comes to securities fraud by Chinese-based companies. "I'm of the view that almost every single one of them is committing fraud to some extent", he said, noting that it is difficult for the SEC to enforce its rules on businesses based abroad.

Victor Riega, head of sustainability at Fidelis Insurance, in an interview for this book, observed that corruption often contributes to greater human misery by exacerbating the social and environmental devastation that unethical business executives or public officials perpetrate. In the same way that those who devastate the environment often abuse human rights in the process and vice versa, so also corrupt individuals are likely to be contemptuous of their other legal obligations and dismissive of wider societal responsibilities in their pursuit of graft.

In a society that seeks to facilitate economic performance and entrepreneurship, and seeks to ensure sufficient regulation to prevent economically, environmentally or socially destructive behaviour by businesses and other organisations there should and will be tension between these two aspirations. As noted, regulation can stifle entrepreneurship, but unregulated economic activity can destroy lives and the environment.

However, the environmental crisis facing the planet and the prevalence of contemporary forms of slavery in diverse international business supply chains suggests that the world is nowhere close to a sufficient level of social and environmental regulation. The depressingly regular recurrence of major corporate corruption scandals suggests it is well short of financial regulation too.

Mason (1959) worried that corporations run by unaccountable and "self-perpetuating oligarchies" are beginning to outgrow in size and resources some states, and the nature of their market power means they cannot be effectively constrained by society.

There are certainly considerable difficulties in holding transnational corporations to legal account. However, a laissez-faire attitude towards business appears to be at large. This means that there is little appetite amongst many political leaders, those charged by Adam Smith with the regulation of corporate enterprises, to even attempt to undertake this vital function.

A new hope?

> Never doubt that a small group of thoughtful, committed citizens can change the world; indeed, it's the only thing that ever has.
> – Margaret Mead

The challenge of saving the planet and advancing the cause of human rights – that is, the challenge of ethical leadership – must fall to that minority of leaders, in business, civil society, government, trade unions, and in the general citizenry, who are morally concerned and professionally conscientious. It must fall to those who recognise that time is running out for the planet. It must fall to those who understand that we as a human society are degraded by our continued toleration of the exploitation of other human beings in the political economic systems that provide us with goods and services.

If this more conscientious group can be empowered – and empower themselves – to provide greater moral example and ethical leadership in the wider community then Milgram's and Zimbardo's work also suggests that they can positively influence others away from more short-sighted or selfish concerns.

As can be seen from discussion of professional maturation, above,[2] the acceptance of responsibility for mistakes that individual professionals feel they have made has been a significant factor in their personal and professional development. This acceptance of personal responsibility may be seen as a core to agency itself. Furthermore, agency itself is leadership. At minimum it can open new discursive spaces. But it can also change the very nature of organisational engagement when the deliberating professional is at a critical conjunction of the rules and resources constraining and enabling an organisation.

The acceptance of personal responsibility is a key source of authority, including moral authority, among professionals. However, the denial of personal responsibility is still common among professionals. This is most serious amongst two groups. First, those who focus on maximising profits for themselves or shareholders through externalising from their businesses the costs associated with their neglect of protection for the environment and for the human rights of workers in their direct operations and supply chains. Second, those in politics and public service who fail to act to ensure that, through legislation, regulation or other action, business enterprises operate in an ethical, life-affirming manner.

Professionalism ends where the denial of responsibility begins. It is at this point where self-reflexivity and personal learning become impossible. The denial of personal responsibility in a situation renders us "fractured reflexives" (Archer, 2020) to that situation: people to whom life merely happens rather than human agents who may have considerable choice in relation to what courses of action will be followed.

Ethical leadership, in which leaders seek to take *personal responsibility* to obtain the most *life-affirming choices* in their professional lives and their roles as citizens, guided by an *appreciation of complexity*, and a willingness to *reflect and learn* from the consequences of their choices offers more positive possibilities. It provides a greater basis for personal growth, a greater capacity to engage with the complexities of a situation and, when doubtful of the rightness of a particular course of action, a reduced likelihood of mere conformity with the majority or the boss. It can also help expand the discursive space necessary to reshape the economic and political systems that currently destroy the lives and livelihoods of millions and imperil the planet.

---

2 See Chapter 6.

By embedding this approach to ethical leadership into diverse leadership teams hitherto ethical blind spots may be illuminated, and narcissistic and destructive cultures reformed.

One place where consideration of ethical approaches to leadership could be introduced is within the management schools of the world's universities. These, at least in theory, provide an opportunity for the discussion of ideas such as personal and professional ethical responsibility in business, and learning from professional ethical misjudgements. Conceptually just as questions of operations management and finance sit in the context of business and corporate strategy so the questions of strategic approach themselves sit in the context of the ethical principles and *moral integrity* (or lack of *moral integrity*) adopted by the business executives deciding strategy.

Given the problems confronting the planet it is necessary to recognise that the questions of business ethics, professional responsibility and personal agency are as fundamental to success and achievement in business as strategy and finance. Indeed, it can be argued that ethics and agency are more important subjects for managerial education than any other core topics of business education. Because where an erroneous strategic choice or limited cash flow can lead to the failure of a business, a failure in ethics can lead to the undermining of entire economies as Wrong's (2009) discussion of the Goldenberg scandal in Kenya demonstrates.

Of course, it would be forlorn to hope that a wholesale reform of the world's political economies could be achieved principally through the efforts of newly minted MBAs. Multiple efforts by multiple leaders in politics, business, trade unions and civil society must be mounted to have any hope of achieving significant change. More robust guidance from the OECD/G20 on corporate governance and how that must attend to obtaining a triple-bottom line within the "doughnut" (Raworth) would be a welcome start. So, also would increased attention by investors into the human rights and environmental practices of the businesses they invest in.

Building on this, governments could introduce more effective law and regulation to advance human rights and environmental restoration in business operations and international supply chains. Governments working collectively, such as the European Union, could do more still, properly fulfilling a role as stewards of a sustainable economy, rather than being cowed by big business, in a way that isolated, weaker nations too often find themselves.

As has been pointed out already in this book, while there is currently insufficient action on either environmental restoration or human rights protections to make significant dents in the challenges, there are signs of possibility. Investigations by journalists and nongovernmental organisations, representations by trade unions, and the advocacy of ethical business leaders have helped expand the law and policy that enables ethical leadership in the wider political economy. For example, as noted in Chapter 2, business advocacy ensured that in 2015 it became a requirement in UK law for businesses to state what they are doing to combat "modern" slavery in their supply chains. In doing this the UK government opened a new discursive space in the business community in which key issues that require ethical leadership for their resolution must be contemplated. From this some new initiatives have grown, such as those also mentioned in Chapter 2: the new contract clause devised by London insurers to keep products of slavery out of export supply chains; and the efforts by the garment retailer, ASOS, working with trade unions and NGOs to establish means of remedy for exploited workers in Mauritius.

Each of these initiatives in turn open new discursive space requiring and empowering others to think about what they are doing or not doing. With continued pressure from ethical businesses, trade unions and civil society, other businesses will translate their thoughts into ideas, and their ideas into action. This in turn can pressure government into new legislation and policy formulation.

Over the years I have found that often leaders who want to do the right thing fail to act simply because they do not know what the right thing actually is. So, in the next chapter I will begin to set out an agenda for action on two inter-related issues currently crying out for ethical leadership: contemporary forms of slavery and global warming.

Points for reflection

- What actions can you, as a citizen or as a professional take to, in small ways or large, make more just the political economic systems with which you engage?
- Are there others, friends or colleagues, who would also be interested in the ideals of ethical leadership and ideas on how to better contribute to environmental restoration and human rights protections?
- How might you encourage more widespread ethical leadership in your community or in your professional sphere?

Chapter 9
Towards an agenda for action

> . . . we all on earth have a commission and a right to defend the weak against the strong, and to protest against brutality in any shape or form.   – Roger Casement

> In which . . . the author explores two major issues requiring ethical leadership in the professional sphere and that of the citizen if universal standards of human rights and environmental restoration are to be achieved: contemporary slavery, and global warming. These inter-related issues exemplify the human costs when human rights protections, and planetary life-support systems are ignored in the world's political economies. They also represent an imperative for action by ethical leaders if the earth and those who dwell upon it are to have any future.

The issues that are explored in this chapter do not represent a comprehensive exploration of all those requiring ethical, life-affirming, action. Rather they are examples of instances in which political economic models fall outside of the "base" and "ceiling" of Kate Raworth's Doughnut Model (2017b). Contemporary forms of slavery illustrate the abuses that emerge when the human rights of millions of vulnerable workers are neither respected nor protected; and global warming shows the planetary consequences when earth's life-supporting systems are trashed.

Chapter 4 described how the thinking processes at the core of the Cruciform of Agency followed the pattern: Reflexive deliberation on the social and the personal in interaction → Reflexive conclusion on options in that situation → Choice of course of action.

This chapter echoes that pattern, beginning with a description of the issues – first contemporary forms of slavery and then the related issue of global warming. This allows the reader to properly deliberate upon those issues in relation to their own personal values. This is then followed by a description of some actual and potential responses to the challenges.

Individuals can embrace ethical leadership and respond to these matters in three principal ways:
- By raising their voices and using their decision-making power as professionals within organisations
- By using their decision-making power to add their organisations' corporate voice in support of justice
- By raising their voices and using their votes as private citizens

This chapter will give examples but will not provide an exhaustive list. Rather it is hoped that individual leaders familiar with their own communities, organisations and countries will conceive of new and imaginative approaches to add to the extant efforts of ethical leadership.

But didn't Wilberforce and Lincoln put an end to all of that?

In Chapter 2 I offered a brief survey of contemporary slavery across the planet. But the ethical distance that so many of us have from the problem means that it is easy to lose sight of both the human impact of this human rights abuse, and what might be done to end it.

So, let us have a closer look now at some of the manifestations of contemporary slavery to consider how ethical leaders can help end them.

A short story from India

In 2010 I supervised research into the forced labour of young women and girls in the cotton spinning mills of Tamil Nadu, India (Anti-Slavery International, 2012). The mother of a young woman who worked in one of those mills spoke to one of our researchers. She described visiting her daughter: "I spoke to her in a room provided for visitors", she said,

> because visitors are not allowed to go inside the mill or hostel. My daughter told me that she was suffering with fever and vomiting often. . . . I met with the manager and requested him to give leave to my daughter because she was unwell. I told him that I would send my daughter back once she was better. But the manager refused saying that there was a shortage of workers therefore they cannot grant leave. He also assured me that they would take care of my daughter and asked me not to worry.

A week later she received a message to say now she could collect her daughter to take her home. She was dead.

Probably the manager who refused to allow this young woman's mother to take care of her was focussed on fulfilling orders, often with tight deadlines, and maximising profits. This young woman was probably just another piece of machinery or livestock to him. She was twenty years old when she died.

One sometimes has the forlorn hope that publicising abuses such as these may change things, that the pen may indeed prove mightier than the sword as a means to obtaining a better world. But despite managing to expose these abuses in the face of considerable corporate resistance in 2012, by 2021 the *Guardian* (Johnson, 2021) reported that a new investigation into the spinning mills of Tamil Nadu by the NGOs SOMO and Arisa had found that little has changed:

> A worker at one of the mills spoken to by the researchers said: "We do not get proper sleep. We always have to work. We often have to work two shifts and sometimes even three shifts. This makes us feel tired and drowsy. But we cannot take any rest." . . . Hundreds of workers had no choice but to live in overcrowded and "unhygienic" hostels, miles from their families and with no paid leave. Workers described severe limitations on their freedom, saying that while they were not working, they had to remain in dormitories and were closely monitored.

Women reported feeling unsafe and that they were subject to sexual harassment in the factories and their accommodation. They described male managers, supervisors, hostel staff and co-workers touching them inappropriately and making sexual comments, often under cover of loud machine noise.

In technical terms these accounts describe *abuse of vulnerability, restriction of movement, isolation, sexual violence* and *intimidation, abusive living and working conditions*, and *excessive overtime*. Each of these individual abuses is regarded by the International Labour Organization as an "indicator" of forced labour (Special Action Programme to Combat Forced Labour, n.d.). The ILO notes, "The presence of a single indicator in a given situation may in some cases imply the existence of forced labour. However, in other cases you may need to look for several indicators which, taken together, point to a forced labour case."

The ILO identifies, in a list that needs updating, eleven indicators of forced labour. The conditions described in the *Guardian* report of Tamil Nadu identifies seven of these eleven indicators. This decisively tips the balance of probabilities towards a conclusion that the report describes a contemporary form of slavery. In other words, the report shows that the contempt for the lives of these workers that I had been involved in identifying over a decade ago in this portion of the garment supply chain remains largely intact. It is also worth noting that the majority of these poor workers are Dalits – the Untouchables whose plight fellow Dalit Kiruba Munusamy[1] endeavours to highlight in the Indian Supreme Court.

As has been noted, the UN Guiding Principles on Business and Human Rights assert that it is the responsibility of businesses to respect the human rights of workers in their operations and supply chains. However, it is plainly the case that it is very difficult to respect the rights of workers if the relevant governments are, either through incompetence or design, failing to protect those workers by facilitating or ignoring abuses even when they occur so openly.

Arundhati Roy (2004) notes that, "There's really no such thing as the 'voiceless'. There are only the deliberately silenced, or the preferably unheard." Silence is facilitated by social exclusion and discrimination practiced wholesale upon the Dalit community as Munusamy's own experience showed. This inhibits the issue of their routine enslavement in enterprises such as spinning mills from becoming a moral outrage and forcing political change: if slavery is being inflicted upon groups and individuals who are denied voice, and who the wider society simply does not like, then that wider community is more likely to tolerate the abuses if they see them and not raise their own voice to demand that governments do their jobs to stop the problem. This is a key reason why, decades after the widespread enslavement of young Dalit women in the spinning mills of Tamil Nadu was first exposed, it continues apparently unabated.

---

1 See Chapter 5.

Advocacy for change

Frequently, in my experience, when businesses are presented with evidence of slavery or other human rights abuses in supply chains their defence is "But we *audit* our supply chains!"

"Ethical auditing", a means by which businesses seek to ensure that there are no labour rights abuses in their supply chains, has been going on for years now. So, it is reasonable to come to some assessment of its effectiveness. One of the things that is increasingly clear is such "audits" have been wholly ineffective in identification and protection of vulnerable workers, and wholly inadequate in bringing about any reform in the systems of production where abuses are so rife (see Sinkovics, Ferdous Hoque and Sinkovics, 2016).

For example,

> The collapse of the Rana Plaza building complex in Dhaka, Bangladesh on April 24, 2013 is one of the most well-known disasters in the textile industry. What not as many people know is that two factories in the building went through the Business Social Compliance Initiative (BSCI, now Amfori) auditing process, the largest labour standard compliance initiative, before the collapse, and that no possible workplace safety risks were identified. Similarly, a few weeks before the fire at the Ali Enterprises textile factory in Pakistan in September 2012, the Italian auditing company RINA issued the factory with a SA 8000 certificate – a marker of high fire safety standards developed by the not-for-profit Social Accountability International (SAI). Yet despite their key role in legitimizing supply chains, the responsibility of social auditing companies and compliance initiatives has too often been overlooked.
>
> (Business and Human Rights Resource Centre, 2019)

This should not be news to anyone because, generally speaking, the purpose of "ethical auditing" is to provide plausible deniability rather than to identify and remediate human rights abuses. Should some diligent journalist or nongovernmental organisation ever expose the sort of exploitation that is routine in, for example, the supply of cheap garments to our high streets, there is little consequence for those businesses or for any business executives who have knowingly made decisions to source from slavery. The Obama administration did empower the US Customs Service to exclude goods tainted with forced and child labour from American markets. In 2021 the European Union is considering a similar measure (Business and Human Rights Resource Centre, 2020). But nowhere are executives held criminally liable for the knowing use of slavery or other egregious labour rights abuses in their supply chains.

However, along with trade unions and civil society, some businesses have begun to add their voices to efforts to eliminate labour exploitation including forced and child labour in their supply chains. It is notable that in the 2021 *Guardian* report highlighting ongoing forced labour of women and girls in Tamil Nadu spinning mills, the businesses Tesco and Next both acknowledged this was a problem that they were trying to deal with. This is progress on my own direct experience. In 2010 when confronted with similar evidence many businesses I spoke to denied that it was their problem despite findings that it did directly relate to their supply chains.

Efforts by international business in alliance with trade unions and civil society delivered the Bangladesh Accord on Fire and Building Safety in the aftermath of the appalling loss of life in the Rana Plaza collapse. As mentioned in Chapter 2, businesses were also vocal advocates for the inclusion of the "Transparency in Supply Chains" clause of the UK's Modern Slavery Act in 2015.

In truth had businesses not added their voices to the demands for these measures it is unlikely that they would have been obtained. As noted, Adam Smith believed that it was the duty of states to regulate businesses. Today it seems that too many national-level politicians regard their responsibility towards business regulation as being to ask businesses how they wish to be regulated. Some business leaders have also come to believe this is the appropriate order of things. Indeed Rupert Murdoch once explained his opposition to the European Union saying, "When I go into Downing Street they do what I say; when I go to Brussels they take no notice" (Hilton, 2016).

So, as we contemplate how we may shape a world in which the human rights of poor workers are protected and the environment is restored we must recognise a hard truth: that in the contemporary world the voice of business carries vastly more weight with national governments than evidence of atrocities or the voice of conscience.

Some businesses do, however act with conscience: a striking example of businesses using their corporate voice for justice occurred in 2020 when "26 companies, business associations and initiatives released a joint statement calling for EU-wide, cross-sectoral mandatory human rights and environmental due diligence legislation" (Business and Human Rights Resource Centre, 2020).

To eradicate contemporary slavery many more businesses will need to raise their voices in this way, joining with civil society to pressure government to act in ways that will compel others to respect and protect the rights of the vulnerable.

Older than Troy

Unfortunately, it is not just governments and private sector that turn blind eyes towards contemporary slavery. Much of the nonprofit sector does as well.

Philip Roth observed in his novel *The Human Stain* (2000), that all Western literature springs from a property dispute over an enslaved girl. The argument between Achilles and Agamemnon over the trafficked girl, Briseis, is at the root of the Iliad. In other words, since the dawn of Western literature the intimate relationship between war and slavery has been explicitly made.

Today thousands of girls and young women are subject to enslavement as a weapon of war by Boko Haram and Islamic State. The experiences of these women and girls are just as brutal and inhumane as anything Agamemnon or Achilles dreamt up. Thousands more, male and female, are subject to state-sponsored forced labour under the guise of military service in Eritrea, and at the hands of the military dictatorship of Myanmar.

Humanitarian emergencies do not just originate from conflict. "Natural" events such as drought, earthquakes, pandemics or floods, are also sources of disasters. Such crises create other slavery risks and a challenge for humanitarian response. For example, an inept response to the tsunami which hit the coast of Tamil Nadu in India in 2004 failed to recognise the specific vulnerabilities of fishing communities arising from the sorts of caste based discrimination that Kiruba Munusamy (Chapter 5) spends her life struggling against. Consequently, the humanitarian response to this disaster actually left many fishing families more vulnerable to enslavement through debt bondage (Human Rights Watch, 2005).

As humans continue to overstress the planetary environment, from the devastation of the world's oceans to the pollution of our atmosphere, such disasters are likely to grow and provoke further conflict over scarce resources.

The history of conflict and "natural" disasters, and the history of slavery are intrinsically bound together. So, one would perhaps imagine that humanitarian actors, those whose very professions includes the support and protection of the victims of war and other calamities, would be amongst the most perspicacious thought leaders and tenacious advocates on the policy and practice measures necessary to reduce the risks of slavery to the disaster affected.

The truth sadly seems something very different.

Viktoria Curbelo (2021) conducted a narrative review of databases for scholarly articles that address the issues of human trafficking and diverse forms of humanitarian crisis. "An initial search", she writes, "produced 59 articles, . . . Once the duplicates were removed, 44 were screened to ensure they met all criteria . . . . Only five articles fulfilled all criteria."

Curbelo acknowledges that a more comprehensive literature review may find additional material. Nevertheless, to find in a narrative review only five papers that fully met her search criteria does indicate a remarkable lack of interest by scholars in the subject area. This in turn corroborates my own observations, as both a humanitarian practitioner and an anti-slavery researcher and advocate: The humanitarian sector is strikingly ignorant of the issue of slavery despite it being intrinsic to the sort of catastrophes to which they routinely respond.

I too was oblivious to it as a young humanitarian practitioner. When I worked on water supply and sanitation in Afghanistan in the 1990s I regularly purchased bricks from kilns that used forced labour without even questioning whether alternative supplies were possible.

When I visited Cox's Bazar in Bangladesh in 2018 I discovered that the slave economy was still being supported in exactly this way. Engineers from international organisations striving to provide secure camps for the Rohingya refugees, with year-round access, were also routinely purchasing bricks from kilns staffed entirely by people enslaved through debt bondage.

The causes of the exploitation and trafficking in the Cox's Bazar camps are not limited to the manner in which humanitarian operations procure supplies. Madmadul Hoque (2021) describes how risks arise from the conjunction of the refugees' vulnerabilities and how the humanitarian response addresses those vulnerabilities.

Hoque notes that,

> Rohingya children are engaged in harmful child labour and become victims of forced labour. . . . National and international agencies struggle to tackle the issue due to several key factors. First, existing social norms and lack of social sanctions make it easy for employers to engage children in commercial and household works. Second, legal and formal institutions fail to tackle the issue as Rohingya children, like many other Bangladeshis, work in informal sectors. Third, parents are forced to give up their children due to a wide range of reasons including lack of access to the formal labour market, limited economic freedom, uncertain future, and poor living conditions in the camps. Fourth, undocumented Rohingya children have become easy targets for forced labour, sex trade, and trafficking through Cox's Bazar. Fifth, the Covid-19 pandemic has contributed to making matters worse since national and international agencies have considerably failed to sustain their regular support.

Hoque quotes a local official stating that, "Some Rohingya children, especially girls after going missing are often found to be forced in prostitution or domestic slavery". This resonates with reports from other humanitarian crises across the world that indicate that daughters may be offered up for various forms of exploitation, including sexual, to enable the survival of other family members.

The issues that Hoque identifies would pose a considerable challenge to any anti-slavery effort. But such efforts are negligible in Cox's Bazar. They seem negligible in all humanitarian practice.

When I was in similar positions as those leading the humanitarian efforts in Bangladesh I know I found plentiful excuses for not thinking much beyond the tyranny of the immediate operations that I was tasked with. But whatever sympathy one may have for the plight of individual professionals in such contexts, it cannot be an excuse for an entire system turning a blind eye on the matter of slavery.

Disasters, Kevin Bales (2021) observes, can disrupt trafficking activities as the infrastructure upon which trafficking operations depend is disrupted by the disaster. For example, the thousands of people who were killed during Cyclone Nargis in 2008 included many shrimp fishermen in bonded labour on Myanmar's Gulf of Motama, hence disrupting the operations of their traffickers for the rest of the season (McQuade and Nyein, 2019).

However, as Bales notes, disasters can also "increase the pool of people who might be exploited through reducing protections and safeguards, and traffickers may be quick to seize upon the opportunities that any chaos provides . . . . Put simply, disasters both terminate and initiate trafficking and slavery, and generally increase the amount and severity of exploitation over time."

Kathryn Bolkovac's experiences in former Yugoslavia,[2] where she uncovered human rights abuses, including complicity in human trafficking by contractors working with the United Nations, is an egregious example of what can happen when humanitarian actors do not make human rights intrinsic to their operational response. Oxfam has also wrestled with some of these issues in its humanitarian operation in Haiti, for example (Ratcliffe, 2019), and that is unlikely to be an isolated example.

Wieltschnig, Muraszkiewicz and Fenton (2021) recognize that trafficking, from child soldiers to financing of conflict through the sale of human beings, to the enslavement of women and girls for sexual exploitation and domestic servitude, pervade the contemporary battlespace – and hence the contemporary humanitarian arena – just as they have done from time immemorial.

However humanitarian actors still seem blissfully unaware of the risks:

"Between April 2020 and March 2021, Delta 8.7[3] convened global expert Working Groups to produce a Policy Guide that seeks to assist policymakers in assessing 'what works' to end modern slavery . . . in the context of Crisis". The resulting guide (Delta 8.7, 2021) published in April 2021, is a robust document that could enrich the depth of understanding of any interested policy maker or practitioner of the risks of slavery posed by humanitarian crises.

Unfortunately, the membership of the Working Groups that produced the guide were composed almost exclusively of long-term anti-slavery researchers and practitioners. Representatives of the big humanitarian policymaking and practitioner agencies were conspicuous by their absence.

Incorporating new ideas, and new responsibilities, such as the need for increased anti-slavery action in humanitarian operations, can be a daunting prospect given that these working environments are already intrinsically difficult and often dangerous. But facing such challenges are fundamental to ethical leadership. History and contemporary research both demonstrate the centrality of slavery risks to human catastrophe. It must be recognized that neglecting human rights and anti-slavery protections in humanitarian response is as professionally negligent as ignoring war- displaced people's need for clean drinking water and shelter.

Reforming the political economy of slavery

Contemporary slavery is sometimes an issue of classic organised crime: the gangs who traffic poor Nigerians in their hundreds into Libyan forced labour in agriculture

---

[2] See Chapter 5.
[3] Delta 8.7 is a project of "the United Nations University – Centre for Policy Research (UNU-CPR) to help policy actors understand and use date responsibly to inform policies that contribute to achieving" the eradication of slavery and forced labour. https://delta87.org/what-is-delta-8-7/.

and construction, for example. Or the Albanian gangsters who entice vulnerable young women abroad with promises of love and marriage only to deliver them into the hands of rapists and years of brutal exploitation in the brothels of Europe.

However, as outlined in Chapter 2, forced labour is more often an issue of the political economy. That is, it is an opportunistic crime practiced by unscrupulous people who see a chance to exploit others to their benefit because of the constraints and enablements that they discern in the law, regulation and custom by which we conduct employment, production and trade. In other words, slavery is a human rights abuse that is conducted by people who see an opportunity to maximise their profits within the laws, policies and customs of the places where they do business.

The risks of forced labour in international supply chains are compounded because, to use a legal metaphor, there is a prima facie case that a number of businesses, countries and regions of the world base their competitive advantage on the use of forced labour. As well as the fishing fleets of Ireland, the agricultural sector in other parts of the European Union is tainted with slavery (see Tondo and Kelly, 2017; Smith, 2017). Across Southeast Asia forced labour is a significant feature of production for export markets, most notoriously perhaps in the supply of prawns and other seafood to supermarkets in the global North. Forced and child labour are recurrent abuses in African agriculture, including, for example, in growing tea for international markets as well as in the mining of rare minerals for electronics (McQuade, 2016).

For migrant workers to Europe, for Dalits in India, for Lao, Myanmar and Cambodian migrants in Thailand, for the children enslaved in the tea estates of Uganda or in the cobalt mines of Democratic Republic of Congo, the idea of protection of their rights by the government, or respect of their rights by business would be laughable notions if the consequences of their absence were not so tragic. It is these absences that create the majority of forced and child labourers in the world today.

However, a conversation is beginning to take hold on how we should seek antislavery reform of the contemporary political economy:

- In 2014 the International Labour Conference, the annual international gathering of member states, business and workers' organisations, adopted the Forced Labour Protocol. This new international law requires the governments of ratifying states to develop, with national level businesses and trade unions, a "policy and plan of action for the effective and sustained suppression of forced or compulsory labour".
- In 2015 the UN made slavery eradication part of one of its Sustainable Development Goals (Ford, 2015) aimed at setting the framework for antipoverty work over the coming fifteen years.
- In 2015 the US Trade Facilitation and Trade Enforcement Act empowered the US Customs and Border Protection to halt the import of goods produced with forced or child labour (Connellan et al., 2019).

- National due diligence and transparency legislation is on the rise (Business and Human Rights Resource Centre, 2017) including, as mentioned, the UK Modern Slavery Act, France's "vigilance" law, and the Dutch Child Labour Due Diligence Law.
- A 2020 initiative by a group of brokers and insurers in the London market (White, 2020) means that cargoes tainted by forced and child labour may have their insurance claims voided.
- By 2021, in addition to plans to prohibit import of goods tainted with forced labour, the EU was set to introduce a mandatory "due diligence" law (Rees, Spath and Grassi, 2021), which would "require companies to carry out effective due diligence of its value chain, which includes its operations, direct and indirect business relations, and investment chains, in relation to . . . Environmental impact contributing to climate change; Potential infringement of human rights; and Good governance to prevent and mitigate corruption and bribery risks".

Each of these laws and initiatives sends out a "ripple" towards other stakeholders who must reconsider their own choices in the light of these. For example, if a manufacturer has based his business model on exploiting the labour of young Dalit women and still wishes to avail of lucrative markets in Europe and the United States, will he have to put greater value on the human rights of the workers now? Or if a government minister wishes to maintain their national revenues from manufacturing exports, will they have to invest in better labour inspection and labour rights enforcement of the manufacturing sectors they have hitherto been studiously ignoring?

These are a promising beginning. But they are only a beginning. To obtain meaningful change across the globe will require sustained and coordinated action by leaders in business, trade unions and civil society to press political leaders to support such initiatives with further reforms in national and international law, policy and practise.

It is this recognition of the need for coordinated action that is at the heart of the 2014 Forced Labour Protocol and its requirement for national governments to work with businesses and trade unions to develop action plans against forced labour and trafficking. This is because obtaining progress against these human rights abuses when they are often so deeply embedded in national and international political economies is something that will demand a sustained demonstration of *leadership as listening*.

Different stakeholders will have to learn from each other to deepen their understanding of the causes of the problems and devise relevant approaches to effectively respond. Trade unions, for example, may be well placed to explain to business leaders the realities of migrant workers' experiences of exploitation in diverse supply chains, and the reasons for their exploitation. International businesses may be well placed to work with their suppliers on improving labour rights standards in factories. In the light of new transnational anti-slavery law, businesses can also help the governments of the countries from which they source to understand the emergent economic risks that may be posed if they do not address systemic failures in labour rights protections.

In the end it is the responsibility of governments to write and enforce laws. They can only do this if they properly understand the complexities of the challenges and the consequences of any failure to respond. This can only be gained by listening to a diverse array of stakeholders beyond government.

The UN Guiding Principles on Business and Human Rights may prompt business leaders to recognise that human rights concerns are an increasing issue in international business. But it is the values and beliefs of leaders which will prompt them to act: to recognise that they should attend to the risks of slavery in their own supply chains and operations; to engage with other relevant stakeholders to try to effectively remedy these issues; and, to recognise that this is not simply a technocratic or managerial challenge but a political one. Hence, this is a process that will demand a sustained demonstration of *leadership as protest* to disrupt the discursive space shaped by contemporary national and international political economies that facilitates the forced labour of at least twenty-five million people across the planet.

Governments, at least within democratic societies, tend to listen to businesses more perhaps than any other stakeholder group. So, as Spiderman teaches us, with this great power comes great responsibility. Given business' power to obtain the attention of politicians it would be an abdication of this responsibility – and hence, by definition, a fundamental failure of ethical leadership – if business leaders do not, across the world, join with trade union and civil society leaders to demand coordinated action to reform the laws, policies and practices that enable so much slavery.

Elements of an agenda for action, part one

When I was the director of Anti-Slavery International, I often got asked by business leaders and policy makers for a "blueprint" to ending contemporary slavery. So, in 2017 as I was preparing to leave after thirteen-year tenure, I drafted the Anti-Slavery Charter (Anti-Slavery International, 2017). This set out the fundamental and interlocking elements of action, national and international, required from governments, businesses and civil society that over a decade of work with the organisation indicated was necessary to make meaningful progress against slavery. Many of the themes may already be familiar to the readers of this book:

The Anti-Slavery Charter

- **Rule of law shall be assured**

National and international systems of rule of law must be established and enforced that protect the human rights of all, which must be administered without fear or favour by a sufficient number of properly trained judges and a similar, professional police force to ensure that the promise of the laws to protect is not an empty one.

- **Discrimination shall be prohibited**

States, businesses and civil society must take meaningful measures to eradicate dehumanising and discriminatory practices from every section of society and to ensure true equality before the law.

- **National legislation shall criminalise all forms of slavery**

National governments, in keeping with international law, must enact and enforce a comprehensive legal framework that specifically criminalises all forms of slavery and defines appropriately prohibitory sanctions for perpetrators.

- **National legislation shall protect individuals from slavery**

Particular attention should be given to measures to protect victims of slavery practices during legal process and prevent the unjust criminalisation of individuals for actions they are forced to commit as a direct consequence of their slavery or exploitation, in keeping with international law. Adequate support and protection, including access to alternative livelihoods, must be provided to victims of slavery.

- **National legislation shall advance access to decent work**

There must be a sufficient and coherent body of law to establish, and realise, minimum criteria for decent working conditions and protection from exploitation, irrespective of the nature of the work, or social opinions regarding that work.

- **Protect vulnerable workers**

Particular attention should be paid [by governments, businesses and civil society] to the specific needs of disadvantaged groups or individuals, such as women, children, migrants, people affected by disability, and people affected by caste discrimination, to achieve equal access and treatment.

- **Freedom of Association shall be guaranteed**

Constraints on establishing democratic trades unions must be removed and the rights of workers and human rights activists to free association upheld.

- **Immigration law and policy which maintains or increases an individual's vulnerability to exploitation and slavery shall be prohibited**

No visa should ever be tied, either explicitly or for all practical purposes, to a specific job or employer. Workers must be able to leave a job or employer without fear of sanction, and they must be entitled to leave a country without fear of criminal or civil penalty for simply doing that.

- **The rights of children shall be upheld**

Measures must be enacted to uphold the rights of children and protect them from child labour and enslavement, including sexual exploitation, forced child begging and domestic servitude. In particular, all nations must ensure universal access to quality and appropriate education up to the age of eighteen, particularly for girls, for groups vulnerable to slavery, and for communities where child labour is endemic.

> – **Forced marriage shall be prohibited**
> All nations must put in place, and implement, laws, policies and effective law enforcement to bring all forms of forced marriage, in particular forced child marriage, to an end.
>
> – **Slavery is a fundamental issue of poverty**
> Humanitarian and development policy makers and practitioners should actively consider how their work can contribute to the reduction of slavery, and develop programmes and strategies to empower slavery vulnerable communities and individuals.
>
> – **Full transparency of national and international business supply chains shall be established and enforced**
> National governments must require, and businesses must establish, transparency of corporate supply chains to identify where risks of slavery, forced and child labour are highest and to help identify the causes of these risks. States must ensure trade agreements fully protect the rights of workers and communities, and establish and enforce robust national systems of professional labour inspection to identify and exclude slavery, forced and child labour from business supply chains.
>
> – **Recruitment agencies and practices shall be appropriately regulated**
> Recruitment agencies, particularly those engaged in international recruitment, must be regulated to ensure that the practices of these agencies do not debt-bond or otherwise render workers vulnerable to slavery and exploitation. Businesses must, through due diligence, ensure that any labour providers they use adhere to basic standards of human rights protections.
>
> – **Goods tainted by slavery, forced and child labour shall be forbidden**
> Where businesses and states have not set robust plans and processes to assess and address slavery and exploitation, powers should be established and executed to exclude goods produced with slavery practices from international markets.
>
> We the undersigned commit to using our power, whatever it may be, to empower those vulnerable to slavery, to advance emancipation, and to promote access to decent work.

Like with so many things, no one individual can do all of this, no matter what their role. But many individuals as professionals can do some of it. For example, a range of organisations from the International Trade Union Confederation, to Marks and Spencer, to Newcastle-under-Lyme Borough Council have already signed the Charter. With their signatures they have used their corporate voices to endorse the need for comprehensive reform of national and international law, policy and practice to combat slavery.

More specifically, organisations, and individual leaders within those organisations, could also lobby government, for specific measures that have been identified as crucial to help eliminate slavery. As well as the demands from businesses for the establishment of an EU due-diligence law,[4] "On 9 December 2015, Owen Tudor of the [Trade Union Congress] and Neil Carberry of the [Confederation of British

---

4 See above, section "Advocacy for change".

Industry] wrote [jointly to the British government] . . . urging the government to ratify the ILO Forced Labour Protocol . . . . On 22 January 2016, the UK Government became only the third government globally to ratify the Protocol . . . . " (Trade Union Congress, 2016).

Within the frame of reference of this Charter, individual professionals can consider further action. For example:
- A business executive working on procurement could review and amend her organisational practices to ensure proper attention is paid to decent work in the business' supply chains.
- A leader working in international business could establish a project to work with other organisations to ensure access to remedy for workers who may experience exploitation or abuse within the supply chain.[5]
- A pension fund manager could prioritise investment in sustainable businesses over unsustainable ones. One test of sustainability could be to enquire of businesses the measures that they have taken to uphold human rights standards in their supply chains and operations.
- A country director for a humanitarian or development organisation could recognise that their programmes do nothing to protect the vulnerable from enslavement or to address the endemic discrimination which underpins slavery within the society with which they work. They could then take steps – such as establishing new programmes, for example, direct cash transfers to support girls' education in families and communities at risk of debt bondage – to rectify such failings.
- Ethical leaders could also work through their organisations to lobby elected representatives or government ministers to protest policies that render workers vulnerable to exploitation. For example, tied visas or other "hostile environment" policies towards migrants pose the considerable risk that slavery facilitated by such state policies may encroach onto business, public sector or not-for-profit supply chains.
- Leaders who are themselves elected representatives may have additional opportunities to work on law, policy or practice to advance some of the specific elements in the letter and spirit of the Charter. For example, poorer countries may be more inclined to ratify the 2014 Forced Labour Protocol if richer nations committed aid funding to finance the action plans that dialogue between government, business and trade unions are meant to formulate.

---

5 Such as the measures, described in Chapter 2, taken by ASOS, in conjunction with national and international trade unions and Anti-Slavery International in response to identified abuses in Mauritius.

Leaders who are in less exalted roles can still raise their voices as citizens in protest. As Ben Phillips (2020) outlines in his book, *How to fight inequality*, even the most progressive senior leaders need a degree of upward pressure upon them to obtain political space for manoeuvre, and to give them the impetus of "public" or "staff" concern to compel them in the right direction.

A fundamental essence of ethical leadership is to do what one can, with what power one has in any given situation. Most of us will never have to sit in the same room as a mother who has lost her daughter in the cause of cheap tee shirts for the wealthy. But we can all still do *something* to protest such contempt for human life and to begin to remake the political economies of the world where such horrors are no longer permitted.

It's getting hot in here

Slavery and the environment

If contemporary slavery represents examples of the ways in which people's lives can be devastated when human rights are not protected within a political economy, then global warming represents how the planet can be devastated when the political economy does not protect adequately the earth's life-sustaining systems.

These two issues, slavery and global warming are interlinked, in relation to humanitarian crises as suggested above,[6] but also in a more endemic vicious cycle described by Anti-Slavery International (2019). For example,

> in Peru, over one-third of the country's glaciers have melted since the 1970s, causing both floods and water scarcity, and rendering the lives of rural peasants highly precarious. . . . Many Peruvians, particularly young people, have been driven to migrate to city areas to find work, placing them at increased risk of exploitation and leaving a deficit in the rural workforce. . . . In Bolivia climate change contributed to the disappearance of the country's second-largest lake in 2015. . . . When Lake Poopo dried up it brought to an end the traditional fishing activities of the Urus-Muratos, forcing at least half of the local population to migrate in search of work.

Researching the links between slavery and environment in this part of South America Chris O'Connell (2021) observed that, "In many parts of the world the effects of climate change are exacerbated by economic activities that cause environmental degradation. Together these factors worsen pre-existing socio-economic vulnerabilities, deepen exclusion and marginalisation, drive displacement and migration, and heighten the risk of contemporary slavery for children and adults." This, in turn exacerbates environmental devastation.

---

6 See section, "Older than Troy".

Kevin Bales, in an interview (Goats and Soda, 2016) to promote his book, *Blood and Earth* (2016), about the relationship between slavery and environmental devastation, noted,

> I was amazed to discover the role that slavery plays in CO2 emissions and in the simple and basic fact of how global warming takes place. . . . When we calculated up, very conservatively, how much CO2 is coming from slavery, it worked out like this: That if slavery were a country it would have the population of Canada, but it would be the third-largest emitter of CO2 after China and the United States. . . . I can point to . . . the gigantic mangrove forests at the bottom of Bangladesh, India, Thailand and Burma that's called the Sundarbans forest, and it's the largest carbon sink in Asia, in other words, a place where carbon is taken out of the air and sequestered by the trees, both into the sea and into the trees themselves, so this is a very important forest for removing atmospheric carbon. This is also a place where slaveholders are using slaves to clear cut these mangrove forests, to put in shrimp farms, to put in rice paddies, to burn the wood, to do a lot of different things with it, but it's almost all slave-based deforestation.

That those who enslave also devastate the environment, and vice versa, should not be a surprise. As noted in Chapter 2, similar phenomena have been observed by Ian Urbina in his investigations of human rights and environmental malpractices in maritime industries. But the increasing precariousness of the lives and livelihoods of vulnerable people that O'Connell, Bales and Urbina describe are also a portent for the rest of us.

Two minutes to midnight

Writing this chapter in October 2021, on the eve of the COP26[7] summit on climate change in Glasgow, there are many unknowns as to how the rules and resources of international industry and trade may be reshaped because of those deliberations. But one thing is blindingly simple: either a sufficient plan to stave off the worst effects of global warming will be achieved, or it will not.

Even in the best case, as with the recent initiatives to combat contemporary forms of slavery discussed above,[8] such a plan will only be the beginning. It will fall to thousands of individual ethical leaders across the globe to transform whatever commitments emerge into actions, and to exceed them if the plans are inadequate.

For those individuals' plans to be optimal it is important to first understand the context in which they are being formed. So, the next sections try to open a "window of knowledge" on these issues to allow for more informed and sophisticated thinking.

Much of this may seem negative. But unfortunately, that also seems inevitable. A slow-motion catastrophe is still a catastrophe, and currently, despite the efforts

---

7 "Conference of the Parties" 26 – the 2021 United Nations climate change conference.
8 See above, "Advocacy for change".

of Pope Francis and Joe Biden (Sherwood, 2021), there is no sign that enough leaders are intending to do enough to stave it off. Plainly too few people seem to fully understand the situation.

The 2015 Paris Agreement (United Nations Climate Change, n.d.) on climate change aims to "limit global warming to well below 2, preferably to 1.5 degrees Celsius, compared to pre-industrial levels". The Intergovernmental Panel on Climate Change (IPCC), the UN body tasked with assessing the science related to climate change, in a 2018 report noted that already, "Human activities are estimated to have caused approximately 1.0 °C of global warming above pre-industrial levels, with a likely range of 0.8 °C to 1.2 °C. Global warming is likely to reach 1.5 °C between 2030 and 2052 if it continues to increase at the current rate." This is why Peruvian glaciers are already melting and Bolivian lakes are drying up, displacing people from their homes and exacerbating the risks of their exploitation.

And it is certain that we have not yet seen the worst that global warming has to offer. Writing on NASA's Global Climate Change website, Alan Buis (2019) warns, based on the work by the IPCC, that,

> At 1.5 degrees Celsius warming, 6 percent of the insects, 8 percent of the plants and 4 percent of the vertebrates will see their climatically determined geographic range reduced by more than half. At 2 degrees Celsius warming, those numbers jump to 18 percent, 16 percent and 8 percent, respectively. The consequences of such range changes could be considerable. Take insects, for example. Pollinating insects, such as bees, hoverflies and blowflies that support and maintain terrestrial productivity, including agriculture for human food consumption, have significantly greater geographic ranges at 1.5 degrees Celsius warming than at warming of 2 degrees . . . risks from forest fires, extreme weather events and invasive species are higher at 2 degrees warming than at 1.5 degrees warming . . . entire ecosystems will transform, with about 13 percent of land areas projected to see their ecosystems shift from one type of biome to another at 2 degrees Celsius warming – about 50 percent more area than at 1.5 degrees warming . . . even if the temperature increase is limited to 1.5 degrees Celsius, sea level will continue to rise, as heat already stored in the oceans from human-produced warming causes them to expand. But that increase is projected to be 0.33 feet (0.1 meters) lower at 1.5 degrees Celsius warming than at 2 degrees. If warming reaches 2 degrees Celsius, more than 70 percent of Earth's coastlines will see sea-level rise greater than 0.66 feet (0.2 meters), resulting in increased coastal flooding, beach erosion, salinization of water supplies and other impacts on humans and ecological systems . . . at an increased level of warming between 1.5 and 2 degrees Celsius, instabilities in the Antarctic ice sheet and/or the irreversible loss of the Greenland ice sheet could lead to multi-meter (greater than 6 feet) sea level rise over a time scale of hundreds to thousands of years.

The consequences of global warming have not yet encroached on the lifestyles of many of our planet's more privileged residents, particularly those of us residing in the temperate zones of the global North. This is perhaps why, despite these looming disasters, in May 2021, citing models developed for the UN's 2021 COP26 climate summit, the *Guardian* reported that they show "that to limit global heating to 2C above pre-industrial levels there needs to be a 25% cut in carbon dioxide emissions by 2030, compared to where they were in 2010. So far the pledges fall far short." It is also perhaps part of the reason why, in 2020, so many US citizens were sanguine about voting for a white supremacist ignoramus who had already trashed the US commitments to halting global warming and squandered years of the limited time needed to obtain this goal. As far as these voters were concerned, global warming was not their problem.

The collapse of civilisations?

In 2014, a study, part-funded by NASA (Ahmed, 2014), into how civilisations collapsed across history posited that two factors – the competition for resources, and the stratification of society into "elites" and "masses" – were key. Essentially, by the time the existential threat to a civilisation from resource competition began to encroach upon the day-to-day lives of the "elites" to such an extent that they were inclined to do something about it, it was already too late.

The study discerned these two factors at play in all the civilisational collapses they studied and noted that the fall of the Roman Empire, "and the equally (if not more) advanced Han, Mauryan, and Gupta Empires, as well as so many advanced Mesopotamian Empires, are all testimony to the fact that advanced, sophisticated, complex, and creative civilizations can be both fragile and impermanent".

In 2020 Miroslav Jenča[9] told the UN Security Council that

> in sub-Saharan Africa, South Asia and Latin America, the changing climate is expected to displace more than 140 million people within their national borders by 2050. In the Middle East and the Horn of Africa, the impacts of climate change have already deepened conflict and provided fodder for extremist organizations. Indeed, it is no coincidence that seven of the 10 countries most vulnerable to climate change already host United Nations peacekeeping or special political missions.

So, the effects of climate change are already making the competition for resources an increasingly fraught aspect of the 21st century.

In 2016 Oxfam reported that the wealthiest 1 percent of the world's population own more than the rest of us combined (Oxfam, 2016a). Or, put another way that " . . . runaway inequality has created a world where 62 people own as much as the poorest half of the world's population" (Oxfam, 2016b).

In his book, *How to Speak Money*, John Lanchester (2014) argued that such inequality emerges from a consensus amongst policy makers that permitting such inequality is the best way to reduce absolute levels of poverty due to the economic activity that it stimulates. In other words, it has been viewed, including by politicians of the centre-Left, as an arrangement of social and economic inequalities that are to the greatest benefits of the least advantaged (Rawls, 1999).

---

[9] Assistant Secretary-General for Europe, Central Asia and the Americas.

However, while there may have been some progress in reduction of absolute levels of poverty because of this policy approach, it opens a different risk. The result has been an extraordinary stratification of society as extreme as anything ancient Rome had to offer when it tottered on the brink of its own collapse. So perhaps it should not be surprising that the world is falling short on the necessary action to limit global warming to 1.5 degrees Celsius: the lives of the elites have not yet been made intolerable by global warming, so they do not regard it as their problem. Instead, four of the world's richest men prioritise making a grotesque spectacle of themselves, joyriding to the edge of space while so many millions remain enslaved, and the planet totters on the edge of ecological catastrophe (Gammon, 2021).

Countering this culture of excess and selfishness must be a priority for ethical leaders in the coming decades.

In the absence of environmental justice

In the global South women and girls are already bearing a disproportionate burden of the effects of global warming. Luke Wilde, chief executive of the human rights and business consultancy *twentyfifty*, observed in an interview for this book, that because tasks such as water gathering and clothes washing are often regarded as women's responsibilities, women have been absorbing its costs and developing a greater awareness of its effects than most of the men with the political and economic power to do something to mitigate its impacts.

For example, in her paper Dalit Women and Water, Janice Lazarus (2015) describes the sorts of prejudices experienced by Dalit women and girls, such as Kiruba Munusamy,[10] and notes that these issues have become more extreme as water supplies have become depleted by environmental degradation.

> Women as the users and fetchers of water are vulnerable to the threat of insults, sexual harassment and ultimately may be denied water. Women as a group have decided to bear the abuse to get access to water, but are conscious of the difficulty and unfairness of the situation that allows for the belittling of a human being because of caste, class and gender.

Such things are likely to get worse. Tim Marshall (2021) notes in his discussion of the geopolitics of the Sahel,[11] that

> since the beginning of the Industrial Revolution global temperatures have risen an average of 1.1 degrees Celsius. The average rise in the Sahel is 50 percent higher . . . the rains now often fall as torrential downpours which can erode what little topsoil there is; and, given the

---

10 See Chapter 5.
11 The Sahel, the "coast" or "shore" of the Sahara Desert, is a semi-arid region that stretches from the Atlantic in West Africa, to the Red Sea.

> warming of the atmosphere, the water on the ground then evaporates more quickly. . . . Such is the picture in a region where over 40 percent of collective GDP depends on agriculture, but in which the FAO[12] says over 80 percent of the land is degraded. (p. 225)

Marshall describes how, in conditions of such impoverishment, the enticements to join fundamentalist paramilitary groups, such as free religious education and US $1,000 for suicide bombers, not to mention the perk of occasionally having the opportunity to kidnap, rape and enslave schoolchildren, can prove irresistible.

Northern hemisphere countries, most notably France, have provided considerable military aid to Sahelian governments to combat the growth of Islamist militancy. But such reactive measures are equivalent to putting a stone on a lid of a dangerously boiling pot rather than turning down the heat.

Efforts to turn down the planetary heat remain sluggish in comparison to the military efforts to suppress the paramilitarism that is growing from the despair and degradation climate change is bringing. For example, the "Great Green Wall", a massive reforestation initiative that is meant to span the Sahel, has been uneven in its achievements.

Such a project will always have technical and social challenges, such as getting the right trees to grow in the right places and reducing losses to the livestock of passing nomads. In Jan 2021 the project received a boost of $14 billion in funding, estimated to amount to about 30 percent of the budget necessary to complete the project by 2030 (United Nations Convention to Combat Desertification, 2021). When one understands that by 2020 this project had only covered 4 percent of its target area, halfway towards its completion date, such funding must be welcomed (Watts, 2020). Still, given the global North's self-interest in the preservation of the carbon sinks of the global South, many will wonder why the project seems to lack urgency and priority amongst many aid donors.

Sarah O'Connor (2021) in the *Financial Times*, observed that "In a decarbonising global economy, metals may be the new oil. Demand for copper, nickel, cobalt and lithium is likely to surge in the next two decades because of their importance to clean energy technologies."

However, without reform of the political economy this is unlikely to spell much hope for mineral rich parts of the world, including Africa's Sahel. As Marshall notes, currently the vast mineral wealth of the Sahel tends to enrich Northern Hemisphere businesses rather than provide funding for local health services, the education of the region's girls and the transition of the region to a sustainable economy to employ those that global warming is currently displacing.

Neither does a mineral bonanza automatically promise decent work for individual workers. As O'Connor goes on to observe, many of the jobs in these industries, from mining to recycling, are often dirty, dangerous and rife with human rights

---

[12] The UN's Food and Agriculture Organisation.

abuses, including child labour and slavery. So, without the measures associated with coordinated national and international anti-slavery work, discussed in the previous section of this chapter, decent work in these "green" supply chains will not be obtained. Instead, the vicious cycle of environmental degradation and human rights abuses will be merely buckled rather than broken.

Elements of an agenda for action, part two

Bleak as this survey of global warming may be, there are glimmers of hope springing from ethical leaders taking upon themselves the moral responsibility to act. In Australia, "eight teenagers and an octogenarian nun" (Morton, 2021) sought an injunction to prevent the federal environment minister from approving the expansion of a coal mine in New South Wales. They argued that the minister had a "duty of care to protect younger people against future harm from climate change". In 2021 Friends of the Earth in the Netherlands (Boffey, 2021) won a case against Royal Dutch Shell in which the court ordered the company to cut its global carbon emissions by 45 percent by the end of 2030 compared with its 2019 levels.

Shell, the ninth biggest polluter in the world in 1988 to 2015 has, of course, stated it will appeal the judgement. Perhaps that business' leaders think they will be immune from any coming crisis.

Ethical leaders do not have the luxury of such delusions. They recognise the imperative to act in the most life-affirming way in the faces of whatever challenges confront them. Sometimes that means they can avert disaster. Sometimes it means that they must make do with managing the risks and mitigating the consequences.

In confronting the challenges posed by climate change, Greenpeace has set out ten elements that it believes are essential (Greenpeace, n.d.):
- "Keep fossil fuels in the ground"
- "Invest in renewable energy"
- "Switch to sustainable transport"
- "Insulate walls and roofs and switch away from oil or gas boilers to heat pumps"
- "Improve farming and encourage vegan diets"
- "Restore nature to absorb more carbon"
- "Protect forests like the Amazon"
- "Protect the oceans"
- "Reduce how much people consume"
- "Reduce plastic . . . Demand for plastic is rising so quickly that creating and disposing of plastics will account for 17% of the global carbon budget by 2050 (this is the emissions count we need to stay within according to the Paris agreement)"

Ethical leaders must contemplate if and how they can advance action on each of these elements to ensure, as Kate Raworth (2017b) has put it, that "we do not overshoot our pressure on Earth's life-supporting systems, on which we fundamentally depend".

As noted, Raworth's idea of "doughnut economics" is for a model of sustainable economic activity that is facilitated between a social foundation that ensures the protection of fundamental human rights, and environmental ceiling that prevents critical planetary degradation. In 2020 Amsterdam formally adopted Raworth's Doughnut Model as "the starting point for public policy decisions" (Boffey, 2020).

In an interview with the *Guardian*, Marieke van Doorninck, deputy mayor of Amsterdam, described how this would be applied. The article noted that,

> Residents' housing needs are increasingly not being satisfied, with almost 20% of city tenants unable to cover their basic needs after paying their rent, and just 12% of approximately 60,000 online applicants for social housing being successful. One solution might be to build more homes but Amsterdam's doughnut highlights that the area's carbon dioxide emissions are 31% above 1990 levels. Imports of building materials, food and consumer products from outside the city boundaries contribute 62% of those total emissions.
>
> Van Doorninck says the city plans to regulate to ensure builders use materials that are as often possible recycled and bio based, such as wood. But the "Doughnut" approach also encourages policymakers to lift their eyes to the horizon . . . [van Doorninck] says "The doughnut does not bring us the answers but a way of looking at it, so that we don't keep on going on in the same structures as we used to".

According to the article, the port of Amsterdam "is looking at how it moves on from dependence on fossil fuels as part of the city's new vision, and [van Doorninck] expects that to naturally evolve into a wider debate over other pressing dilemmas brought to the forefront by the doughnut model".

In other words, van Doorninck describes using Raworth's Doughnut Model as a fundamental basis upon which the city will conduct its strategic and operational planning and decision-making in order to ensure not just that the basic needs of the city's population are met, but that they are met in an environmentally sustainable fashion.

Amsterdam is a world city. So, the choices that it makes, will ripple forth across the world, for example, requiring international businesses which wish to use the port to also contemplate how well they are fitting into the "doughnut" between the "floor" of human rights and the "ceiling" of environmental protections.

This is an approach which other businesses, nongovernmental organisations and government agencies could also take, adopting the Doughnut Model as a fundamental strategic planning tool. This then would make explicit the need to consider environmental costs and human rights protections when developing all plans for the future. The Doughnut Model would demand that leaders have conversations on developing measures to reshape operations and organisations to meet the environmental and human rights challenges with the urgency that the impending planetary crisis requires. This approach would then ripple forth from the new practitioners, increasing the discursive space within which others can also consider and act upon these imperatives.

Some human consequences of inaction

> Through various hazards and events we move.   – from the *Aeneid*, by Virgil

Abebi[13] dreamed of working in Europe. She heard stories in her Nigerian community in Edo State of the opportunities that existed there for hard working Nigerians. So, rather than continue living in an area wracked with insecurity and with limited economic opportunities, she contracted an "agent" to help her travel overland to Libya where she was assured she could take a boat to Europe.

What happened to her next was highly typical of the experiences of overland migration for young Nigerians hoping for better lives in Europe:

> I had a terrible experience on my way to Libya. I was subjected to emotional, physical and mental torture. I drank the urine of my friend due to dehydration. On my arrival at the Niger border, we were attacked by Niger security personnel and spent two days in the forest. The truck I was transported in was attacked in the desert and I and the group of people I travelled with spent 7 days in the desert. We were forced to dress [in full body cover] to disguise ourselves. We were packed in a truck and tomatoes placed on top of us to hide our identities because we had no visas. I was not spared in Libya as my hut was attacked . . . which led to me running for my life before I met a woman who put me to work as a prostitute in a brothel.

Another migrant, Idris,[14] describes similar experiences:

> In January 2018, I left Nigeria with the hope of crossing the Mediterranean Sea to Germany. I left Benin [City] for Kano, travelling through Agadez – Niger, the Sahara Desert before arriving in Libya. The journey was tough, stressful and dangerous. I suffered dehydration, starvation, fell ill and was also tortured by bandits. I saw people drink their urine when they were thirsty. On our journey through the desert, we were attacked by bandits and lives were lost – mainly little children who could not run: they were buried in the desert. My best friend was shot and killed on one of the occasions that we were attacked. Five people died from my Hilux truck, their valuables such as phones and money were stolen. The men who had nothing on them were beaten while the girls and young women were raped. On my way, I was sold by my connection man called Mr James and my mother had to send [money] so I could regain my freedom. In Libya I worked as a labourer and slept on the streets for two months before I was able to rent an apartment.

Neither Idris nor Abedi ever managed to get as far as the sea let alone Europe.

---

13 Not her real name. Abebi participated in a research project funded by the UK Department for International Development that I led at the end of 2019.
14 Not his real name.

David,[15] an Eritrean national fleeing, like hundreds of others, state-sponsored forced labour in his own country, also sought to travel to Europe via Libya. After enduring similar violence and enslavement in Libya to that suffered by Idris and Abebi, in about 2014 David did manage to get onto a wooden boat along with, he reckons, 300 other people. In the middle of the Mediterranean somewhere Italian authorities found the boat and saved them. David believes that he would not have survived but for the Italian navy.

Thousands of others do not make it. Writing in the *Guardian* in 2018 Kenan Malik noted

> In October 2013, a ship carrying migrants sank off the Italian island of Lampedusa. Some 300 people drowned. . . . It was not the first time that migrants had drowned in the Mediterranean. In fact, at that time it was estimated that in the previous 25 years at least 20,000 people had died trying to reach the shores of Europe. The real figure was most likely much higher. But that sinking in October 2013 was the first time that such a tragedy had truly impressed itself upon the conscience of Europe.

There are tens of thousands of stories like those of Abebi, Idris and David emerging from Africa alone. Others continue to flee war in the Middle East, and the tide of refugees from Afghanistan is set to rise since the departure of the United States and its allies in 2021.

Abedi, Idris and David are among the lucky ones in that they survived. Nevertheless, their stories are still typical in that they describe an experience of migration that is spurred by desperation and marked by appalling levels of violence. These stories represent the human face of the consequences of slavery and global warming, and the economic decline and political upheavals that these prompt.

Few of these migrants stated that they were expecting the horrors that awaited them. But nevertheless, it is difficult to imagine them setting out on such perilous journeys if they had satisfactory prospects at home.

As noted, Eritrea has a comprehensive system of state sponsored forced labour ensnaring its young. In Nigeria the economic collapse arising from global warming and environmental degradation has, amongst other indignities, prompted a rise in kidnappings for ransom of both local people and foreigners, by both Islamists and local militias. Neil Munshi in the *Financial Times* on 26 April 2021 quoted Zainab Usman, of the Carnegie Endowment for Peace, who observed that "Banditry has flourished in an economy that has been crippled by two recessions in six years. It has spread across the entire country partly because it has become a viable career option for some of the millions of young Nigerians thrown each year into an economy that cannot create enough jobs to accommodate them."

---

15 Not his real name.

The *Financial Times* article went on to note that,

"For now kidnapping remains a career path because there are virtually no consequences for doing it", says Chris Kwaja[16] . . . "You will see instances of groups arrested by security agencies but in all these arrests we haven't seen prosecutions . . . so we see how they are emboldened", says Kwaja, adding that under-resourced security forces rife with corruption are incapable of addressing the problem.

Tim Marshall (2021) notes, "When the rains fail so do the crops. When the lakes shrink so does the food supply. When this happens people move, and when people move, the places they move to are often not ready for them" (p. 206). But it must be remembered that people undertaking such perilous journeys are not just survivors of ecological collapse, state failure or repression. They are also political actors, giving the world a stark reminder of the human consequences of our collective failure to deal with climate change and slavery. That the relatively privileged citizens of the global North have generally, until now at least, been trying to studiously avoid thinking about and responding adequately to all but the most immediate threats is no guard against what is coming.

Conclusion

It is now plain that the way economic activity has been practiced since the onset of the Industrial Revolution is not sustainable. It has too often treated human beings as expendable and natural resources as inexhaustible. It has generated considerable levels of carbon, which has warmed the atmosphere and so made unsustainable the livelihoods of millions and threatens the livelihoods of millions more, particularly in the global South. This in turn threatens further violent insurgency and involuntary migration that will open more to the risks of enslavement and contribute to further environmental destruction.

So, if what currently passes for human civilisation is to survive the next century, and avoid the fate of ancient Rome and so many other lost civilisations, it is essential that the elites – those with their hands on the levers of power – exercise sufficient moral courage and ethical leadership to ensure fairer distribution of resources for everyone. This means, in particular, compelling those with excess to share through just systems of taxation, forcing those who are greedy to desist from their grasping with sensible law, policy and practice, including more effective legislation on businesses implementing the Doughnut Model to obtain a "triple bottom line", and investing properly in health, education and environmental justice across the planet.

---

16 A senior lecturer at the Centre for Peace and Security Studies in Yola, a city in the Nigeria's northeast.

Of course, other historical lessons, from the Roman Empire to the decolonisation of the British Empire, show that if the elites do not act with justice the masses will take it for themselves anyway. And there are too many sanguinary examples that demonstrate that a clamour for justice too long unrequited can result in unconstrained and indiscriminate vengeance when anger and frustration finally boil over.

Such outcomes are failures of ethical leadership *on the part of the elites* who have not risen to their "moment of truth" when they had the opportunity. So, to endeavour to avoid that there is an urgent need to reduce the absolute levels of inequality in the world. Environmental justice is a fundamental part of this challenge. So too is ensuring fundamental standards of human rights for all.

It is often the case that decisive human action is only prompted by immediate imperatives such as a military threat, rather than by a sense of common humanity or even careful contemplation of long-term self-interest. This lack of a strategic perspective in relation to the impact of climate change is a fundamental failure of ethical leadership.

Ray Anderson understood this when he sought to transform his business into a "restorative" enterprise.[17] The rest of the world now needs to race to catch up before the calamities already experienced by poor people in places such as the Sahel, Peru and Bolivia become more general.

The pace of global warming, and its dreadful consequences including hunger, impoverishment, the growth of forced human migration and violent insurgencies already cry out the need for urgent action. As it stands, things are set to get worse to an extent in which even the most obdurately ignorant will be confronted with its consequences: If even a portion of the changes predicted by the IPCC come to pass, the disastrous situation in places like the Sahel and the Andes will become catastrophic, and the currently tolerable situations in other places will become disastrous. This will contribute further to that vicious circle of destroyed lives and undermined livelihoods. It will also see growth in new violent insurgencies, drive new forced migrations, and render the affected populations vulnerable to trafficking and exploitation, both by armed factions and in industries that will contribute further to the disaster of global warming.

The examples discussed in this chapter are demonstrations of what can happen when the social foundations and the environmental ceiling of economic activity are ignored. In the immediate term the costs are borne in brutal terms by poor people. But, as they continue to be ignored the problems morph and multiply, degrading human rights standards and the living environment in every corner of this fragile planet.

However, action is possible, as described above, and if a critical mass of ethical leaders around the globe take it upon themselves to act and encourage others to

---

17 See Chapter 5.

act, it would help break the vicious cycles of human rights abuses and environmental degradation in which we are currently spiraling.

None of this is necessarily easy. But action of some sort by every leader is possible, either directly changing practice and policy, or loudly protesting injustice and prejudice.

There is no longer anywhere to hide. So, it is instead necessary to lead.

Points for reflection

- On reflection, do you think the operations or supply chains of your organisation or your community is implicated in any of the issues described in this chapter?
- Are there other issues which you feel are a particular urgent challenge in need of ethical leadership?
- What actions might you be able to take over the coming year, in either your professional sphere or your sphere of citizenship, that might contribute to addressing the causes or consequences of some of the issues identified in this chapter or which you have identified from your personal experience and reflection?

Chapter 10
Final reflections

> Ever try. Ever fail. No matter. Try again. Fail again. Fail better.   – Samuel Beckett

> In which . . . the author offers final reflections on ethical leadership, including how even doing the "right" thing can lead to regret; why it's important not to use personal values to justify reprehensible behaviour, and, revisiting Bobby Kennedy's reflections on "numberless diverse acts of courage and belief", how with hard work, sometimes, we can make "hope and history" rhyme.

The consequences of leadership

> Act if it is beneficial, desist if it is not.   – from *The Art of War*, by Sun Tzu

By 2000 in Angola we had expanded our humanitarian operations to two additional cities in the central highlands of the country: Huambo and Malange. The triangle between these cities and Kuito continued to be bloodily contested, even as the major set-piece battles of late 1998 and early 1999 evolved into guerrilla conflict.

As in Kuito the city of Malange was also thronged with civilians fleeing UNITA. Here, however, the government controlled, at least for most of the time, a larger enclave around the city that included several outlying villages. Consequently, they established some of the new settlements of war-displaced people in these villages.

One such village was called Cangandala, about 20 km south of Malange along a heavily pitted, narrow asphalt road. There were about two poorly functioning wells in the village – barely sufficient for the original population of the village and woefully inadequate for the thousands more families crammed into the poorly sanitised camps that had quickly grown up there. The Oxfam team in Malange made remediating the water and sanitation situation in Cangandala their priority, such was the extremity of the situation. They moved their drilling equipment into the village and started opening new wells, to ensure safe drinking water became rapidly available, and promoting safe sanitation and hygiene practice.

Shortly after this operation began, I received a phone call one morning in my office in Luanda, the Angolan capital, from a colleague in another agency. Our Malange team had travelled to Cangandala without incident that morning, but after they had reached their destination a subsequent vehicle on the same road had hit a landmine with casualties. Aside from the immediate human suffering the implications of this information were very troubling. The heavy usage of the road to Cangandala suggested that the mine must have been laid very recently, probably during the previous night. There was no way of knowing if a single mine had been laid or if there were more. And, if a UNITA unit had breached security of the

Malange pocket to do this, how often could they do this again, particularly on the long, isolated road to Cangandala?

The next hours were very tense as I waited for a report from Malange on whether the team had managed to safely negotiate the return leg of their journey to the relative safety of the city proper. When the call came it was a huge relief to hear that everyone was back safe.

In the intervening time waiting for the call I had made a decision, and when I spoke to Jamie, the programme manager, that afternoon I communicated it. "You are to shut down operations immediately in Cangandala and shift them to a less exposed part of the enclave", Jamie protested. He was conscious of the need in the place and the consequences in terms of, particularly, infant morbidity and mortality if the work he had started was not finished. I dismissed his argument. In terms of the big picture, I said, death or injury of our staff would be a huge blow to the entire national operation as well as the provincial one that he was leading. This in turn could mean that the ambitious objectives we had set ourselves for the provision of public health measures for the people in the besieged cities of the central highlands would not be met. In other words, the possibility of death or injury to my staff outweighed the probability of death and illness to the ordinary, war-displaced families in Cangandala.

That ended the debate and the operation in Cangandala. Some months later, with no more incidents reported on the road, we reassessed the security situation and restarted the operation in Cangandala. It proceeded without further security incident.

I have always felt that my decision to suspend humanitarian work in Candangala was right and easily defensible from both moral and practical operational perspectives. Like Dr Robert's decision to refuse to renew a lost prescription,[1] I felt that my priority had to be protection of the integrity of the service we offered rather than assistance to a particular individual or group in need. I also for some years after was awakened in the night by the thoughts of how many children died in the village because of my choice.

Years later I read an essay by Schlick (1951), which posited that if a person was compelled to do something negative – for example, betray a friend – as a result, say, of torture, then he should not feel guilt for any of the consequences of the betrayal.

The essay struck me as complete nonsense. In this experience, the external compulsion to act, the security threat to my staff, had little impact on subsequent feelings of guilt and regret, which plagued me for years and polluted almost every aspect of my life and relationships. Simply because I can make rational claim to have acted morally and to have managed the security of the situation wisely does

---

1 See Chapter 6.

little to assuage the thought that I condemned to death women as old as my mother and children who, when I saw them playing in the Cangandala camps, reminded me of my nieces and nephew

As most leaders will already know, and as this book demonstrates, making a choice can often be very difficult. This is as true for ethical choice-making as any other variety. But it should also be remembered that even if the choice is the best and most moral that could be achieved in a particular circumstance, it does not guarantee an easy conscience.

Nevertheless, ethical choice-making remains not only vital but urgent when the challenges of the contemporary world are considered. Worry and regret are often the price of leadership, but these can be a spur to better leadership when they prompt learning and empathy. It may be some further small consolation if they are earned in a decent cause.

Summing up

In the previous chapters I have defined human agency as individuals' capacities for free choice within whatever social context, personal, professional or both, that they find themselves. As we reflect on how human beings make choices we can discern a trinity of elements within agency composed of reflexive deliberation, conclusion and then initiation of a course of action.

Sometimes the choice of a course of action may be contingent on a particular set of circumstances pertaining that allow for the choice to be translated into action. That is, if an individual is not implicated in a relevant social situation, then it may be impossible to translate choice into action: For example, in 2020 a European may have been convinced that Joe Biden would make a better president than Trump. However, unless they had dual nationality, and a vote in the United States, the range of action into which that opinion could be translated would be heavily constrained.

Sun Tzu, in the *Art of War*, noted that "All strategy is choice". So, as agency is choice, it is analogous with strategy. Agency is to the personal as strategy is to the organisational. Hence, agency is also leadership: it can be self-leadership, deciding for oneself what one is going to do, taking account of the social pressures but also taking personal responsibility for the consequences of the choice. It can also be organisational leadership either through protest, endeavouring to create new discursive space for the contemplation of different ideas and alternate courses of action or through policymaking, if the choosing individual is at a conjunction of rules and resources that are critical to the shaping of organisational or political action.

Leadership requires listening. In an interview for this book, Jo Berry, observed that individuals often have a lack of willingness to empathise beyond their "tribe". This leads to short-term perspectives on problems and a lack of care for others. At its worst this can also lead to self-righteousness, something that further undermines empathy and willingness to listen.

An individual who uses their capacity for choice to ensure that they are learning from the example and experiences of others, one who, indeed, tries to empathise with others in the struggles that they are facing, is also demonstrating moral and professional integrity and opening themselves to the opportunity for personal growth through deeper understanding of others. For this reason, doubt is an important leadership attribute in that it increases leaders openness to learning and revision of past decisions.

Agency – leadership – can be enriched by penetrative understanding of a social situation gained through experience or reading. This may allow a leader to discern a greater range of options than those for whom a situation is wholly unfamiliar. Or it may allow the leader to comprehend how issues are interconnected and interrelated. But it is personal values and hopes that drive leadership rather than calculations of rational expediency. It is specifically moral values that provide the basis for a personal critique of the choice posed by the social situation either in relation to those values alone or in relation to how they affect other valued relationships. It is the personal that allows the individual the capacity to problematise a situation and hence move it to a status other than taking-it-for-granted, in which the individual simply conceives of not having a choice and does what everyone else is doing. Instead, agency opens the possibility for taking personal responsibility for the contemplation of a variety of courses of action.

Considering the ethical dilemmas of doctors discussed in Chapter 6, or the assertions of dissent described in Chapter 5, reminds us that doing the "right" thing is often about privileging one moral code over another. The flipside question, "Why do 'good' people do 'bad' things?" paradoxically also leads to the same answer. They do "bad" things because they also often believe they are doing good things. Or more specifically because they believe they are privileging one set of "goods" over another. The soldiers who murdered children at My Lai, for example, believed they were doing their duty by following orders.

This is not to assert that everything is morally relative. I believe there are certain moral absolutes. Many would argue that these are unknowable, but whether they are or not is beyond the scope of this book. But a reasonable place I would start would be to take as a basic assumption that causing death or injury to other human beings is always a bad thing. I hold this irrespective of the number of people involved in a decision, the distance between cause and effect, or the cause in which violence is being considered: even just wars are evil things. However, as I attempt to illustrate with the description of my decision to end a humanitarian operation in Angola in the face of a security threat, it is clear that social and situational pressures can be brought to bear, which can lead individuals to believe, rightly or wrongly, that this is indeed the lesser of evils.

Denying responsibility for a choice among the lesser of evils does seem to be unacceptable. This can occur in, at least, two ways – if reflexive assessment and taking responsibility for and learning from such a choice, right or wrong, simply does not happen. Or if it is argued that the lesser of evils is in fact a moral good. Friedman's assertion that the only moral responsibility of business executives is to make profits for shareholders within the law allows for both delusions to flourish.

As Descartes (Fearn, 2001) showed, doubt is the one thing we can be truly certain of. Review of Chapter 6 in this book, on the ethical choices of doctors, indicates the importance of doubt, *reflexive assonance*, in the management of complex ethical questions. It is important because it is a strong basis for learning, but also, as Montaigne argued, because it contributes to tolerance, and tolerance can engender the basis of civilisation, in the best sense of the word.

The notion of free will is fundamental in allowing individuals the capacity to find meaning in their lives – life is not something that simply happens to you, but something with which you have the choice of how to engage. Frankl (1985) argued that this search for meaning is fundamental to the human experience and that the possibility of finding meaning in even the most extreme situations is the freedom that can be denied by only oneself.

Comte-Sponville (2004) asks, "Are we free to choose what we want?" He describes the question of the extent and nature of freedom of choice as the most philosophically problematic aspect of the concept of freedom. I would argue the other way – that it is choice itself that defines and delineates our freedom. As I described in Chapter 4, there is no such thing as autonomous free will. All free will is rooted in the social world that poses choices, ethical and otherwise, to us. Our agency is determined by the nature of our values, particularly our moral values, the questions that these lead us to pose to the challenges we are confronted with in the social world, and the questions the "moments of truth" we meet pose to us. At that point are we the leader who denounces corrupt practices, or the timeserver to takes the path of least resistance?

We can also choose to change: For example, the Abraham Lincoln of 1860 was a racist. By the time of his death, a mere five years later, his engagements with the likes of Frederick Douglass and, in particular, the troops of the Union's black regiments had turned him into a much more mature and enlightened man (Kearns Goodwin, 2005). Chapters 5 and 6 of this book suggest other examples of people whose experiences have changed or accentuated their values to bring new dynamics of reflexivity to their encounters with the social world, and hence to themselves. This is something that will happen to all of us because of life, of falling in love, sometimes from professional success, more often perhaps from experiencing failure, bereavement, romantic disappointment, sometimes from brushes with violence and death.

This does not necessarily mean that we are more or less free. This is merely the essence of freedom.

A word of advice

A year or so ago, an organisation that I was once a board member of, RedR (UK), the Register of Engineers for Disaster Relief, asked me, on quite short notice, to speak to one of their training sessions. The previous speaker they had arranged had to drop out for some unavoidable reason. The course they were running was for engineers and associated professions preparing for their first deployment into humanitarian operations.

I spent a day or two preparing for the session thinking about what would be the key lessons that I would give my twenty-five-year-old self in a similar situation. So, I prepared my notes to talk about some of the difficult ethical choices that might arise and how to cope with the distress and trauma their work might bring.

But, at the end of the day, I told them, the single piece of advice I would like them to remember, if no other, was: "Don't be an arsehole".

At its best, any workplace can be a stressful environment. The workplaces that these young people were heading for were not at their best. But, more pernicious than that, they were off into diverse parts of the world to do "good". Unfortunately, too often in human history "good" has been the most seductive excuse imaginable for some of the most shameful things ever perpetrated by human society.

So perhaps this is the right moment to mention *Star Wars*. Much of the *Star Wars* universe is brilliantly executed fantasy. Some of it – think ewoks and bleeding Jar Jar Binks – is execrable. But in the midst of all of this there is at least one important philosophical point: Obi Wan and Vader follow the same religion. The only difference is that Vader's path is on the "Dark Side".

Many belief systems have similar "Dark" and "Light" sides. An atheist, for example, can follow the "Light Side" by viewing life as something precious that they had better do right because they will only get one shot at this. Or they can decide that they can do what they like, given that there are no immortal consequences for even the worst of actions.

Similarly, a Christian could follow the "Light" by seeing each of us as human beings in the image of God despite our flaws and differences. Or they could take to judging how poorly everyone else appears against their subjective standards and inflicting their notion of condemnation and righteous vengeance at every opportunity.

As mentioned in Chapter 7, Martha Nussbaum, in *The Fragility of Goodness*, argues that humans often do evil not because they transgress a moral system, but because they privilege one moral system, or perhaps a particular interpretation of a moral system, over another. Christopher Browning demonstrates the depth of depravity that can emerge from such thinking when one group of "Ordinary Men" from diverse backgrounds and political outlooks in Eastern Poland during the Second World War decided to uphold their perceived duties to following their orders over their more fundamental human duties not to butcher unarmed children, women and men in cold blood.

But, despite the power of well demonstrated social pressures in such circumstances, human agency, the choices in the social world that we make based on our beliefs and values, is still at the core of human action. A person can still choose to be decent despite the social pressures to the contrary. Or, indeed, despite their underlying belief system: two of the great "rescuers" of the Second World War, Oskar Schindler (Keneally, 1982) and John Rabe (Chang, 1998), were both card-carrying members of the Nazi party. So, decency, even heroism, does not depend simply on the belief system that we choose. It also depends on how we choose to interpret it and which beliefs to privilege.

I have known great and humane atheists. I have known great and humane Christians, Hindus, Muslims, Jews and Buddhists. I have also known people who use their noisy public commitment to vital human rights issues as a cloak to disguise the immense depth of their moral cowardice and venality. And then there are the murderous Crusaders of history, the Nazis, the Maoists and Stalinists, the Ku Klux Klan and their ideological cousins in Islamic State – those who use their beliefs as excuses to choose the darkest and bloodiest paths through life.

Richard Dawkins (2007) and his fellow travellers like to blame religion for so many of the world's ills. But the sprawling silliness of Star Wars, and the mythical universe that it has created, has hit upon a much wiser understanding of human nature. As Shakespeare, the great chronicler of human folly and human evil, also understood: the faults are in ourselves.

But so are the solutions.

Numberless diverse acts of courage and belief

This book has probably raised more problems than solutions in relation to some of the major issues facing humans in the 21st century. Some of the solutions to these issues are straightforward: for example, the ending everywhere of systems tying the work visas of migrants to specific employers would radically reduce their risk of enslavement; or a more rapid transition to noncarbon energy technologies and protection of the world's carbon sinks would help impede global warming. Some of the solutions, such as how to end humanity's toxic love-affair with casteism and other forms of "othering", are certain to be complex.

However, attending to the planet's existential threats is less a technical question than a political one. In the contemporary political economy certain stakeholders are privileged by decision-makers more than others. The resulting laws, policies and practices that have emerged to date are ones that, for the most part, facilitate the destruction of the environment and the exploitation of vulnerable people.

The world is this way because too many of us allow it to be so. Social movements have made considerable advances in social and environmental justice over the course of history. But every movement begins with individuals, reflecting, alone and with others, on the state of the world and choosing that it should be different.

In other words, the choices and actions of individuals matter, both in their roles as professional leaders and as citizens. When individuals believe otherwise they are creating a self-fulfilling prophesy: if they don't think their choices and actions matter then they probably won't.

In setting out how individuals in difficult situations make ethical choices, this book hopes to empower more leaders and citizens to understand how, at the "moment of truth", they can also act in a more life-affirming way and pressure others with power to do the same.

This book opened with Bobby Kennedy's memorable description of how protest creates discursive space and how that in turn brings change: Each time a person

> stands up for an ideal, or acts to improve the lot of others, or strikes out against injustice, [they send] forth a tiny ripple of hope, and crossing each other from a million different centers of energy and daring, those ripples build a current that can sweep down the mightiest walls of oppression and resistance.

While a focus of this book has been on the importance of moral values, rather than rational calculation, as the source of human agency, we should not ever abandon our logical thinking capabilities. In the face of the contemporary crises confronting the planet we have two options: to acquiesce and ensure the loss of everything, or to lead ethically and strive to end up some place better.

Given the starkness of this choice the only rational option is to engage our moral values and relentlessly demand change to the political economies that threaten the future of our planet and those we love who live upon it.

After all, as Seamus Heaney put it in The Cure at Troy, "sometimes hope and history rhyme". Heaney's former schoolmate John Hume, who himself made this rhyme once with his contribution to Irish peace, might add, " . . . when you put the hard work and sweat in".

This is the urgent challenge of ethical leadership facing each of us today. The future depends upon it.

References

> . . . at least a lengthy catalogue of authors will give the book an unexpected authority.
> – from *Don Quixote* (Prologue), by Miguel de Cervantes

Ahmed, N. (2014). Nasa-Funded Study: Industrial Civilization Headed for 'Irreversible Collapse'? *The Guardian*, 14 March, https://www.theguardian.com/environment/earth-insight/2014/mar/14/nasa-civilisation-irreversible-collapse-study-scientists

Anti-Slavery International. (2012). Slavery on the High Street: Forced Labour in the Manufacture of Garments for International Brands. *Anti-Slavery International*, June, https://www.antislavery.org/wp-content/uploads/2017/01/1_slavery_on_the_high_street_june_2012_final.pdf

Anti-Slavery International. (2017). Anti-Slavery Charter. *Anti-Slavery International*, July, https://www.antislavery.org/anti-slavery-charter/

Anti-Slavery International. (2019). Climate Change and Modern Slavery. *Anti-Slavery International*, 14 June, https://www.antislavery.org/climate-change-slavery/

Applebaum, S. (2012). Insight: Kathryn Bolkovac, Whistleblower. *The Independent*, 19 January, https://www.independent.co.uk/news/people/profiles/insight-kathryn-bolkovac-whistle blower-6291533.html

Archer, B. (2020). Sunday Independent attacks on John Hume Over Adams Talks 'Went too Far' – Senior Executive. *The Irish News*, 10 August, https://www.irishnews.com/news/northernire landnews/2020/08/10/news/sunday-independent-attacks-on-john-hume-over-adams-talks-went-to-far–senior-executive-2030598/

Archer, M.S. (2003). *Structure, Agency and the Internal Conversation*. Cambridge: University Press.

Ariely, D. (2008). *Predictably Irrational: The Hidden Forces That Shape Our Decisions*. London: Harper Collins.

ASOS. (2021). ASOS Modern Slavery Statement, February 2020 to January 2021. *ASOS*, https://www.asosplc.com/~/media/Files/A/Asos-V2/ASOS%20Modern%20Slavery%20Statement%202020-21.pdf

Associated Press. (2014). Gay Man Jailed in Cameroon Has Died, Says Lawyer. *The Guardian*, 13 January, https://www.theguardian.com/world/2014/jan/13/gay-man-jailed-cameroon-died-lawyer-mbede

Bales, K. (2016). *Blood and Earth: Modern Slavery, Ecocide and the Secret to Saving the World*. New York: Random House.

Bales, K. (2021). What Is the Link Between Natural Disasters and Human Trafficking and Slavery? *Journal of Modern Slavery*, vol. 6, no. 3.

Barnett, A. and Hughes, S. (2001). British Firm Accused in UN 'Sex Scandal'. *The Guardian*, 29 July, https://www.theguardian.com/world/2001/jul/29/unitednations

BBC. (2011). Timeline: Lord Black on Trial, *BBC*, 24 June, https://www.bbc.co.uk/news/world-us-canada-10721541

Berminghan, F. and Jiangtao, S. (2021). EU to Ban 'Forced Labour' Products Taking Aim at China's Treatment of Uygurs. *South China Morning Post*, 15 September, https://www.scmp.com/news/china/diplomacy/article/3148881/eu-ban-forced-labour-products-taking-aim-chinas-treatment

Bilton, M. and Sim, K. (1992). *Four Hours in My Lai: A War Crime and Its Aftermath*. New York: Penguin.

Bingham, T. (2010). *The Rule of Law*. London: Allen Lane.

Boffey, D. (2020). Amsterdam to Embrace 'Doughnut' Model to Mend Post-Coronavirus Economy, 8 April, https://www.theguardian.com/world/2020/apr/08/amsterdam-doughnut-model-mend-post-coronavirus-economy

Boffey, D. (2021). Court Orders Royal Dutch Shell to Cut Carbon Emissions by 45% by 2030. *The Guardian*, 26 May, https://www.theguardian.com/business/2021/may/26/court-orders-royal-dutch-shell-to-cut-carbon-emissions-by-45-by-2030

Bowcott, O. (2011). Cameroon Gay Rights Lawyer Warns of Rise in Homophobia. *The Guardian*, 16 November, https://www.theguardian.com/world/2011/nov/16/cameroon-gay-rights-laywer-alice-khom

Brammer, S. and Millington, A. (2003). The Effects of Stakeholder Preferences, Organisational Structure and Industry Type on Corporate Community Involvement. *Journal of Business Ethics*, no. 45: 213–226.

Bravin, J. (2007). The Conscience of the Colonel. *The Wall Street Journal*, 31 March, https://www.wsj.com/articles/SB117529704337355155

Browning, C.R. (2001). *Ordinary Men: Reserve Police Battalion 101 and the Final Solution in Poland*. London: Penguin.

Buis, A. (2019). A Degree of Concern: Why Global Temperatures Matter. *Nasa Global Climate Change*, 19 June, https://climate.nasa.gov/news/2865/a-degree-of-concern-why-global-temperatures-matter/

Business and Human Rights Resource Centre. (2017). Modern Slavery in Company Operations and Supply Chains. *International Trade Union Confederation*, September, https://www.ituc-csi.org/IMG/pdf/modern_slavery_in_company_operation_and_supply_chain_final.pdf

Business and Human Rights Resource Centre. (2019). Social Audits in the Textile Sector: How to Control the Controllers? *BHRRC*, 4 February, https://www.business-humanrights.org/en/blog/social-audits-in-the-textile-industry-how-to-control-the-controllers/

Business and Human Rights Resource Centre. (2020). 26 Companies, Business Associations, and Initiatives Make Joint Call for EU Mandatory Human Rights & Environmental Due Diligence. *BHRRC*, 2 September, https://www.business-humanrights.org/en/latest-news/eu-mandatory-due-diligence/

Chandler, G. (2009). The Amnesty International UK Business Group: Putting Human Rights on the Corporate Agenda in McIntosh, M. (ed.) (2009) *Landmarks in the History of Corporate Citizenship: A special theme issue of The Journal of Corporate Citizenship*, Issue 33, Apr.

Chang, I. (1998). *The Rape of Nanking*. London: Penguin.

Chikudate, N. (2002). Collective Myopia and Disciplinary Power Behind the Scenes of Unethical Practices: A Diagnostic Theory on Japanese Organization. *Journal of Management Studies*, no 39.

Comte-Sponville, A. (2004). *The Little Book of Philosophy*. London: Vintage.

Connellan, C., Hussain, T., Barclay, D. A., Holland, E., and Kepkay, A. (2019). US Customs & Border Protection Enforces Forced Labor Prohibition in First Action Against Vessel, *White & Case*, 8 April, https://www.whitecase.com/publications/alert/us-customs-border-protection-enforces-forced-labor-prohibition-first-action

Cragg, W. and Greenbaum, A. (2002). Reasoning About Responsibilities: Mining, Company Managers on What Stakeholders Are Owed. *Journal of Business Ethics*, no 39: 319–335

Curbelo, V. (2021). Exploring the Relationship Between Humanitarian Emergencies and Human Trafficking: A Narrative Review. *Journal of Modern Slavery*, vol. 6, no. 3.

Dawkins, R. (2007). *The God Delusion*. London: Black Swan.

Dean, C. (2007). Executive on a Mission: Saving the Planet. *The New York Times*, 22 May, https://www.nytimes.com/2007/05/22/science/earth/22ander.html

Delta 8.7. (2021). Crisis Policy Guide. *United Nations University*, http://collections.unu.edu/eserv/UNU:8065/Delta87_CrisisPolicyGuide.pdf

Department of Labour. (2020). *List of Goods Produced by Child Labor or Forced Labor*. USDOL, Washington DC, https://www.dol.gov/sites/dolgov/files/ILAB/child_labor_reports/tda2019/2020_TVPRA_List_Online_Final.pdf

Economist. (2004). The Chronicles of Greed. *Economist*, 2 September, https://www.economist.com/business/2004/09/02/the-chronicles-of-greed

Economist. (2009). A Chill in the Boardroom. *Economist*, 10 December, https://www.economist.com/business/2009/12/10/a-chill-in-the-boardroom

Edwards, P. and Pap, A. (1965). *A Modern Introduction to Philosophy*. New York: The Free Press.

Edwards, P. (1965). Determinism, Freedom and Moral Responsibility: Introduction. In Edwards, P. and Pap, A. (ed.), *A Modern Introduction to Philosophy*. New York: The Free Press.

Ellis, D. (2011). "The Arc of the Moral Universe is Long, But it Bends Toward Justice". *The White House: President Barack Obama*, 21 October, https://obamawhitehouse.archives.gov/blog/2011/10/21/arc-moral-universe-long-it-bends-toward-justice

Emirbayer, M. and Mische, A. (1998). What Is Agency? *American Journal of Sociology*, January, vol. 103, no. 4: 962–1023.

Fearn, N. (2001) *Zeno and the Tortoise: How to Think Like a Philosopher*. London: Atlantic Books.

Flanagan, P. (2019). How Woman, 60, Has Saved Thousands of Child Brides in Malawi and Helped Girls Finish Education Amid Death Threats. *inews*, 2 August, https://inews.co.uk/news/world/malawi-tribal-chief-child-brides-underage-marriage-death-threats-education-321625

Ford, L. (2015). Sustainable Development Goals: All You Need to Know. *The Guardian*, 19 January, https://www.theguardian.com/global-development/2015/jan/19/sustainable-development-goals-united-nations

Fortune Editors. (2020). The Biggest Business Scandals of 2020. *Fortune*, 27 December, https://fortune.com/2020/12/27/biggest-business-scandals-of-2020-nikola-wirecard-luckin-coffee-twitter-security-hack-tesla-spx-mcdonalds-ceo-ppp-fraud-wells-fargo-ebay-carlos-ghosn/

Frankl, V.E. (1985). *Man's Search for Meaning*. New York: Washington Square Press.

Freeman, R.E. (2000). *Strategic Management: A Stakeholder Approach*. Cambridge: Cambridge University Press.

Freeman, R.E. and Liedtka, J. (1991). Corporate Social Responsibility: A Critical Approach. *Business Horizons*, July–August, vol. 34, no. 4: 92–99.

Friedman, M. (1970). The Social Responsibility of Business is to Increase Its Profits, *New York Times Magazine*, September 13: 122–126.

Gammon, K. (2021). How the Billionaire Space Race Could Be One Giant Leap for Pollution. *The Guardian*, 19 July, https://www.theguardian.com/science/2021/jul/19/billionaires-space-tourism-environment-emissions

Giddens, A. (1984). *The Constitution of Society*. Cambridge: Polity Press.

Gidla, S. (2017). *Ants Among Elephants: An Untouchable Family and the Making of Modern India*. New York: Farrar, Straus and Giroux.

Gillam, C. (2021). 'A Sip Can Kill': Did a Chemical Company Misrepresent Data to Avoid Making a Safer Product? *The Guardian*, 24 March, https://www.theguardian.com/environment/2021/mar/24/syngenta-paraquat-deadly-john-heylings?CMP=Share_iOSApp_Other

Global Slavery Index. (2018a). India Country Study. *Global Slavery Index*, https://www.globalslaveryindex.org/2018/findings/country-studies/india/

Global Slavery Index. (2018b). Asia and the Pacific Regional Analysis. *Global Slavery Index*, https://www.globalslaveryindex.org/2018/findings/regional-analysis/asia-and-the-pacific/

Global Witness. (1998). *A Rough Trade: The Role of Companies and Governments in the Angolan Conflict*. London: Global Witness.

Global Witness. (1999). *A Crude Awakening: The Role of the Oil and Banking Industries in Angola's Civil War and the Plunder of State Assets*. London: Global Witness.

Goats and Soda. (2016). Today's Slaves Often Work for Enterprises That Destroy the Environment. *National Public Radio*, 20 January, https://www.npr.org/sections/goatsandsoda/2016/01/20/463600820/todays-slaves-often-work-for-enterprises-that-destroy-the-environment?t=1622711760561&t=1632044111650

Goldsworthy, A. (2006) *The Fall of Carthage*, London: Phoenix.

Gonzalez, E. (2002). Defining a Post-Conventional Corporate Moral Responsibility. *Journal of Business Ethics*, no. 39: 101–108.

Greene, M. (2019). Trump Signs Full Pardon for Former Media Mogul Conrad Black, Who Wrote Flattering Bio of President. *Chicago Tribune*, 16 May, https://www.chicagotribune.com/news/breaking/ct-met-conrad-black-pardon-donald-trump-20190515-story.html

Greenpeace. (n.d.). What Are the Solutions to Climate Change? *Greenpeace*, https://www.greenpeace.org.uk/challenges/climate-change/solutions-climate-change/

Guardian. (2021). The Guardian View on Climate Change Lawsuits: Big Oil Is in the Dock. *The Guardian*, 28 May, https://www.theguardian.com/business/commentisfree/2021/may/28/the-guardian-view-on-climate-change-lawsuits-big-oil-is-in-the-dock?CMP=Share_iOSApp_Other

Haney, C., Banks, C. and Zimbardo, P. (1973). Interpersonal Dynamics in a Simulated Prison. *International Journal of Criminology and Penology*, no. 1: 69–97.

Hilton, A. (2016). Stay or Go – The Lack of Solid Facts Means it's All a Leap of Faith. *Evening Standard*, 25 February, https://www.standard.co.uk/comment/comment/anthony-hilton-stay-or-go-the-lack-of-solid-facts-means-it-s-all-a-leap-of-faith-a3189151.html

Hoque, M. (2021). Forced Labour and Access to Education of Rohingya Refugee Children in Bangladesh: Beyond a Humanitarian Crisis. *Journal of Modern Slavery*, vol. 6, no. 3.

Human Rights Watch. (2005). After the Deluge: India's Reconstruction Following the 2004 Tsunami. *Human Rights Watch*, May, https://www.hrw.org/reports/2005/india0505/india0505.pdf

Human Rights Watch. (2019) India: Growing Crackdown on Activists, Rights Groups. *Human Rights Watch*, 17 January, https://www.hrw.org/news/2019/01/17/india-growing-crackdown-activists-rights-groups

Human Rights Watch. (2020). *Yemen: Events of 2019*, https://www.hrw.org/world-report/2020/country-chapters/yemen#

Humber, J.M. (2002). Beyond Stockholders and Stakeholders: A Plea for Corporate Moral Autonomy. *Journal of Business Ethics*, no. 36: 207–221.

International Labour Organization. (2017a). *Promoting Decent Work and Protecting Fundamental Principles and Rights at Work in Export Processing Zones*. International Labour Office (ILO), Geneva.

International Labour Organization. (2017b). *Global Estimates of Child Labour: Results and Trends, 2012–2016*. International Labour Office (ILO), Geneva, https://www.ilo.org/wcmsp5/groups/public/@dgreports/@dcomm/documents/publication/wcms_575499.pdf

International Labour Organization. (2017c). *Global Estimates of Modern Slavery: Forced Labour and Forced Marriage*. International Labour Office (ILO), Geneva, https://www.ilo.org/wcmsp5/groups/public/-dgreports/-dcomm/documents/publication/wcms_575479.pdf

International Transport Workers Federation. (2019). ITF Wins Protection for Migrant Workers in Ireland's Fishing Industry. *ITF*, 26 April, https://www.itfseafarers.org/en/news/itf-wins-protection-migrant-workers-irelands-fishing-industry

International Transport Workers Federation. (n.d.). Flags of Convenience. *ITF*, https://www.itfglobal.org/en/sector/seafarers/flags-of-convenience

IPCC. (2021). Summary for Policymakers. In: *Climate Change 2021: The Physical Science Basis. Contribution of Working Group I to the Sixth Assessment Report of the Intergovernmental Panel on Climate Change* [Masson-Delmotte, V., P. Zhai, A. Pirani, S. L. Connors, C. Péan, S. Berger, N. Caud, Y. Chen, L. Goldfarb, M. I. Gomis, M. Huang, K. Leitzell, E. Lonnoy, J. B. R. Matthews,

T. K. Maycock, T. Waterfield, O. Yelekçi, R. Yu and B. Zhou (eds.)]. Cambridge University Press. In Press.

Jackson, K.T. (2000). The Polycentric Character of Business Ethics Decision-Making in International Contexts. *Journal of Business Ethics*, no. 23: 123–143.

Johnson, S. (2021). Tesco and Next Among Brands Linked to Labour Abuses in India Spinning Mills. *The Guardian*, 28 May, https://www.theguardian.com/global-development/2021/may/27/tesco-admits-to-finds-evidence-of-labour-abuses-in-india-supply-chain

Jones, M.T. (1999). The Institutional Determinants of Social Responsibility. *Journal of Business Ethics*, no. 20: 163–179.

Jones, T.M. (1991). Ethical Decision Making by Individuals in Organizations: An Issue Contingent Model. *Academy of Management Review*, no. 16: 366–395.

Junger, S. (2011). *War*. London: Fourth Estate.

Kaye, L. (2016). How Bonded Labor Fuels India's Garment Industry. *Triple Pundit*, 6 December, https://www.triplepundit.com/story/2016/how-bonded-labor-fuels-indias-garment-industry/56541

Kapelus, P. (2002). Mining, Corporate Social Responsibility and the 'Community': The Case of Rio Tinto, Richards Bay Minerals and the Mbonambi. *Journal of Business Ethics* 39: 275–296, https://doi.org/10.1023/A:1016570929359

Kearns Goodwin, D. (2005). *Team of Rivals: The Political Genius of Abraham Lincoln*. New York: Simon & Schuster.

Keneally, T. (1982). *Schindler's Ark*. London: Hodder and Stoughton.

Krog, A. (1999) *Country of My Skull*, London: Vintage.

Lanchester, J. (2014). *How to Speak Money: What the Money People Say – And What They Really Mean*. London: Faber and Faber.

Lantane, B. and Darley, J.M. (1968). *The Unresponsive Bystander: Why Doesn't He Help?* New York: Appleton-Century-Crofts.

Lazarus, J. (2015). 'Dalit Women and Water', wH2O: *The Journal of Gender and Water*, vol. 4, no. 10, https://repository.upenn.edu/wh2ojournal/vol4/iss1/10

Lowth, M. (2017). Does Torture Work? Donald Trump and the CIA. *British Journal of General Practice*, March, https://www.ncbi.nlm.nih.gov/pmc/articles/PMC5325643/

Maas, P. (1974). *Serpico*. London: Fontana.

Malik, K. (2018). How We All Colluded in Fortress Europe. *The Guardian*, 10 June, https://www.theguardian.com/commentisfree/2018/jun/10/sunday-essay-how-we-colluded-in-fortress-europe-immigration

Marshall, T. (2021). *The Power of Geography – Ten Maps That Reveals the Future of Our World*. London: Elliott & Thompson.

Mason, E.S. (1959). *The Corporation in Modern Society*. Harvard: University Press.

Mason, P. (2011). Ray Anderson Obituary. *The Guardian*, 26 August, https://www.theguardian.com/environment/2011/aug/26/ray-anderson-obituary

McClements, F. (2018). Greysteel Massacre, 25 Years on: 'The Smell of Gun Smoke Has Never Left Me'. *The Irish Times*, 30 October, https://www.irishtimes.com/news/ireland/irish-news/greysteel-massacre-25-years-on-the-smell-of-gun-smoke-has-never-left-me-1.3679685

McQuade, A. (2015). Combatting Child Marriage to Save Girls from Slavery. *Thomson Reuters Foundation News*, 21 May, https://news.trust.org/item/20150521143909-fxl8s/

McQuade, A. (2016). Miners, Tea Pickers, Brides: These Children Are Slaves, Not Labourers. *The Guardian*, 10 February, https://www.theguardian.com/global-development/2016/feb/10/miners-tea-pickers-brides-these-children-are-slaves-not-labourers

McQuade, A. and Nyein, Y. (2019). We Can't Allow Myanmar's Slavery-Tainted Shrimp to Land on Our Plates. *The Guardian*, 12 November, https://www.theguardian.com/global-development/2019/nov/12/we-cant-allow-myanmars-slavery-tainted-shrimp-to-land-on-our-plates

McNeish, H. (2016). Malawi's Fearsome Chief, Terminator of Child Marriages. *Al Jazeera*, 16 May, https://www.aljazeera.com/amp/features/2016/5/16/malawis-fearsome-chief-terminator-of-child-marriages

Mellema, G. (2003). Responsibility, Taint, and Ethical Distance in Business Ethics. *Journal of Business Ethics*, no. 47: 125–132.

Mercurio, J. (2002). *Bodies*. London: Vintage.

Milgram, S. (1992). *The Individual in a Social World: Essays and Experiments*. New York: McGraw Hill.

Moriarty, G. (2021). John Hume: 'We Did Not Quite Realise How Significant He Was Until He Died'. *The Irish Times*, 31 July, https://www.irishtimes.com/news/ireland/irish-news/john-hume-we-did-not-quite-realise-how-significant-he-was-until-he-died-1.4634906

Morton, A. (2021). Australian Court Finds Government Has Duty to Protect Young People from Climate Crisis. *The Guardian*, 27 May, https://www.theguardian.com/australia-news/2021/may/27/australian-court-finds-government-has-duty-to-protect-young-people-from-climate-crisis

Munshi, N. (2021). Why the Kidnapping Industry Is Thriving in Nigeria. *Financial Times*, 26 April, https://www.ft.com/content/d8d9bf8f-0aa2-405f-b3f7-2a3e7e7b297c

Ní Chonghaile, C. (2015). Cameroonian Lawyer Urges World to Join Her in Fight Against Anti-Gay Legislation. *The Guardian*, 10 March, https://www.theguardian.com/global-development/2015/mar/10/cameroon-lawyer-campaign-against-anti-gay-legislation

Nussbaum, M.C. (2001). *The Fragility of Goodness: Luck and Ethics in Greek Tragedy and Philosophy*. Cambridge: University Press.

O'Connor, F. (2020). John Hume Obituary: Nationalist Leader Who Championed 'Agreed Ireland'. *The Irish Times*, 3 August, https://www.irishtimes.com/life-and-style/people/john-hume-obituary-nationalist-leader-who-championed-agreed-ireland-1.4320556

O'Callaghan, M. (2020). Finding a Way Out of the Darkness Was Hume's Mission. *RTE*, 4 August, https://amp.rte.ie/amp/1157086/

O'Connell, C. (2021). From a Vicious to a Virtuous Circle. *Anti-Slavery International*, https://www.antislavery.org/wp-content/uploads/2021/04/ASI_ViciousCycle_Report_ExecSummary2.pdf

O'Connor, S. (2021). Not All Green Jobs Are Safe and Clean. *Financial Times*, 26 October, https://www.ft.com/content/111f9600-f440-47fb-882f-4a5e3c96fae2?accessToken=zwAAAXzCsl6Qkc8RH5YA9EBH-9OIL0pePJb64g.MEUCIQDPaSWVHP3oUdmx0xFc5Nbpk4hWwxi_DUcB-KVgEsZkhAIgX78GZjayUNZEkmOOGSgZ3Pt2ZviBxXl_-7-DQqjKKfU&sharetype=gift?token=894ba3e6-310b-4749-ade6-94356ac59bb0

OECD. (2015). G20/OECD Principles of Corporate Governance. *OECD Publishing*. Paris. http://dx.doi.org/10.1787/9789264236882-en

OECD. (2021). OECD Corporate Governance Factbook 2021, https://www.oecd.org/corporate/Corporate-Governance-Factbook.pdf

Okeowo, A. (2012). The Eight Most Fascinating Africans of 2012. *The New Yorker*, 7 December, https://www.newyorker.com/news/news-desk/the-eight-most-fascinating-africans-of-2012

O'Malley, P. (1983). *The Uncivil Wars: Ireland Today*. Belfast: Blackstaff Press.

Oxfam. (2016a). An Economy for the 1%, *Oxfam*, 18 January, https://oi-files-d8-prod.s3.eu-west-2.amazonaws.com/s3fs-public/file_attachments/bp210-economy-one-percent-tax-havens-180116-summ-en_0.pdf

Oxfam. (2016b). 62 People Own Same as Half World. *Oxfam*, 18 January, http://oxfamapps.org/media/prhow

Perrigo, B. (2020). The Fatal Gang Rape of a Young Woman Is Forcing a Reckoning in India Over the Caste System. *Time*, 15 October, https://time.com/5900402/hathras-rape-case-india-violence/

Phillips, B. (2020). How to Fight Inequality (and Why That Fight Needs You). London: Polity.

Post, F.R. (2003). The Social Responsibility of Management: A Critique of the Shareholder Paradigm and Defense of Stakeholder Primacy. *Mid-American Journal of Business*, no. 18: 57–61.

Quazi, A.M. and O'Brien, D. (2000). An Empirical Test of a Cross-national Model of Corporate Social Responsibility. *Journal of Business Ethics*, no, 25: 33–51.

Ratcliffe, R. (2019). Oxfam Failed to Report Child Abuse Claims in Haiti, Inquiry Finds. *The Guardian*, 11 June, https://www.theguardian.com/global-development/2019/jun/11/oxfam-abuse-claims-haiti-charity-commission-report

Rawls, J. (1999). *A Theory of Justice*. Oxford: University Press.

Raworth, K. (2017a). *Doughnut Economics*. London: Random House Business.

Raworth, K. (2017b). What on Earth is the Doughnut? *Kate Raworth Exploring Doughnut Economics*, https://www.kateraworth.com/doughnut/

Rees, G., Spath, P. and Grassi, P. (2021). EU Set to Introduce Mandatory Environmental and Human Rights Due Diligence Law. *Morrison and Foerster LLP*, March 23, https://www.lexology.com/library/detail.aspx?g=ab945361-e236-405d-8193-4d4088373bf4

Robinson, K. (2021). What Is the Kafala System? *Council on Foreign Relations*, 23 March, https://www.cfr.org/backgrounder/what-kafala-system

Roth, P. (2000). *The Human Stain*. Boston: Houghton Mifflin.

Roy, A. (2004). Roy's Full Speech: The 2004 Sydney Peace Prize Lecture Delivered by Arundhati Roy, at the Seymour Theatre Centre, University of Sydney – Peace and the New Corporate Liberation Theology. *The Sydney Morning Herald*, 4 November, https://www.smh.com.au/national/roys-full-speech-20041104-gdk1qn.html

Schlick, M. (1951). When Is a Man Responsible? In Edwards, P. and Pap, A. (ed.) (1965), *A Modern Introduction to Philosophy*. New York: The Free Press.

Shahinian, G. (2009). Report of the Special Rapporteur on Contemporary Forms of Slavery Including its Causes and its Consequences. *Human Rights Council*, July, https://idsn.org/wp-content/uploads/user_folder/pdf/New_files/Key_Issues/Bonded_Labour/A-HRC-12-21_E.pdf

Sheehan, M. (2020). London Market Adds Modern Slavery Clause for Marine Cargo. *Reinsurance News*, 22 June, https://www.reinsurancene.ws/london-market-adds-modern-slavery-clause-for-marine-cargo/

Sherwood, H. (2021). Pope Francis Urges Leaders to Take Radical Climate Action at Cop26. *The Guardian*, 29 October, https://www.theguardian.com/world/2021/oct/29/pope-francis-world-leaders-climate-action-cop26

Singh, A. (2021). Exclusive: Raab Says UK Wants Trade Deals with Nations That Violate Human Rights. *Huffington Post*, 16 March, https://www.huffingtonpost.co.uk/entry/raab-trade-deals-human-rights_uk_6050d75bc5b605256ebeaca6

Sinkovics, N., Ferdous Hoque, S. and Sinkovics, R.R. (2016). Rana Plaza Collapse Aftermath: Are CSR Compliance and Auditing Pressures Effective? *Accounting, Auditing and Accountability Journal*, vol. 29, no. 4, 16 May, https://www.emerald.com/insight/content/doi/10.1108/AAAJ-07-2015-2141/full/html

Smith, H. (2017). Bangladeshi Fruit Pickers Shot at By Greek Farmers Win Human Rights Case, *The Guardian*, 30 March, https://www.theguardian.com/world/2017/mar/30/bangladeshi-strawberry-pickers-shot-at-by-greek-farmers-win-european-rights-case

Special Action Program to combat Forced Labor (n.d.). *ILO Indicators of Forced Labor*. Geneva: International Labor Organization, https://www.ilo.org/wcmsp5/groups/public/–ed_norm/–declaration/documents/publication/wcms_203832.pdf

Stoney, C. and Winstanley, D. (2001). Stakeholding: Confusion or Utopia? Mapping the Conceptual Terrain. *Journal of Management Studies*, no 38: 603–626.

Stormer, F. (2003). Making the Shift: Moving from 'Ethics Pays' to an Inter-System Model of Business. *Journal of Business Ethics*, no. 44: 279–289.

Sudworth, J. (2020). China's 'Tainted' Cotton. *BBC*, December, https://www.bbc.co.uk/news/extra/nz0g306v8c/china-tainted-cotton

Tondo, L. and Kelly, A. (2017). Raped, Beaten, Exploited: The 21st Century Slavery Propping Up Sicilian Farming. *The Guardian*, 12 March, https://www.theguardian.com/global-development/2017/mar/12/slavery-sicily-farming-raped-beaten-exploited-romanian-women

Trade Union Congress. (2016). ILO Protocol of 2014 to the Forced Labour Convention, 1930, Trade Union Congress, 22 January, https://www.tuc.org.uk/research-analysis/reports/ilo-protocol-2014-forced-labour-convention-1930

Trevino, L. and Brown, M. (2004). Managing to Be Ethical: Debunking Five Business Ethics Myths. *Academy of Management Executive*, no. 18: 69–83.

Unicef. (2018). Child Marriage in Malawi. *Unicef*, https://www.unicef.org/malawi/media/526/file/Child%20Marriage%20Factsheet%202018.pdf

United Nations Climate Change. (n.d.). The Paris Agreement. *United Nations Climate Change*, https://unfccc.int/process-and-meetings/the-paris-agreement/the-paris-agreement

United Nations Convention to Combat Desertification. (2021). Great Green Wall Receives of $14 Billion to Regreen the Sahel – France, World Bank listed Among Donors. *United Nations Convention to Combat Desertification*. 11 January, https://www.unccd.int/news-events/great-green-wall-receives-over-14-billion-regreen-sahel-france-world-bank-listed-0

Urbina, I. (2019). *The Outlaw Ocean: Crime and Survival in the Last Untamed Frontier*. London: The Bodley Head.

VanSandt, C.V. and Neck, C.P. (2003). Bridging Ethics and Self Leadership: Overcoming Ethical Discrepancies Between Employee and Organizational Standards. *Journal of Business Ethics*, no. 43: 363–387.

Van Wersch, P. (2018). Kuruba, Fighting Caste Cruelties in India. *Justice and Peace*, https://justiceandpeace.nl/en/stories/kiruba/

Vulliamy, E. (2012). Has the UN Learned Lessons of Bosnian Sex Slavery Revealed in Rachel Weisz Film? *The Guardian*, 15 January, https://www.theguardian.com/world/2012/jan/15/bosnia-sex-trafficking-whistleblower

Ward, A. (2006). *Kant: The Three Critiques*. Cambridge: Polity Press.

Warnock, G. and Magee, B. (1987). Kant. In Magee, B. (ed), *The Great Philosophers*. Oxford: University Press.

Waters, J.A. (1978). Catch 20.5: Corporate Morality as an Organizational Phenomenon. *Organizational Dynamics*: 3–19.

Watt, J. (2020). Africa's Great Green Wall Just 4% Complete Half Way Through Schedule. *The Guardian*, 7 September, https://www.theguardian.com/environment/2020/sep/07/africa-great-green-wall-just-4-complete-over-halfway-through-schedule

White, B. (1984). *John Hume – Statesman of the Troubles*. Belfast: Blackstaff.

White, M. (2020). Insurers Introduce Marine Cargo Clause Against Forced Labour. *Global Trade Review*, 8 July, https://www.gtreview.com/news/europe/insurers-introduce-marine-cargo-clause-against-forced-labour/

Whittington, R. (1989). *Corporate Strategies in Recession and Recovery: Social Structure and Strategic Choice*. London: Unwin Hyman.

Wieltschnig, P., Muraszkiewicz, J. and Fenton, T. (2021). Without Data We Are Fighting Blind: The Need for Human Security Data in Defence Sector Responses to Human Trafficking. *Journal of Modern Slavery*, vol. 6, no. 3.

Wilkerson, I. (2020a). America's Enduring Caste System. *New York Times*, 1 July, https://www.nytimes.com/2020/07/01/magazine/isabel-wilkerson-caste.html

Wilkerson, I. (2020b). *Caste: The Lies That Divide Us*. London: Allen Lane.

Women's International League for Peace and Freedom. (2014). 'The Whistleblower' 15 Years on; Where Are We Now? *WILFP*, https://www.wilpf.org/the-whistleblower-15-years-on-where-are-we-now/

Wrong, M. (2009). *It's Our Turn to Eat: The Story of a Kenyan Whistleblower*. London: Fourth Estate.

Wrong, M. (2021). *Do Not Disturb: The Story of a Political Murder and an African Regime Gone Bad*. London: 4th Estate.

Zimbardo, P. (2007). *The Lucifer Effect: How Good People Turn Evil*. London: Rider.

Further reading

> There are more things in heaven and earth, Horatio,
> Than are dreamt of in your philosophy. — from *Hamlet*, by William Shakespeare

Anderson, G. (2009). *'Cityboy': Beer and Loathing in the Square Mile*. London: Headline.
Angell, M. (2004). *The Truth About the Drug Companies: How They Deceive Us and What to Do About It*. New York: Random House.
Bolkovac, K and Lynn, C. (2011). *The Whistleblower: Sex Trafficking, Military Contractors and One Woman's Fight for Justice*. New York: Palgrave Macmillan.
Brady, F. N. and Logsdon, J. M. (1988). Zimbardo's Stanford Prison Experiment and the Relevance of Social Psychology for Teaching Business Ethics. *Journal of Business Ethics*, September 1988, vol. 7 no. 9.
Carroll, A.B. (1991). The Pyramid of Corporate Social Responsibility: Towards the Moral Management of Organizational Stakeholders. *Business Horizons*, no. 34: 39–48.
Carroll, A.B. and Buchholtz, A.K. (2000). *Business and Society: Ethics and Stakeholder Management*. Cincinnati: Southwestern College.
Cockburn, A. (2007). *Rumsfield: An American Disaster*. London: Verso.
Daley, R. (1978). *Prince of the City*. Boston: Houghton Mifflin.
Damasio, A. R. (2006). *Descartes' Error: Emotion, Reason and the Human Brain*. London: Vintage Books.
Dutton, J.E. and Dukerich, J.M. (1991). Keeping an Eye on the Mirror: Image and Identity in Organizational Adaptation. *Academy of Management Journal*, no. 34: 517–554.
Fogelman, E. (1994). *Conscience and Courage: Rescuers of Jews During the Holocaust*. New York: Anchor Books.
French, J.R.P and Raven, B.H. (1959). The Bases of Social Power. In Cartwright, D. (ed.), *Studies in Social Power*. Ann Arbor: Institute for Social Research.
Friedman, M. (1990). The Suicidal Impulse of the Business Community. *Business Economics*, vol. 20, no. 1: 5.
Friedman, M. (2002). *Capitalism and Freedom*. Chicago: The University of Chicago Press.
Gourevitch, P. and Morris, E. (2008). *Standard Operating Procedure: A War Story*. London: Picador.
Hardin, G. (1968). The Tragedy of the Commons. *Science*, no. 168: 1243–1248.
Hardy, C. Palmer, I. and Phillips, N. (2000). Discourse as a Strategic Resource. *Human Relations*, September, vol. 53, no. 9: 1227–1248.
Hart, S.L. and Christensen, C.M. (2002). The Great Leap: Driving Innovation from the Base of the Pyramid. *MIT Sloan Management Review*: 51–56.
Matten, D. and Crane, A. (2002). Theorizing Corporate Citizenship. *Management Research News*, no. 25: 8–10.
Matten, D., Crane, A. and Chapple, W. (2003). Behind the Mask: Revealing the True Face of Corporate Citizenship. *Journal of Business Ethics*, no. 45: 109–120.
McKenna R. and Tsahuridu, E. (2001). Must Managers Leave Ethics at Home? Economics and Moral Anomie in Business Organizations, *Reason in Practice*, no. 1: 67–76.
Mead, G. H. (1964). *On Social Psychology: Selected Papers*, Strauss, A. (ed.). Chicago: The University of Chicago Press.
Moore, G. (1999). Corporate Moral Agency: Review and Implications. *Journal of Business Ethics*, no. 21: 329–343.
Roy, A. (2014). The Doctor and the Saint, an Introduction to *The Annihilation of Caste*, by B.R. Ambedkar. New Delhi: Navayana Pub.

Soares, C. (2003). Corporate Versus Individual Moral Responsibility. *Journal of Business Ethics*, no. 46: 143–150.
Sridharan, U.V., Dickes, L. and Caines, W.R. (2002). The Social Impact of Business Failure: Enron. *Mid-American Journal of Business*, no. 17: 11–21.
Wood, D.J. (1991). Corporate Social Performance Revisited. *Academy of Management Review*, no. 16: 691–718.
Wulfson, M. (2001). The Ethics of Corporate Social Responsibility and Philanthropic Ventures. *Journal of Business Ethics*, no. 29: 135–145.

About the author

Aidan McQuade is a writer and independent human rights consultant. He comes from South Armagh in the North of Ireland.

Aidan was director of Anti-Slavery International from 2006 to 2017. Prior to that he worked extensively in development and humanitarian operations, including from 1996 to 2001 leading Oxfam GB's emergency responses to the civil war in Angola.

He is a recognised expert on forced labour and trafficking, with an honorary OBE for his work on the elimination of modern slavery, and he regularly advises businesses, international and non-governmental organisations.

He holds a PhD from the University of Strathclyde, and is the author of a novel, The Undiscovered Country.

Photo source: Jakub Sobik/ Anti-Slavery International.

About the series editor

Bernd Vogel is a Professor in Leadership and Founding Director of the Henley Centre for Leadership at Henley Business School, UK.

Bernd has more than 20 years of global experience in research, educating, speaking, and consulting with outstanding companies, business schools and universities. He supports organisations and people in life-long learning journeys that transform lives, organisations, and society. He bridges academia with practice and is an executive coach.

His expertise is in leadership and leadership development; future of work and leadership; strategic leadership to mobilise and sustain healthy energy and performance; developing leadership and followership capability; healthy and performing senior management teams; change, transformation and culture; leadership development architectures.

Bernd features regularly in media. He publishes in top-tier global academic journals and has written and edited several books, case studies and industry reports.

Throughout his career Bernd has had academic roles at the Leibniz University Hannover, Germany, and University of St. Gallen, Switzerland. He has held global visiting positions at Claremont Graduate University, USA; IESE Business School, Spain; and Marshall School of Business, USC, USA.

Index

"This ball [of thread] Ariadne gave to Theseus, and instructed him to follow it until he reached the sleeping monster . . ."
– Robert Graves, *The Greek Myths*

9/11 Commission 48

abortion 67
accountability 14
Achilles 106
Adivasi 12
Aeneid, The (epic poem by Virgil) 124
Afghanistan 48, 63, 107, 125
Africa 4, 32, 35, 58, 84, 110, 119, 121, 125
Agamemnon 106
agriculture 11, 109–110, 118, 121
Al Jazeera 53–54
al Qaeda 48
Albania 110
Amnesty International 89
Amsterdam 123
Anderson, Ray 17, 46–47, 55, 62–63, 83, 86, 89, 96, 127
Andes 127
Angola 1–4, 9, 84, 128, 131
– Cangandala 128–130
– Kuito 1–3, 128
– Luanda 9, 128
– Malange 128–129
Antarctic 118
Anti-Slavery Charter 112–115
Anti-Slavery International 3, 10, 16, 103, 116
Archer, Margaret 33–34, 37–38, 78, 99
Ariely, D. 81
Aristotle 14
arseholes 133
Art of War, The 130
Asia 89, 110, 117, 119
ASOS 16, 101
Association for the Defence of Homosexuals 57–58
assonance 7, 64, 68–75, 87, 132
Australia 122
– New South Wales 122

Bahrain 11
Bales, Kevin 108, 117
banditry 125

Bangladesh 106–108, 117
– Cox's Bazar 107–108
Bangladesh Accord on Fire and Building Safety 106
basic rules of society 10, 13–14
basic structure of society 14, 87
bastinado 58
Beckett, Samuel 128
Belleeks 50
Berlin 29
Berry, Jo 75, 130
best interest of patient 72
Biden, Joe 118, 130
Bilton, Michael 22–23, 47
Bingham, Tom 14–16, 90
Black, Conrad 95
black regiments of Union army 132
Blood and Earth (book by Kevin Bales) 117
Boko Haram 106
Bolivia 116, 127
– Lake Poopo 116, 127
Bolkovac, Kathryn 55–57, 62–63, 109
Borodino 24
Bosnia 55–57
bottom trawling 13
Brazil 14
Brexit 53
Briseis 106
British Army 50
British Empire 127
British Journal of General Practice 48
Brown, M. 28, 82
Browning, Christopher 22–26, 28, 47, 77–78, 84, 133
Buis, Alan 118
business 6, 9–11, 13–21, 23, 26–28, 30, 35, 40–41, 47, 83–93, 95–100, 104–106, 110–112, 120–122, 126–127, 132
– international 8, 13, 16, 83, 85–87, 90, 92, 98, 106, 112
business executives 13, 16–17, 26, 84–86, 88, 100, 105, 132

Index

Cambodia 110
Cameroon 57–59
carbon sink 117
Casablanca 42
Casement, Roger 102
caste 10, 12, 59–62, 107, 120, 134
Catholics 52
Cervantes, Miguel de 80, 137
Chandler, Sir Geoffrey 89
Chicago 95
Chikudate, N. 27
child labour 10–13, 19, 89, 105, 108, 110–111, 113–114, 122
child marriage 53–55
child protection 7, 65, 71, 74
China 11, 117
choice 4–7, 9, 14, 21, 24–25, 29, 31–32, 34, 39, 41–42, 44–45, 47, 57, 61–65, 69–70, 73–81, 83–86, 88, 91, 93, 99, 130, 132, 134–135
choice-making 6, 31, 33, 36–37, 43, 45, 80, 82, 87, 130
Cicero 50
citizens 102, 135
citizenship 5, 7–8, 14, 21, 92, 98–99, 119, 126
civil society 23, 95, 98, 105–106, 111–112
Clausewitz, Carl von 14
climate change 8, 13, 35, 85, 89, 111, 116–122, 125–127, 134
cobalt 12, 110
code of conduct for ethical leadership 5, 7, 20, 80, 91
Cold War 2
coltan 12
Comte-Sponville, A. 132
Confédération des Travailleurs des Secteurs Publique et Privé (CTSP) 16
Confederation of British Industry (CBI) 115
confidentiality 71, 74–75
conformity 28, 76, 84, 99
conscience 20–21, 37, 41, 49, 61, 63, 74, 78, 106, 125, 130
contemporary slavery 112
COP26 117–118
coral bleaching 13
cotton 11–12, 103
Couch, V. Stuart 48–50, 57, 62–63
Country of My Skull (book by Antjie Krog) 32
Cragg, W. 28–29, 33, 85

Cruciform of Agency 6–7, 32, 34, 37, 39, 42, 44–46, 49, 61–62, 65, 69–70, 77, 80–82
Curbelo, Viktoria 107

Dalits 12, 29, 59–60, 104, 110, 120
Darley, J. M. 22, 25–26, 29, 40–41, 76–78, 84
Dawkins, Richard 134
debt bondage 11
decent work 113–115
decision-making 4–7, 19, 22–23, 30, 32, 44, 46, 64, 73, 76, 86–87
Delta 8.7 109
Democratic Republic of Congo (DRC) 12, 110
Descartes, Rene 132
determinism 6, 22, 24, 33–35
diamonds 2, 15, 19, 84, 86
Dickens, Charles 89
direct cash transfers 115
discrimination 10, 60, 64, 89, 104, 107
discursive space 29–30, 35, 45, 47, 49, 53, 55, 61, 63, 65, 83, 99, 112, 130, 135
displaced people 1–3, 109, 128–129
dissent 7, 23, 30–31, 41–42, 45, 49, 55–56, 61, 63–64, 69, 131
Do Not Disturb (book by Michela Wrong) 74
Don Quixote (book by Miguel de Cervantes) 80, 137
doubt 7, 59, 64, 69, 73–75, 82, 98, 131–132
doughnut economics 90, 123
Doughnut Model 90–91, 96, 102, 123, 126
Douglass, Frederick 132
Dublin 29, 48, 52
due diligence 111

ecological sustainability 19
Economist, The 95
Emirbayer, M. 34, 36–38, 40, 42, 62, 77
end of life 7, 65–66, 69–70
Enron 18, 97
environment 1, 4–6, 13, 17, 20, 23, 25, 27–28, 31, 34–35, 46–47, 58, 61–62, 72, 75, 82, 84–87, 89–90, 97–99, 106–107, 116–117, 122, 127, 133–134
environmental degradation 85, 116, 120, 122, 125, 128
environmental justice 127
environmental restoration 1, 7–8, 17, 20, 47, 85, 91, 96–97, 101–102
environmental standards 7, 20, 83–84, 92, 94

Eritrea 107, 125
Ethical auditing 105
ethical choice 6, 25, 62, 69, 74–75, 132–133
ethical complexity 74, 86
ethical distance 29, 30, 84, 103
ethical leadership 1, 5, 7–8, 20, 25, 30, 32, 44–45, 47, 61–63, 65, 69, 78, 80, 82–84, 86–88, 93–95, 98–102, 109, 112, 116, 126–128, 135
ethical principles 69, 76, 88, 100
ethical responsibility 6, 19
Ethical Trading Initiative (ETI) 17, 91
ethics 7
Europe 47–48, 55, 58, 110, 119, 124–125
European Union 45, 53, 100, 105–106, 111
ewoks 133
Export Processing Zones (EPZs) 11

Fabius 33
Fanon, Franz 74–75
female genital mutilation 75
Fenton, Toby 109
Fidelis Insurance 85, 97
Financial Times 121, 125–126
fishing boats 11
Food and Agriculture Organisation (FAO) 121
forced labour 10–13, 83, 89, 103–105, 107–112, 125
– state-facilitated forced labour 11
– state-sponsored forced labour 11
– state-tolerated 12
Forced Labour Protocol (2014) 110–111, 115
forced prostitution 55
Foreign, Commonwealth and Development Office (FCDO) 10
Fortune Magazine 97
France 111, 121
free will 6, 21–22, 24–25, 32–33, 35, 81, 132
Freeman, R. Edward 17
Friedman, Milton 9–10, 13–14, 16–17, 19–21, 23, 71, 83, 85–86, 88–90

G20 96–97
Ganguly, Meenakshi 61
garments 12–13, 15–17, 84, 92–93, 101, 104–105
Germany 48, 59, 95, 97, 124
Giddens, Anthony 36, 41

Gidla, Sujatha 59
girls' rights 55, 62
Glasgow 84, 117
Global Slavery Index 11–12
global South 30, 120–121, 126
Global Witness 2, 19, 84
Gonzalez, E. 19
Goree 32
government 35
Great Green Wall 121
Greenbaum, A. 28–29, 33, 85
Greenland 118
Greenpeace 122
Guantanamo Bay 47–48
Guardian, The 55, 56, 58, 103–105, 118, 123, 125
Gulf countries 11
Gupta Empire 119

Hamlet 63, 147
Han Empire 119
Hannibal 33
Heaney, Seamus VII, 22, 135
Holbach, Baron d' 24
Hollinger International 95–96
Hoque, Madmadul 108
Horn of Africa 119
Horrocks, Michael 48
human agency 6, 28, 31–38, 40–42, 49, 51, 57, 77–78, 80, 82–83, 95, 99–100, 128, 130–132, 134–135
human rights 1, 7–8, 10, 12–13, 15–17, 19–20, 29, 45, 58–62, 64, 83–84, 89–92, 94, 96–106, 109–117, 120–121, 123, 127–128, 134
human rights abuses 90, 105, 109, 111, 122, 128
Human Rights Watch 14, 61, 107
human trafficking 11, 55, 93, 107–109, 111, 127
– maritime trafficking 11, 13
– sexual exploitation 55
humanitarian crisis 2
humanitarian response 1–3, 5, 9, 65, 107–109, 128, 133
Hume, David 24, 30, 41, 49
Hume, John 50–53, 62–63, 135
Hume, Mo 52
Hume, Pat 53
Hungary 14

ideas and thoughts 33
Iliad, the (epic poem by Homer) 106
Independent, The 55–56
India 12, 14, 59–61, 84, 103, 107, 110, 117
– Tamil Nadu 12, 103–105, 107
individual choice 6, 36–37
Industrial Revolution 120, 126
IndustriALL 16
Intergovernmental Panel on Climate Change 8, 118
International Committee of the Red Cross (ICRC) 1
international conventions 13
International Labour Conference 110
International Labour Organization (ILO) 12, 89, 96, 104
international law 10–11, 16, 80, 89, 110
international markets 11, 13, 110
international standards 13
International Trade Union Confederation (ITUC) 114
International Transport Workers Federation (ITF) 11
Ireland 4, 10–11, 35, 50–53
– Derry 52–53, 62
– Greysteel 53
Irish Republican Army 50, 52
Irish Times, The 53
Islamic State 106, 134
Islamist militancy 121

Jar Jar Binks 133
Jenča, Miroslav 119
Jones, M. T. 29–30
Jones, T. M. 26–27
judgement 17, 34–36, 42, 66, 72–74, 78, 122
Junger, Sebastian 63
Justice and Peace Netherlands 60–61

Kachindamoto, Theresa 53–55, 62–63
kafalah 11, 16
Kagame, Paul 57
Kant, Immanuel 18, 25, 81–82
Kapelus, Paul 11, 18
Kennedy, Robert Francis 1, 135
Kenobi, Obi Wan 133
kidnapping 126
King, Martin Luther 4

Klein, Jacques 56
Kohlberg, Lawrence 28, 85
Krog, Antjie 32, 34
Ku Klux Klan 134
Kuwait 11
Kwaja, Chris 126

labour inspection 11
Lanchester, John 119
Lantane, B. 22, 25–26, 29, 40–41, 76–78, 84
Laos 110
law 3, 10–11, 13–16, 20, 28–29, 46, 56, 71, 74, 82–84, 86–90, 110–111, 126, 132
Lazarus, Janice 120
leadership IX, 1–2, 4–10, 13–17, 19–21, 23–32, 35–36, 39, 41, 43, 45, 47, 49, 52–53, 59, 61–65, 69, 72, 75–76, 78–79, 82–93, 96–100, 106–107, 111–112, 118, 122, 128, 130–132, 135
legitimate authority 22, 47, 55, 76, 84
Libya 109, 124–125
life-affirming choices 1, 29–30, 43, 99
Lincoln, Abraham 132
London 10, 16, 84, 92, 111
Lowth, Mary 48
Luanda 9
Luckin Coffee 97

Maas, P. 27
Machiavelli, Niccolo 18
Magee, B. 23, 32, 81
Malawi 53, 62
– Zomba 53–54
Malik, Kenan 125
Marks and Spencer 114
Marshall, Tim 120–121, 126
Martin Luther King 5
Marx, Groucho 9
Mason, E. S. 98
Mathias, Charles 85
Mauritania 48
Mauritius 16
Mauryan Empire 119
Mbédé, Roger Jean-Claude 58
McGrath, Paul 35–36
medical profession (doctors) 7, 43, 64–67, 69–70, 72–79, 82–83, 86–88, 95, 131–132
– anaesthetist 66
– general practitioner (GP) 65, 67

– psychiatrist 70
– surgeon 66, 74
Mediterranean, the 41, 124–125
Mellema, G. 29, 84
Micawber principle 89
Middle East 11, 89, 119, 125
migrants 10–11, 29, 110, 125
migration 8, 116, 124–127
Milgram, Stanley 22–23, 25–26, 28–29, 40, 76–78, 84, 99
military aid 121
Mills, John Stuart 24, 27, 30, 41, 49
Mische, A. 34, 36–38, 40, 42, 62, 77
Montaigne, Michel de 132
moral courage 20, 59, 63–64, 126
moral cowardice 13, 134
moral decision-making 6
moral guidance 13, 27, 69, 86, 88
moral outrage 104
moral resonance 7, 15, 43, 45, 65–66, 79
moral responsibility 7, 13–14, 20, 22–25, 28–30, 62, 80, 84, 86
moral values 44, 82, 86, 88, 131–132, 135
Munshi, Neil 125
Munusamy, Kiruba 60–63, 104, 107, 120
Muraszkiewicz, Julia 109
Murdoch, Rupert 106
My Lai 22, 47, 131
Myanmar 7, 17, 91–93, 107–108, 110, 117
– Gulf of Motama 108

Namibia 2
Napoleon 24
NASA 118–119
Neck, C. P. 27–28, 30
Netherlands, the 122
New York 27, 46–47
New York Times 46–47
New Yorker, The 57
Newcastle-under-Lyme Borough Council 114
Nigeria 109, 124–126
– Edo State 124
Nkom, Alice 57–59, 62–63
non-governmental organisations 35, 92
not-for-profit sector 17
Nussbaum, Martha 69, 86, 133

O'Connell, Chris 116–117
O'Connor, Sarah 121

O'Mara, Shane 48
Obama, Barack 105
Observer, The 57
obstetrics 67–68
Oedipus the King (play by Sophocles) 14
oil 2
Oman 11
Ordinary Men (book by Christopher Browning) 133
Organisation for Economic Co-operation and Development (OECD) 96–97
Oxfam GB 1, 3, 109, 119, 128

Pakistan 48
Paris 58, 118
Pascal, Blaise 32
penetration 36, 41, 78
Perle, Richard 95
personal moral values 6–7, 21, 32, 80, 82, 89
Peru 116, 127
pharmaceutical industry 43
Phillips, Ben 116
physical courage 63
points for reflection 8, 21, 31, 44, 63, 79, 94, 128
Poland 22, 47, 133
police 12, 55–58, 71
political economy 6–7, 8, 11, 14–15, 25, 29, 47, 55, 86, 98, 101, 109–110
pollinating insects 118
Pope Francis 58, 118
Post, F. R. 18
professional maturation 76, 81, 99
professional principles 74
profits 13–14, 19, 26, 60, 84, 89, 91, 106
protest 30, 47, 49, 57, 59, 61, 63, 65, 67, 102, 112, 130, 135
public sector 17

Qatar 11

Raab, Dominic 10, 12–13
Rabe, John 134
Rana Plaza 106
Rawls, John 14, 87
Raworth, Kate 90, 123
REDR, the Register of Engineers for Disaster Relief 133
refugees 108, 125

religion 133–134
Riega, Victor 97
Rohingya 107–108
Roman Empire 119, 127
Romania 56
Rome 33–34, 120, 126
Rose, Richard 50
Roth, Philip 106
Roy, Arundhati 104
Royal Dutch Shell 89, 122
Ruggie, John 20
Rule of Law 14–17, 20, 49, 83–84, 90, 96
Rumsfeld, Donald 48
Russell, Willy 64
Russia 58
Rwanda 57

Sahel 32, 120–121, 127
Sarajevo 55
Saudi Arabia 11, 14, 20
Savimbi, Jonas 2, 9
Schindler, Oskar 23, 134
Schlick, M. 129
Second World War 22–23, 47, 87, 133–134
Senegal 32, 34–35
Serpico 27
sex working 72
sexual abuse 55, 57
Shakespeare, William 134, 147
shareholder theory 18
shrimp 12, 108, 117
Sim, Kevin 22–23, 47
Slahi, Mohamedou Ould 47–49
slavery 3, 8, 10–13, 15–16, 18, 20, 45, 54, 60, 98, 100–117, 122, 125
Smith, Adam 10, 98, 106
social complexity 40, 78, 82
Social Democratic and Labour Party (SDLP) 52
social pressures 23–24, 28–29, 31, 43, 76, 80–82, 89, 130, 134
Sophocles 14
South Africa 2, 10, 32, 85
South America 116
South Asia 12, 29, 60–61, 119
Special Air Service 50
Speer, Albert 23
Spiderman 112
spinning mills 12, 103–105

SS 22, 25
stakeholder theory 9, 17–21, 85, 88
Star Wars 133–134
states 11, 15–16, 19, 89, 98, 106, 110
Stauffenberg, Claus von 23
Stoney, C 17–18
Strathclyde University 10
Sudan 10
– Darfur 10
Sun Tzu 128, 130
Sundarbans 117
Sunday Independent (Ireland) 52
supply chains 4, 13, 15–16, 29, 88–91, 98–101, 104–105, 110–112, 114–115, 128
Sustainable Development Goals 110
sustainable economy 100, 121
system integrity 72–73

Thailand 12, 110, 117
The Fragility of Goodness (book by Martha Nussbaum) 69, 86, 133
The Human Stain (novel by Philip Roth) 106
The Mauritanian 47
Thebes 14
tied visas 11, 115
Tolstoy, Leo 24
torture 48, 58, 129, 124
totalitarianism 45
Trade Union Congress (TUC) 114–115
trade unions 89, 92, 95, 98, 105, 110–111
trans-Atlantic slave trade 2
transnational corporations 15–16, 98
transparency 111
treatment of drug addicts 72
Trevino, L. 28, 82
Troubles, the 50, 52
Troy VII, 106
Trump, Donald 95, 130
Turkey 14
Turkmenistan 12

UK Modern Slavery Act 16, 111
– Transparency in Supply Chain Clause 16
– Transparency In Supply Chain 106
Ukraine 56
UN Guiding Principles on Business and Human Rights 19, 21, 89, 96, 104, 112
Unicef 53

UNITA 1–2, 14, 19, 65, 84, 128
United Arab Emirates 11
United Kingdom (Britain) 10, 13–14, 53, 55, 79
United Nations 19, 21, 55–57, 89, 92, 96, 104, 110, 112, 118–119, 121
United States of America 2, 14, 47–48, 59, 117, 130
– Pennsylvania 25
Universal Declaration of Human Rights 15, 20, 89
Untouchables 12, 104
Urbina, Ian 11, 13, 117
Urus-Muratos 116
Usman, Zainab 125

Vader, the Dark Lord Darth 133
van Doorninck, Marieke 123
VanSandt, C. V. 27–28, 30
veil of ignorance 87–88
Virgil 124

Wall Street Journal 48
war 1–3, 5, 9–10, 14, 19, 49–50, 52, 57, 65, 93, 106–107, 109, 125, 128–129
– just war 131

War and Peace 24
War (book by Sebastian Junger) 63
Ward, A. 81
Warnock, G 23, 32, 81
Waters, J. A. 25–27, 30
whales 13
White, Barry 52
Whittington, R. 31
Wieltschnig, Peter. 109
Wilde, Luke 120
Wilkinson, Isabel 59
window of knowledge 88
Winstanley, D. 17–18
Wirecard 97
Women's International League for Peace and Freedom (WILPF) 57
World Trade Center 48
Wrong, Michela 20, 57, 74, 100

Yeats, William Butler 64
Yemen 14
Youssou N'Dour 35

Zenica 55
Zimbardo, Phillip 22–23, 25–29, 41, 77, 81, 84, 99